Signaling Goodness

Economics, Cognition, and Society

This series provides a forum for theoretical and empirical investigations of social phenomena. It promotes works that focus on the interactions among cognitive processes, individual behavior, and social outcomes. It is especially open to interdisciplinary books that are genuinely integrative.

Editor: Timur Kuran

Editorial Board: Tyler Cowen   Avner Greif
                 Diego Gambetta   Viktor Vanberg

Titles in the Series

Signaling Goodness

Social Rules and Public Choice

Phillip J. Nelson and Kenneth V. Greene

The University of Michigan Press
Ann Arbor

2006   2005   2004   2003   4   3   2   1

A CIP catalog record for this book is available from the British Library.

Library of Congress Cataloging-in-Publication Data

Nelson, Phillip J., 1929–
    Signaling goodness : social rules and public choice / Phillip J.
Nelson and Kenneth V. Greene.
        p. cm. — (Economics, cognition, and society)
    Includes bibliographical references.
    ISBN 0-472-11347-X (alk. paper)
    1. Charities.   2. Altruism.   3. Social norms.   4. Social
perception.   5. Political sociology.   6. Public interest.
I. Greene, Kenneth V.   II. Title.   III. Series.

HV31 .N45   2003
361.2'5—dc21   2003005038

Contents

CHAPTER I

Overview

Political, intellectual, and academic discourse in the United States has been awash in "political correctness." It has been both berated and defended, but there has been little attempt to understand it. We do so by looking at a more general process: adopting political positions to enhance one's reputation. Long before "political correctness" came to American colleges, Reilly, a character in T. S. Eliot's *Cocktail Party* (1950), observed,

> Half the harm that is done in this world
> Is due to people who want to feel important.
> They don't mean to do harm—but the harm does not interest them.
> Or they do not see it, or they justify it
> Because they are involved in the endless struggle
> To think well of themselves.

Obviously, Reilly was not too happy with precursors to "correctness." Our focus, however, is on successful prediction of political behavior. While standard analyses ignore reputation seeking, we argue that it is essential to understanding such behavior.

As we shall argue later, Reilly's version of reputation seeking is not quite right (but, then again, we cannot speak in blank verse). Much about the behavior Reilly berates is really quite sensible. Why should a person be worried about the consequences of the policies he advocates, when his advocacy has virtually no impact on whether those consequences will be realized? Many other people are also engaged in advocacy, so any one person's advocacy, or vote, has a miniscule impact on policy.

This is an example of the *free-rider problem.*[1] It creates a fundamental difficulty for economists' standard analyses of political and charitable behavior, both of which concentrate on the consequences of policies. By and large, public choice economists assume that people maximize their narrow *self-interest:* that is, people advocate policies that do the most good for them. But Reilly's people are actually acting more reasonably.

Economists focusing on charity traditionally assume that *altruism* is the reason for charitable contributions. In defining altruism these economists look at the motivation for behavior rather than its results. Altruism is defined as concern for the well-being of others, or in the language of economics, having the utility of others in one's own utility function. We shall use altruism in that sense throughout this book. But it makes sense to leave the charitable giving to others rather than to give oneself if altruism is the sole motivation for charitable giving. Others can improve the lot of the poor as well as I can. If they do so, my desires for the poor to be better off can be satisfied at no cost to me. This free-rider problem is analyzed in detail in chapter 2. So most modern analyses of charity recognize that altruism cannot be the sole motivation for charity (again, examined in chapter 2). Yet people give to charity, just as a majority of eligible voters in most countries trek to the polls in national elections. Again, we argue that such behavior can only be explained by reputation seeking.

It may seem strange that an altruist would leave the charitable giving to others when the altruist has some concern about the welfare of these others too. But actual behavior requires that at most people are limited altruists—that they are more concerned with their own well-being than that of others outside their family. In consequence, they only give to the poor because the *marginal* utility of a dollar to the poor is greater than its marginal utility to them. Given their greater concern with themselves than with others, they would prefer that others with comparable marginal utilities of money do the charitable giving.

While this free-rider problem is extremely serious for both voting and charity, the standard approaches used to explain these phenomena have had some modest empirical successes. At least superficially, narrow self-interest seems to govern some voting decisions. People with higher incomes, for example, are more likely than others to vote for candidates who advocate political positions good for people with higher incomes. Similarly, altruism seems to have something to do with charity. On the whole, charity tends to go to those activities that serve some social purpose: aid to the poor, education, health, and the environment, for example. It is incumbent on any alternative theory of either charity or voting to also predict these results.

On the other hand, the standard approaches also have glaring failures. As shown in chapters 5 and 8 narrow self-interest variables—income and related variables—are not nearly as important in determining voting behavior as are ethnic and religious variables. Nor does altruism successfully predict the charitable behavior of donors, a question examined in chapter 3. The theory we develop does a much better job on both counts.

The deficiencies of standard economic models in dealing with many social interactions have been the subject of a considerable literature. Surveys of that work are provided by Elster (1998), Fehr and Gachter (2000), Manski (2000), Ostrom (2000), Rabin (1998), and Robson (2001). But as important as they are, these criticisms are insufficient. One cannot predict behavior just by knowing that standard economic models do not always successfully predict behavior. A new theory is required to understand social interactions, or standard theory must be so modified that it works better. The theory we propose is consistent with many of the ideas of the critics of the standard analyses. (Other researchers have expressed similar ideas, but in somewhat less usable form. Our specific debts are indicated in references throughout this book.)

The core of our theorizing rests on two kinds of behavior. A person is interested in his reputation for *trustworthiness*. In consequence, he behaves in such a way as to signal to others that he is trustworthy. A person is also interested in whether she herself thinks she is trustworthy, whether she behaves in accordance with certain internalized social norms because she feels better by so doing. The latter is what is generally labeled *conscience*. As we shall see, the two behaviors have enough in common to generate many similar implications.

This book focuses on three propositions about reputation-seeking behavior. First, charity and voting participation increase a person's reputation for trustworthiness. (In this and the other propositions about reputation, reputation to oneself—a conscience—is always relevant.) Chapters 2–4 develop and test this proposition. Others have also proposed this idea (Posner 2000; Alexander 1987), but our model and tests are somewhat different and more fully developed than theirs. This idea is supported by a growing literature on the importance of investments in reputation—social capital, including participation in community organizations (for example, Glaeser, Laibson, and Sacerdote 2000). There is a lot of evidence that reputation seeking is at least one of the motivations for charity. For example, charities like the American Cancer Society and United Way try whenever possible to use solicitors that know potential donors. We believe that the predictions generated by a model of reputation seeking work more generally because we expect conscience motivated charity to behave quite similarly to reputation *signaling,* an idea developed in chapter 2. The success of our tests lends credence to such a belief.

A person is interested not only in another person's general trustworthiness, but in how trustworthy that other person would be for him. The other two propositions about reputation focus on for whom a person is trustworthy. Our second proposition is developed in chapter 5. We maintain that a person signals that he is trustworthy to some group by imitating its members' behavior. In particular, he imitates their political behavior. This *imitation* is why ethnic groups and religious groups play such an important role in political behavior and civil strife. A person by definition belongs to the same ethnic group as his parents. He is also quite likely to belong to the broadly defined religious group of his parents. In the United States the percentage of people who say their religion is the same as their parents is 86 percent among Catholics, 85 percent among liberal Protestants, and 86 percent among conservative Protestants (Lawton and Bures 2001). Our model predicts that lags are an extremely important part of behavior, and the data concur. In consequence, these long-lasting association patterns play a particularly important role in determining political positions. The close correlation between friendship patterns and political positions can be confirmed by a visit to any college campus.

Our third reputation hypothesis requires a much more elaborate rationale than can be provided easily in a paragraph or two. We maintain that by adopting a particular strategy one can signal generalized trustworthiness at the expense of trustworthiness to the group to which one belongs. The strategy is to advocate more expenditures for the poor, for education, for health, and for the environment than one's group advocates. We call this *asymmetric "goodness"* because the opposite behavior, advocating less of these expenditures, does not signal generalized trustworthiness. The most obvious evidence for this phenomenon is attitudes about the environment. Many people who do not intend to use an environmental amenity, such as Glacier National Park, are willing to be taxed for that amenity. Most environmental economists attribute this phenomenon to altruism, an attribution we reject. They believe that such nonusers are concerned with the well-being of the users of the park. At the same time the economists ignore the apparent unconcern of users with the welfare of those who will be taxed for the amenity but have no use for it. This kind of asymmetric behavior is demonstrated over and over again in our data. For example, demonstrations are held in favor of the poor and the environment, but there are no similar promarket demonstrations, in favor of less government regulation of economic activity.

The obvious explanation for these asymmetries will not work. While there are some *externalities* associated with each of the "good" expenditures, there is no reason to expect public expenditures to fall below the appropriate levels. These externalities to the individual are internalized when governments force everybody to finance an activity. At the level of expenditures produced by a democracy supposedly correcting for the externalities, why is it "good" to advocate more rather than less?

We believe there is a reasonable evolutionary defense for this behavior. To get there, however, requires a kind of analysis increasingly used by psychologists but not frequently employed by economists.

Sociobiology

It is hard to disagree with the basic premise of sociobiology: that there is a higher survival rate for traits and preferences that maximize the probability of their own survival. For example, we prefer to eat bread rather than stones because we would not survive with the opposite preference. This proposition holds for both genetic and cultural transmission of preferences.

The problem with sociobiology lies with putting it to work. First of all, the maximization is constrained rather than unconstrained. There are limits on how man can change given the stuff of which he is made. We are human rather than superhuman. Survival processes produce local maxima rather than a global maximum, so starting points matter (Elster 1984).

Without prior knowledge of the constraints or of the particular local maximum, the predictive power of sociobiology is limited. Elster emphasizes this reason for the predictive difficulties of sociobiology. He believes that at best one can find an evolutionarily stable solution among many such possible solutions. However, if one can find reasonable constraints that yield a variety of testable implications, sociobiology can do more than explain events a posteriori. In particular, we defend in chapter 2 the proposition that because of our animal origins individuals are less future oriented than would be required to maximize the survival of their genes. This constraint does lead to behavioral predictions. When for simplicity we write *maximizing survival,* we always mean *maximizing survival with constraints* or *an evolutionarily stable solution that is a function of those constraints.*

Second, survival processes take a long time to affect preferences. Preferences appropriate for survival in one period can persist in periods when they are no longer appropriate, and a temporary existence in terms of survival processes can be a long time. Evolutionary psychologists such as Barkow (1992) stress the stage of development relevant for survival processes—the hunter-gatherer stage. Man was in that stage long enough, two million years, for survival to determine behavior, and the post-hunter-gatherer stages have not been long enough to have a substantial survival impact—ten thousand years. We believe that there are enough of the hunter-gatherer preferences surviving to have an important impact on contemporary behavior. Whether that belief is confirmed or not is an empirical question, which we will try to answer the only way such questions can be answered—empirically.

Furthermore, there can be genetic or cultural drift: nonrandom changes in preferences that do not contribute to survival. If their rate of change is slow enough, they, too, will be eliminated by their evolutionary inadequacies, but even more slowly than other processes. While we do not know about nonrandom processes in genetic variation, our data strongly suggests nonrandom cultural changes. In chapters 6 and 8 we maintain that "compassion" has seemed to grow beyond its evolutionary roots. This phenomenon seemingly affects a wide enough variety of behavior, so it is not simply another "just so" story.

Finally, one must face the question of the relative roles of individual and group selection. While the dominant views of sociobiologists emphasize individual over group selection, a growing number of sociobiologists believe that group selection is important. We believe both views are right, though about very different aspects of behavior. We argue in chapter 2 that individual survival determines individual behavior in response to social rules. But the story is quite different when it comes to the social rules themselves. Any *operational social rule* must be structured so that there is on average a net return to individuals within the society to follow those rules. But many alternative social rules can satisfy that requirement. The rules "Thou shalt not kill" and "Murder at will" can both be operational in different societies if in the former case a sufficiently powerful enforcement mechanism is at work.

Of course, it must pay enforcers evolutionarily to enforce these rules. In the absence of a government with police power, there are two operative mechanisms. (1) Those who do not punish are in turn punished. By its logic this requires an infinite extension. Those who do not punish the nonpunishers are punished, and so forth. (2) As we show in chapter 3, it can be in the self-interest of enforcers not to do certain things with those who break the social rules because the latter are not trustworthy. It is this second mechanism that is particularly important in modern societies.

Which operational social rule will survive? In this case it is group survival rather than individual survival that determines the answer. If an operational rule maximizes group survival, then the society with that rule grows relative to others. Given the enforcement mechanism associated with an operational rule, those who disobey the rule do not increase within the society relative to those who do not. Hence, the society can continue that social rule indefinitely. As that social group grows relative to others, that rule eventually becomes the dominant social rule.

We would, therefore, expect social rules to develop that cause societies to grow, but not to have individual behavior oriented to that goal. Adam Smith's "invisible hand," then, is no evolutionary surprise. Social institutions tend to develop that generate favorable social consequences from individual self-interested behavior, at least in long-run equilibrium.[2] But individual behavior must be consistent with self-interest *evolutionarily defined,* though not necessarily with self-interest as economists use that term. (We will explore the differences between those two concepts later.) Evolutionary processes will insure that individual altruism—one of the standard explanations for charitable and political behavior—is not very important. But it is easy to see how charity will be given to causes that benefit society even though individual donors are not altruistic. It costs the individual no more to give to "good" causes than others. Hence, the social rule that charity should be focused on "good" causes can be easily enforced and clearly has group survival value.

Besides altruism, the other standard explanation for charity is *warm glow* (Andreoni 1990). This is the idea that people get an unspecified private return from acts that benefit others. Operationally, warm glow often has been defined simply as nonaltruism, so the rejection of altruism necessarily implies that warm glow must be the explanation of a phenomenon incompatible with altruism or narrow self-interest. However, not all versions of warm glow will do. All versions are self-interested behavior as economists define that term, but not all are self-interested behavior in an evolutionary sense. To use warm glow to explain charity requires an explanation of why giving to charity translates into higher survival probabilities for one's genes. None of the warm-glow advocates have asked that question, let alone answered it. We do.

It must be emphasized, however, that there is nothing automatic about this process of creating social rules that maximize group survival given individuals interested only in individual survival. The social rules are themselves the results of individual decision making. In chapter 6 we show that a very special individual behavior is required to produce mores that maximize group survival.

There is no guarantee that this evolutionary approach to reputation-seeking behavior will work. The best evidence that we have of the usefulness of this survival approach lies in the success of the standard assumptions of economics, for their ultimate rationale does require survival logic.

The Assumptions of Economics

For the most part, economists have employed a pragmatic defense for their underlying assumptions: They work. However, in some cases these assumptions, as usually applied, do not work. Economists have not been very successful in dealing with certain human interactions, a contention defended in detail in the chapters that follow. We shall show how those assumptions and their application can be revised to work and still be consistent with their survival foundations.

The most important assumption of economics is that of self-interest: an individual is interested in maximizing his own well-being and his family's. A behavior that has some features seemingly inconsistent with that assumption is charity, especially anonymous charity. The explanation for why the assumption of self-interest works so frequently is not hard to find: survival. Survival provides the rationale of all of the underlying assumptions of microeconomics. The critical behavioral assumptions economists make in deriving the downward sloping demand curve are that (1) at the margin more is better than less (scarcity), (2) an individual consumes two or more goods (the basis for what economists call the convexity assumption), and (3) price is not an argument in the utility function.

Each specification of preferences makes sense in terms of survival. (1) Over the period when preferences were being formed, survival increased with levels of total consumption. (2) We consume more than one good because that increases our survival chances. (3) Price is *not usually* in the utility function because survival usually depended upon quantities consumed, not prices. (A possible exception was first discovered by Veblen: the status impact of price. Under the appropriate circumstances, that status effect can be important because survival probabilities can be related to status.)

While the assumption of self-interest does not enter directly into the proof of the downward sloping demand curve, it is crucial in making that proposition operational. Price is defined in terms of the costs to individuals and their families of buying an additional unit of the good. (That insight is behind the inclusion of time costs in the definition of price.) That definition only works if people are self-interested.

Even a more recent addition of fundamental assumptions (Bailey, Olson, and Wonnacott 1980) has its roots in survival: risk aversion. Increases in income yield diminishing marginal survival probabilities. In consequence, a 50 percent chance of a loss of x dollars must be rewarded by a 50 percent chance of a gain of more than x dollars for a person to be willing to undergo the risky strategy. In terms of survival rather than income, however, a person would be risk neutral.

Furthermore, economists find that on the whole those goods that are close substitutes in a survival sense will also be close substitutes in a demand sense. For example, foods that are nutritionally close substitutes tend to be close economic substitutes.

Sociobiology and Reputation Seeking

It appears, then, that sociobiology provides a unifying basis for the assumptions of microeconomics in the usual areas where it has been applied. But that does not exhaust the uses of sociobiology. As detailed in chapter 6, group selection provides the underlying defense for our third proposition about reputation seeking. Individuals signal general trustworthiness at the expense of less trustworthiness to their group by advocating more expenditures for the poor and for education among other causes because that leads to greater group survival—an increase in the long run of the number of people with the preferences that produce those results. (We call this *goodness* signaling.) Social rules that produce a more equal distribution of income lead to more survivors in a society because of the diminishing marginal survival value of income. So too do social rules that generate more child care because individuals tend to underweight, in a survival sense, future generations, a proposition defended at length later. It is no wonder that social rules in hunter-gatherer societies encourage both food sharing and the family, the main institution of child care. At the same time reputation-seeking behavior of individuals does not reduce individual survival given the belief of others that such behavior in fact signals greater trustworthiness. We discuss the origins of such beliefs in chapter 6.

In long-run equilibrium, social rules must be able to survive. Such a requirement changes considerably the nature of the social rules we expect. Standard economic analysis would maintain that social rules are the product of summation of individual decisions, with economists divided over whether those decisions are motivated simply by self-interest or by some combination of self-interest and altruism. In our analysis survivable individual decisions are motivated by self-interest. But something else is required to go from these decisions to group survival. That something else is "goodness" signaling: the advocacy of causes that promote group survival. This is a way of getting social rules that maximize group survival out of individual behavior that maximizes individual survival. This "goodness" signaling combines with the standard model in a way described in chapter 6. The behavior predicted is substantially different from the predictions of the standard economic model with or without altruism.

CHAPTER 2

Charity and Evolution

Why do people give to charity? Our thesis is that charity is a signal that a person can be trusted in interpersonal relationships. People signal by engaging in socially approved activities at some cost to themselves. We also recognize a "conscience" motivation, where conscience is defined as the internalization of social norms, a desire to follow social rules because one feels better by so doing. Given these motivations, charity has a different meaning in different societies to the extent that social rules vary.

Our thesis differs considerably from the traditional view that charity is determined by altruism, defined as concern for the well-being of others, or in the language of economics, having the utility of others in one's utility function.[1] We use a somewhat narrower definition, but, in fact, the one that economists operationally employ. Altruism means being concerned with the utility of people who can be directly affected by one's actions. It thus does not include helping somebody because of the approval of some other person whom one loves.

This standard definition is different from another definition of altruism sometimes used—any action benefiting others at some material cost to oneself. To avoid confusion please remember we are *not* using this latter definition. Given that definition, charity is of necessity altruistic.

The focus of this chapter is this battle of ideas—altruism versus signaling and conscience. It has important consequences not only for charity but for the political behavior we examine in later chapters. We show in this chapter the assorted deficiencies of altruism. Even if it were an important part of individual behavior, it won't work for contributions to charity because of the free-rider problem. Altruism is not evolutionarily stable. A lot of cooperative behavior cannot be explained by altruism. In contrast, we show that none of these deficiencies are shared by our hypothesized combination of signaling and conscience. We further show that this combination leads to implications that we test in later chapters.

Altruism versus Self-Interest: The Free-Rider Problem

Much of the current economic literature on charity is dominated by the issue of how much of charity is attributable to altruism and how much is the result of "warm glow"—some return to the donor other than through altruism. It is generally recognized that altruism by itself cannot explain the totality of charitable contributions. The argument is simple. Altruism implies that an increase in government expenditures in an activity reduces by the same amount charitable contributions for that activity, yet such perfect "crowding out" is not observed. (See, for example, Andreoni 1990.) Suppose, for example, that a person initially gives one hundred dollars to a charity. Then the government taxes that person fifty dollars and uses that money for the same charitable activity. The rational response of that person if he were altruistic would now be to give only fifty dollars to charity. Perfect crowding out should occur. In fact, it does not.[2]

But a far stronger proposition also holds. Altruism, at best, explains only a miniscule amount of charity. If one person helps a poor person, he increases the utility of all others who have that poor person in their utility function. Given widespread altruism, charity is a *public good.* But in the altruism case something more is required to produce the standard free-rider problem associated with public goods. To be even vaguely related to actual behavior altruism must be a very limited kind of altruism. People must value the utility of themselves and their family more than the utility of others. Otherwise, they would make sure that others had more income than they. Given this limited altruism, a person wishes to help the poor only because the marginal utility of a dollar to them is so much higher than the marginal utility of a dollar to that person and his family. While he might also be concerned with the well-being of his fellow donors, this will not be enough to offset his preference that others with the same marginal utility of income as he do the helping in his place. It is this preference that creates a free-rider problem in the public goods case whether one is dealing with a limited altruist or with a totally self-interested person.

To determine the amount of altruistically determined charity, we must guess the percentage of income a typical person would give to a single charity for altruistic reasons if he were the sole contributor to charity. Since that last clause is contrary to fact, such a guess is not easy. Fortunately, the guess does not have to be precise. The actual total charity-to-income ratio is an upwardly biased estimate of the hypothetical ratio for a single charity, if for no other reason than people give to many charities. In the United States the actual ratio is less than 3 percent (U.S. Census 1999). As will become obvious below, our case against altruism as the explanation of charity could easily withstand charitable contributions to a single charity in the order of magnitude of 95 percent of income. At that level of giving most donors would become poorer than the beneficiaries they are trying to help. It is not quite clear what actual amount of charity would be produced if this limited altruism were the only source of charity. On the one hand, because of his altruism a person would like to see some charity. On the other hand, because his altruism is limited, he would prefer that others do the contributing. The person would also realize that if others were similarly motivated, the more he contributes to charity, the less others will contribute. The marginal utility of their charitable contributions would fall because this person's charitable contributions would reduce their needs to give to charity.

As in many strategic games, there is no single solution. But, as we shall see below, all the possible solutions are confined to a limited range—somewhere between no charity and some small multiple (in the order of magnitude of 1.03) of the charity that a person who most wants to contribute to charity would contribute if he were the sole contributor to charity.

One possible outcome is no charity. That occurs if everybody simply waits for somebody else to make the first move. However, a person aware of this possible outcome unless he contributes might be willing to make the first move. The most that person will contribute is the amount that makes the marginal utility of his so doing just equal the marginal utility to him of his alternative purchases. But these contributions reduce the incentives of anybody else to make a charitable contribution. The crowding out will not be perfect, as it is in the case of government expenditures that Andreoni (1990) discusses. In the fellow contributors' case other potential donors' real income is increased by one's charitable contributions. Their utility is increased by, say, the poor being better off, because the utility of the poor is in their utility function. These others are, then, faced with the option of giving more to charity (because their utility function would so dictate given their higher income) or waiting for somebody else to do so. The most another person would give would be less than the amount the person who most wants to contribute would give if he were the sole contributor. Suppose this second person does so. That act, then, has the same joint effects as the initial charitable contribution: a crowding out and an increase in real incomes. Others might also give now, but less than they would have given had current donors not given. But they also might wait for others. At most, this process continues until the pool of potential donors is exhausted. We can show that at most the total amount of charitable contributions will be 3 percent more than the greatest amount any one individual would make if nobody else contributed to charity.[3]

Given the indeterminacy associated with the strategic considerations involved in the private provision of a public good, there are other possible solutions. The solution above is the least egalitarian solution among donors. The most egalitarian solution is one where every donor gives the same amount up to the point that their utility is maximized by the amount of their charitable contributions. We can show that the result of this process is approximately the same as the outcome of the least egalitarian solution.[4] This is far less charity than the total contributions to many specific charities that are many times the average income of the actual donors, so necessarily many times the amount that individuals would wish to contribute to charity for altruistic reasons if they were the sole donor. In 1999 the American Red Cross, for example, collected \$817 million in direct donations (American Red Cross 1999). This is thousands of times greater than the average income of its contributors.

Not only do we expect small total contributions to charity if altruism were the total story. We expect even a smaller amount of contributions attributable to altruism if some charity is generated by warm glow, that is, any motivation other than altruism. A contribution from somebody else has the same crowding-out effect on a person's altruistic charitable contributions whether somebody else made his contributions for altruistic or warm-glow motives (with, of course, the same income effects on the altruistic component). The already insignificant amount of charity that could be attributable to altruism will probably become negligible for all reasonable specifications of altruism.[5]

An obvious objection to this analysis is the question, "How can one donor's charity 'crowd out' another's when for most charities donors do not know how much others give?" First of all, crowding out does not require knowledge of individual contributions, just knowledge of total contributions. So the question has to be rephrased in terms of information about the total contributions of a given charity, rather than individual contributions. While ignorance of total contributions among potential donors is also rampant, it need not be. The expense of including that number in a charitable solicitation is minimal. That charities largely do not do so is evidence that potential donors do not demand such inclusion.[6] But if altruism were motivating charitable contributions, we would expect all charities to publicize their total contributions.

For the analysis of this section to be relevant, actual crowding out is not required. The analysis only requires potential crowding out if altruism were important. That potential donors do not care about total contributions is further evidence that altruism is not motivating charity.

This analysis requires the hypothetical charity/income ratio for altruistically motivated charity for a person if nobody else contributed to charity. However, for our estimates we used the actual ratio. The absence of much crowding out because of lack of information strongly suggests that the actual ratio is at most biased downward a minimal amount by crowding out.

There are, indeed, some charities, such as the United Way, that do publicize their total contributions. Even in these cases we believe that these charities are not driven to do so by altruistically motivated donor demand. Charities can have another interest in this publicity. With reputationally motivated charity there is likely to be a "bandwagon" effect rather than "crowding out." Chapter 3 shows that people are sometimes interested in their reputation for trustworthiness *relative* to others. As a result, they want to keep up with others in their charitable contributions. In chapter 3 we develop the necessary theory and present regression evidence that supports the "bandwagon" effect, though, admittedly those tests are not overwhelmingly convincing.

How do we distinguish between donor-demanded disclosure of total contributions for a charity and "bandwagon" reasons for disclosure? For the "bandwagon" effect the important reputational competition is among members of the same group. Donor-demanded disclosure is disclosure about total charitable contributions over all people making contributions. Hence, the "bandwagon" effect predicts disclosure about specific group contributions when such disclosures do not reveal implicitly to others that their group made less contributions. Disclosures about total United Way contributions within a firm fit that bill, since these disclosures are made only to those who work for the firm. So our university tells us what fraction of employees contribute and how much the university has collected, but does not reveal the total contributions in the county.[7]

It should be emphasized that the crowding out whose publicity implications are not observed is the crowding out of one individual's charity in response to another's. This is quite different from the possible crowding out of private charity by government. Our theory of charity developed in chapter 3 predicts big differences between the two phenomena. As chapter 3 shows, the "bandwagon" effect is produced by a reputational contest. Individuals vie with one another to be considered more trustworthy. There is no similar reputational contest between individuals and government.

Economists often test for the proportion of altruism to warm glow by looking at crowding out of private charity by government. They usually find some crowding out and conclude that some substantial part of charity must be due to altruism. But this is not good evidence for the existence of altruism. We will see later that this same sort of crowding out is also consistent with our reputational theory of charity. So the presence of crowding out does not confirm the presence of altruism.

Altruism makes another prediction about charity that is inconsistent with the evidence. If altruism motivated charity, it would pay most individuals to give to only one charity. The contribution of any one individual to any one charity is usually a very small part of total contributions to that charity. As a result, the marginal benefit to the cause of the giver's first dollar of contributions to a charity is virtually the same as the marginal benefit of his last dollar. Suppose, for example, one is providing as much as ten thousand dollars to famine relief in Ethiopia. There are more than ten thousand Ethiopians in approximately the same degree of distress, and a dollar is not going to make that much difference in the marginal utility of dollars to any given Ethiopian.

If, then, a donor were determining his charity by these marginal benefits, it would be in his interest to devote all his dollars to the same cause. The only exception would be the case where his marginal utility of the first dollar from so giving were approximately the same for more than one charity, which one would expect to be a quite unusual occurrence. In fact, people give to many charities—a phenomenon easily explained in terms of the theory developed in chapter 3.

In sum, altruism does not do a very good job of explaining charity.

Altruism versus Self-Interest: Evolution

We have shown in the previous section that if altruism existed, it would not have a significant effect on charity. In this section we show that we would expect evolution to make altruism a very minor phenomenon at best even were there no free-rider problem. That sounds like double kill. But the issue is so important that double kill is well worthwhile.

More importantly, this section also shows that warm glow must be so specified that it is consistent with self-interest in an evolutionary sense.

The paragraph above made an important assumption: that the survival that counts in evolution is individual rather than group survival. Such an assumption accords with the dominant view of sociobiologists that emphasizes individual over group selection. But there is a growing group of sociobiologists who believe that group selection is important.

The advocates of the importance of group selection base their case on the Price equations (Price 1972). In terms of those equations, the amount of group relative to individual selection increases with an increase in two ratios: (1) the ratio of group benefits in survival terms relative to individual benefits in the same terms, and (2) the ratio of intergroup variances in the trait relative to within-group variances. Most of the group selection advocates concede that if groups are just random collections of individuals, then individual selection would dominate because the intergroup variance (a variance of the means) would be small relative to intragroup variances. They find, however, three sources of nonrandomness in the formation of groups.

1. Conformity (Bowles 1998; Boyd and Richardson 1985). There is an obvious self-interest in conformity. But, in criticism, there seems no obvious way in which self-interested conformity generates any behavior that is not self-interested.
2. Assortative interactions (Wilson and Dugatkin 1997). If altruists associated predominantly with altruists, and the relevant group effects are confined to association groups, then one expects group selection to become important. (In terms of the Price equations, the intergroup variance becomes large relative to the intragroup variance.) But altruists will not do as good a job restricting their associations as do self-interested reciprocators. The latter are more motivated to avoid moochers than are altruists, with their love of humanity, including moochers. Not only will self-interested reciprocators do better than altruists in terms of individual survival, but they will form groups with fewer moochers, facilitating group survival of these reciprocators relative to the mixed bag of altruists and moochers.
3. Kin selection (Hamilton 1963). During the hunter-gatherer stage, when man's preferences were evolving, groups were small enough that all members of the group were kin, and so shared genes. Hence, genetic selfishness would generate some

altruism toward members of the group. But can kin selection explain altruism among nonkin, especially nonkin that are strangers to one another? It is this latter kind of altruism that is required if altruism is the motivation for most charity. It would pay hunter-gatherers to vary the altruism by the degree of relationship, rather than treating the group as one homogenous happy family. There surely was far greater altruism within the immediate family than between clan members than between other tribal members than between strangers. It is hard to see how altruism toward strangers can be generated by kin selection.[8]

However, some human and animal behaviors seem difficult to explain except by altruism: volunteer warriors facing high probabilities of death, for example. Two things should be noted, however. First, what one observes is progroup behavior rather than altruism as we define it. As discussed below, there are alternative explanations for progroup behavior. However motivated, though, this progroup behavior would still be bothersome to our approach if it were inconsistent with the evolutionary interests of the individuals engaging in such behavior. But there are genetic returns to warriors: rape and the abduction of women of the enemy and more and better sexual partners within the group. It is not clear, however, that this is enough to compensate genetically for the shorter time period available for the production and raising of children. In any case, we must admit that in terms of the Price equations, there can be circumstances where the group return is so enormous compared to the individual costs, that group selection will operate. The exceptions that we have discussed and these troublesome cases are irrelevant to the issues examined in this book. Charity is not usually defined as aid to relatives and friends.

Self-Interest and Conscience

In the next chapter we develop a simple self-interest explanation for charity. One of the big returns to social interactions is receiving favors from others. To get those favors, one must be considered likely to reciprocate. Charity can increase one's reputation for being trustworthy, that is, likely to reciprocate.

Obviously, reciprocity is not the sole possible return from social interactions. There are emotional returns and costs. We like others to smile at us rather than frown. Yet our emotional responses to others are closely related to the nonemotional consequences of their behavior toward us. A smile from a boss or a spouse is more important emotionally and otherwise than the same expression from a casual acquaintance. In this context, emotionally controlled behavior might very well lead to similar implications as behavior determined only by nonemotional consequences. Of course, emotions might often be nonfunctional, as Elster (1999) maintains. But since neither Elster nor anybody else has derived any implications from such a position, we have no option but to treat such emotions simply as noise, and to hope that a theory that ignores nonfunctional emotions will successfully predict behavior.

An obvious problem with this explanation is the existence of anonymous contributions, which provide no signal to anybody. The magnitude of anonymous charity can be exaggerated, since there usually is somebody, maybe one's spouse, who knows that one has given to charity. But certainly, there are charitable contributions of which very few people are aware.

Moreover, people believe that charity is not simply a response to "what others think." Morgan (1977) asks: "Do you think a person is likely to give more if the amount he gives is made public?" 45 percent answered "Yes," while 29 percent said, "No," with the rest giving equivocal answers. The way the question is phrased assumes that there is something other than reputation involved in charity. The answers suggest that both reputation and something else motivates charity.[9]

More generally, reciprocal activities are not totally explained by simple self-interest, as most economists use that term. Fehr and Gachter (2000) provide an excellent summary. So, for example, they construct a one-shot experimental employer-employee game where it is in a rational employer's interest to pay low wages (because of excess labor supply and low opportunity costs of labor), and in the rational employee's interest to shirk (because they cannot be observed and punished for it). The average employer offers wages above the competitive level and the average employee works more than required to maximize income.

How is almost anonymous charity and the Fehr and Gachter behavior consistent with self-interest evolutionarily defined? Frank (1988) provides one answer. He both explicitly and implicitly uses a conscience concept. His implicit definition is the same as ours: conscience is an internalized desire to follow the social rules even in cases where so doing would be unobserved by others. Such a definition accords with the dominant view of sociologists and social psychologists, for example, Coleman (1990).

Frank sees two possible ways a conscience can help its possessor evolutionarily. First, a conscience might generate an aura that others can detect. In consequence, others will be more likely to trust those with a conscience. Second, a conscience might lead a person to act more in her self-interest than she would otherwise by bringing a future cost into a decision process that might otherwise weight immediate rewards too highly. Without rejecting the first process, we defend the second. Its existence plays an important role in our analysis beyond the role of conscience.

A person's evolutionary self-interest can be served by a conscience only if that interest is not maximized by conscience-free behavior. Self-interest as the behavior posited by economists need not lead to evolutionary self-interest. Look at evolutionary self-interest's stringent demands on behavior. Only the future is of importance (albeit it is the future of past generations).[10] Present consumption has no value in its own right. It is simply productive consumption, contributing to the future: the reproduction of traits.

That is not man's utility function. Our behavior arose out of animal roots where the animal moves toward favorable immediate experiences and away from unfavorable immediate experiences. There is a standard animal solution to this discrepancy between the present as motivator and the future as survival engine: make the immediate experiences favorable that have favorable future consequences. The squirrel need have no sense of the future to squirrel nuts. The instinct is built into what he wants to do in the present.

But such simple solutions take many generations, reducing survival probabilities for some environmental changes. Fortunately, human beings can conceptualize the future. In their thoughtful decisions they explicitly take the future into account. They balance future joys against present joys when the latter have not fully incorporated the former. But this still does not give the future the proper survival weight: everything.

Thoughtful decisions are also hard work, fighting bodily tendencies to simply maximize present utility. Witness the struggles people have to lose weight who have thoughtfully decided that they would be better off if they did so. Both Elster (1984) and Thaler and Shefrin (1981) provide evidence for the existence of this problem.

Conscience also incorporates the future into present decisions. By definition, a conscience makes an individual follow social rules more than he would in its absence. There are two sources of gain to an individual in his following social rules: (1) avoiding the response of others to the individual violating those rules (he might, for example, be ostracized for misbehavior); (2) the evolutionary interests of the individual in following the rules independently of the social response to his behavior.

This second process works for reasons developed in chapter 1 and amplified in chapter 6. In long-run equilibrium there will be a tendency for social rules to maximize group survival. Part of this process of maximizing group survival is to help individuals maximize individual survival, a goal that is only imperfectly achieved by individual decision-making, as we have seen. Social rules that are directed to help the individual rather than society as a whole are designed to protect that individual against present temptation. For example, being "good" by staying away from drugs generates favorable future consequences to the abstainer.

On the other hand, social rules develop to maximize group survival rather than individual survival. By doing what others want or what would serve them, one can act against one's own evolutionary interests. But one's fitness can be maximized by giving conscience the appropriate weight in one's behavior.

Conscience reflects the dual character of social rules. One can feel guilty about not helping others, or one can feel guilty about behavior, like drinking too much alcohol or neglecting one's children, that is harmful to one's long-run interests. Wilson (1993) provides evidence for a connection between beneficent (his sympathy) and future-oriented behavior (his self-control) by way of a conscience. Psychopaths show by their behavior no concern about others, nor do they show any concern about the future.

Conscience has another advantage over thoughtful decision-making. The former is built in to allow it to compete directly with other bases for spontaneous decision-making. The case for a conscience is particularly strong for the hunter-gatherer stage of development, when our innate preferences were formed. Throughout this stage there was close social contact, so that the probability of others actually finding out what one did was extremely high. It paid to assume that they would, in fact, do so and to have such an assumption built into present preferences.

Altruism versus Being "Good"

There are reasons besides those previously discussed to believe that altruism is not an important phenomenon in predicting behavior outside of the kin and friendship relationships that have been previously discussed. It must be stressed, however, that our theoretical needs do not require a demonstration that altruism is insignificant. All we need to show is that altruism is sufficiently unimportant that reputation and conscience have predictive power.

Consider a society trying to determine efficient ways to enforce its rules. It can try to admonish its members to be altruistic or to be "good," that is, follow the social rules. The society is, then, free to impose whatever sanctions it chooses to enforce its will. There are two reasons why a society will choose the "be good" strategy. First, in discussing individual selection we saw that a conscience could promote survival of an individual's genes, whereas altruism was not so conducive. So we would expect a greater built-in predisposition toward being good than being altruistic.

Second, there is a far more serious monitoring problem associated with imposed altruism. When the individual is not being observed by others, he might be bad or not love without loss of social approval. However, even in this case, unobserved badness can often be discovered through observed consequences. The relative monitoring deficiencies of altruism are even greater when others observe a person's behavior. It is obviously easier to observe deeds than emotions. We, therefore, expect greater returns to the individual in "being good" than in being altruistic. These greater returns make it easier for others to convince a person to "be good." In consequence, we would expect society to concentrate on the "be good" strategy.

That proposition can be tested directly. We predict that others will try to influence individual behavior by admonitions to "be good" or to act in an approved way rather than encouragements "to love." Our own unsystematic observations of child rearing support that contention. A nonrandom sample of five mothers, when asked individually, agreed that they used sentences such as, "Be good," "Don't be naughty," "Good girl" much more often than sentences like "Love mommy," "Do not hate Johnny." The probability of chance agreement to such a proposition would be less than 5 percent if this were, indeed, a random sample. These results support common observation. Focusing on this common observation is important, however, because it is inconsistent with the standard views of economists who attempt to explain prosocial behavior by altruism rather than "being good."

Furthermore, altruism is insufficient. One needs the "Be good" rule in any case. For example, tithing was the biblical formula for charity. Jews were encouraged to give between one-tenth and one-fifth of their income to public causes, including charity (Domb 1980), a practice continued in many Christian congregations. The tithing lumps charity to the poor in with religious and other contributions. It is hard to see how altruism by itself could generate a comparison between the well-being of others and religious duties. Obviously, the rules determining how to be good could do so. In general, social rules often involve much more than interpersonal comparisons. For example, "Go to church" and "Salute the flag" were social rules in the old days. Altruism is insufficient to enforce such rules.

There has been considerable emphasis in the literature on social rules. Most of that literature does not concern itself directly with altruism versus warm glow. Neither is relevant if the social rule is enforced by police power. But to affect individual behavior in any other fashion, either altruism or warm glow must operate. Altruism would do the job by the prescription, "Love and, therefore, obey the social rules." In terms of our version of warm glow the social rules would be enforced by, "You will be considered good by others if you follow the rules" or "You will consider yourself good if you do so." Since altruism is irrelevant for a great many social rules, the importance of these rules is significant evidence for the operation of warm glow.

Hoffman and Spitzer (1982) ran an interesting experiment that sheds some light on these issues. Essentially, one person, the controller, decided among alternative payoffs to himself and another person. This decision was made after consulting the other person, who could offer side payments to influence the first person's decisions. This experiment was run under all the combinations of two dichotomous variables. The first variable was how the controller was chosen: in one case by a flip of a coin, in the other case by the winner of a game that required a modicum of skill. The second variable was a moral authority variable. In the no-moral-authority case the instructions specified, "If you win the game (or the coin toss) you are designated controller." In the other, moral authority, case the instructions stated, "If you win the game (or the coin toss) you have earned the right to be controller." Hoffman and Spitzer found significant differences in results between each combination of the variables. The differences were particularly large between the coin toss, no-moral-authority combination and the game, moral-authority option. In the first case 61 percent of the outcomes were nearly equal splits, while in the second case only 32 percent of the choices fell within this range.

This difference in results can be explained by the social rules. One social rule is that it is all right not to share equally money that one has earned. The simple substitution of the word *earned* for *designated* suggests that the experimenters do not regard a nonsharing controller as a bad person. The message that one has "earned" the right to be controller is fortified if, in fact, one has. Winning a game that does not entirely depend upon luck provides a justification for the controller's getting more than his share of the payoff. As we shall see later, there are group survival reasons for both the social rule that encourages sharing and that which provides incentives for effort by larger returns to those who have earned them. These social rules will have an impact on the controller's behavior either through conscience or by the prospects of meeting his fellow player later.

In contrast, altruism does not explain this behavior. Clearly, altruism cannot explain the differences in behavior among options. As far as altruism itself is concerned, all the options are the same, yet there are exceedingly large differences in outcomes between these options.

Even more importantly, the overwhelming altruism required to explain the dominance of equal sharing in the no-moral-authority, coin-tossing game is unbelievable. The payoffs in these experiments are small relative to the incomes of the participants, and controllers have the same average income as the other players prior to the experimental payoffs. In consequence, controllers would have approximately the same income as their fellow players after the payoffs even if these controllers kept all of the gains in the game for themselves. To get equal sharing by way of altruism under these circumstances requires controllers' decisions to give the same weight to the utility of their fellow player as they give to themselves.[11] Yet 61 percent of the controllers behaved in this saintly way. However the rule of equal sharing arose, it is clear that it is not altruism that is enforcing that rule. Rather it is some combination of externalized and internalized returns to following social rules.

It should be emphasized that this particular experiment is one in which the players communicate with one another. There is less egalitarianism in experiments with no communication between players (Ostrom 2000). Altruism cannot explain that difference. Wanting the approval of your fellow player can.

There is a rather interesting contrast in the behavior of economists and others that cannot be simply explained by altruism differentials. Beginning with Marwell and Ames (1981), many studies look at prisoner's dilemma games where cooperating and cheating are the options and simple self-interest is maximized by the cheating. They find that economics students cheat more than do others. Frank, Gilovich, and Regan (1993) confirm this. (They also show that after an economics course students give higher subjective estimates that both they and others will not return clearly marked envelopes with cash to their rightful owners or will not pay the full amount rather than a clearly understated invoice.)[12] However, Laband and Beil (1999) show that economists do not cheat more than political scientists and cheat less than sociologists in voluntarily paying income-based dues to the American Economic, Political Science, or Sociology Associations, respectively. Altruism would not produce this difference in behavior for economists relative to others in the Maxwell and Ames and the Laband and Beil cases. But a desire to follow the "rules of the game" will. Economists are often taught that self-interested behavior in business or business-like games is all right. Others are often taught the opposite. Neither economists nor others are taught that lying is all right or that not voting or failure to give to charity is acceptable behavior. None of this evidence demonstrates that altruism among nonkin, nonfriends does not exist. The evidence does show, however, that altruism by itself cannot explain the behavior examined. Something else is required. It is this "something else" on which this book focuses.

Palfrey and Prisbrey (1997), however, run experiments in which they observe no altruism effect. Players are given the option of contributing however much they like to a public good, which is the equally shared product of a fund to which all who wish can contribute. Palfrey and Prisbrey vary both the sacrifice required of the players to contribute to the public good and the productivity of the public good, that is, how much a dollar contribution translates into a return to all players. They find that players are willing to make sacrifices for the public good, but that contributions do not increase with increases in the productivity of the public good except to the extent that the player's own returns are a function of this productivity. (In their experiments group size is sufficiently small that there is a significant return to the player from his own public good's contribution.) Since altruism predicts this latter relationship, they conclude that no altruism is observed where it should be observed if it existed.

However, it should be noted that players within any one experiment do not have the option of choosing between public goods. Since there is a social rule, "Help others," one expects some tendency for higher productivity public goods to be chosen more frequently than less productive public goods. This seeming "altruism" is perfectly consistent with no real altruism, as observed by Palfrey and Prisbrey.

Brandts and Schram (2001) get similar results. Again, altruism has no impact on contributions. However, they show that contributions to public goods are also increased by an increase in returns from reciprocity. Since reciprocity plays a fundamental role in our analysis, this finding is of some importance.

There are, however, social psychologists who do believe that there is some altruism. But most of them concede that there is some helping behavior that cannot be explained without warm glow, and they do not provide any evidence that warm glow is not important. And because of the free-rider problem, none of their tests are relevant to the charitable or political behavior that we examine in this book.[13]

Reciprocity and Other Social Pressure

Most people are aware at least to some extent that social pressure is one of the determinants of charitable contributions, as revealed in the Morgan (1977) data previously discussed. That social pressure can take several forms. Eskimos were willing to kill the nongenerous (Posner 1980). Ostracism of those who broke social rules was also frequently practiced in primitive societies. Yet we concentrate on a particular form of punishment—refusal to engage in reciprocity.

The reason for this focus is that the information requirements for the other punishments of the noncharitable are rarely satisfied in modern society. The information requirements to make them work are much more severe than the requirements for trustworthy signaling. One is much more likely to know that another person has contributed to a particular charity than that a person has made no charitable contributions at all. The latter knowledge is required for ostracism to operate, while the former knowledge is all that is usually required for charity signaling to work. Ivan's charitable contribution that signals that he wishes to be friends with John is the charitable contribution that John is most likely to know about—a charity that both are interested in. However, to ostracize a person for being noncharitable demands that one knows that the person hasn't made the required charitable contributions among all possible charities. That knowledge existed in closely knit primitive communities for the prosocial acts that were the equivalent of today's charity, but is rare in modern societies.

There is one case, however, where ostracism will be quite common in present societies: ostracism for antisocial acts as opposed to prosocial acts. That ostracism can be triggered by knowledge of a single antisocial act, so one does not need to know the whole history of a person to practice ostracism. For example, Parnell led boycotts of Irish landlords in the 1880s, and his movement ostracized those who did not participate (Keneally 1998); and people are likely to avoid pedophiles even when they have no young children.

We will assume, henceforth, that the social pressure encouraging charity in modern societies is simply the response of others' reciprocity decisions to that charity. There is, however, an important role for ostracism and other punishments in our analysis. In chapter 1 we saw how group survival would be a crucial determinant of operational social rules. But in our analysis of charity in the next chapter we use group selection only in one way: to determine the beneficiaries of charity. The amount of charity produced by signaling is not determined by group selection. In the model of chapter 3 that amount is uniquely determined by individual behavior. However, in primitive societies group selection can operate through determining the extent of the other punishments of not following the social rules—ostracism and violence.

CHAPTER 3

Charity and Reciprocity

Can Reputation Explain Charity?

This chapter contains a simple reputational model of charity. That model not only applies to charity as usually defined but to voting participation, which we examine in the next chapter. Both are cases of socially approved behavior, and both involve costs to participants. A reputation for good deeds requires others to know about them. Relatively few people know about many donations, and fewer still about the voting participation of others. How, then, can charity or voting participation enhance reputation?

Glazer and Konrad (1996) provide evidence of the reputational character of charity when charitable contributions are known. They find that the proportions of donors who make anonymous contributions to charities is exceedingly small, between 0.2 and 1 percent. They also find that when charitable contributions are published by size category, contributions tend to be near the minimum amount necessary to get into a category. Consider the contributions to a fund established by the Cameron Clan at Carnegie Mellon University for 1988–89 and published as donations in the $1,000–$4,999 category. Of the eighty-two contributions, fifty-six (68 percent) gave exactly $1,000. Another seventeen (21 percent) gave contributions somewhere between $1,000 and $1,100. In contrast only four gave between $900 and $1,000 and thus got published in the $500–$999 category. (The average size of the gift in the latter category was $525.) Similarly, the 1993–94 Harvard Law School Fund reported that of those in the $500–$999 category, 93 percent gave exactly $500.

Lying

Additional direct evidence that charity has a reputational effect is that people often lie about their charity. People would not lie about their charity unless they were concerned about what others think. For example, if people gave to charity solely for altruistic reasons, there would be no return to them from others believing that their charitable contributions were larger than they actually were. Yet Parry and Crossley (1950) found that of a sample of 920, 34 percent said that they had given to the Community Chest but were not listed as donors in the Community Chest files. That is a lot of lying.

It is conceivable, of course, that the sole reason for lying in this case is to get smiles rather than frowns from others. But as discussed in chapter 2, those smiles must be more important when they are associated with other favorable consequences. As the analysis of this chapter shows, it makes sense for people to do more than smile at charitable donors. They will behave in a more trusting manner toward them. Indeed, one suspects that the smiles themselves are produced by a belief in the greater trustworthiness of donors. Both the emotional response to an act and concern with that emotional response will be at least somewhat related to the nonemotional consequences of each. As discussed in chapter 2, in modern societies the important nonemotional payoff to what others think is in acquiring reciprocity partners. In consequence, lying does provide evidence that charity yields a reputational return in terms of more or better reciprocity partners.

In the Parry and Crossley study there also were a lot of people, 31 percent, who did not give to Community Chest and who admitted that fact. This latter result suggests a cost to lying even under circumstances, such as those in the study, where the probability of being unmasked is virtually zero. The source of that cost is conscience, discussed in chapter 2. Can anybody doubt that there is a social rule, "Thou shalt not lie," and that conscience is the internalization of such rules?

Furthermore, the standard catchall explanation for any prosocial activity, altruism, will not work here. Just as altruism cannot explain a return to lying, it cannot explain not lying when there is a return to lying. As discussed in chapter 2, altruists, if they exist, must be limited altruists, ones who in valuing the utility of others value their own utility more. They, therefore, would not engage in any activity that harmed themselves more than it benefited others. But seemingly, not lying about not contributing to charity harms the would-be liar more than it benefits his listener.

The costs of lying have been documented. The whole basis for the polygraph test is the visible discomfort—sweat, and so forth—generated by lying.

If there were no costs of lying, one could explain this combination of liars and nonliars by hypothesizing that there also was no return to lying. People would, then, be indifferent between lying and nonlying, and some random process would determine their behavior. But this story is contradicted by the other obvious finding in the Parry and Crossley study. There were no cases of giving to charity and then lying about it. On the "no return, no cost" theory of lying, there should be little or no difference between the lying behavior of charitable donors and nondonors. The totality of Parry and Crossley's results can only be explained by some kind of reputational gain from charity and a cost to lying.

There is similar evidence on lying about voting participation, another behavior with individual costs. Three different methods have been used to estimate the amount of this lying, with substantially different results. The first technique compared actual voter participation to self-reported voter participation of the same group of voters. There was some uncertainty associated with this procedure because it was impossible to determine whether a small group of the self-reported voters actually voted. (This was because of lack of cooperation on the part of local election officials.) Ignoring that group, Harbaugh (1996), using data from Miller (1989), estimated that the percentage of nonvoters who claimed they voted in the 1988 general election was 25 percent with a sample size of seven hundred nonvoters. If the group whose voting was undeterminable were counted as nonvoters, that percentage went up to 28.4 percent. Counting that same group as nonvoters, Silver, Anderson, and Abramson (1986) got lying rates for nonvoters between 27.6 percent and 31.4 percent for the 1964, 1978, and 1980 presidential elections and 22.6 percent for the nonpresidential elections of 1976.

In contrast, Bernstein, Chadha, and Montjoy (2001) estimated the lying rate for each of the presidential elections between 1972 and 1996 to vary between 38 percent and 45 percent. They used the percentage of respondents who reported voting from the National Election Studies (also used by Harbaugh and by Silver, Anderson, and Abramson), comparing this percentage to the percentage of the total age-eligible population actually voting. This procedure has the advantage of avoiding determining whether the small group of uncertain reported voters actually voted. However, there is a real problem with the Bernstein, Chadha, and Montjoy procedure that is produced by a peculiarity of the National Election Studies. The same people who are asked after the election whether they voted are asked before the election whether they intend to vote, and they know in advance of voting that they are likely to be asked afterward whether they voted. Either case produces an increase in the expected cost of lying if one does not vote and says that one has either voted or will vote. In these cases the lie is certainly required, while in other cases it is less certain at the time of voting whether one will be asked whether one has voted or has been asked whether one will vote. This extra expected cost of lying can be avoided by actually voting. This cost of lying not only affects verbal behavior, but changes voting behavior so that lies are not required to avoid embarrassment. In 1988, 60 percent of the respondents to the National Election Study actually voted as compared to a 50 percent national voting rate. Later, in chapter 8, we will use this property of lies.

There is yet one more technique to estimate the lying percentage for nonvoters: to compare the actual total percentage of nonvoters to the percentage of people who are asked after the fact whether they have voted or not. For the four presidential elections between 1976 and 1988 the percentage of lying nonvoters as determined by this technique varied between 11.7 and 12.9 percent (U.S. Census 1992). There is an obvious explanation for the difference between these results and produced by the other methods. The culprit is the same peculiarity of the National Election Studies noted earlier. In the latter those who were asked whether they voted or not were already asked whether they intended to vote. This not only increases their actual voting rates, but it increases the number of respondents who lie about having voted. Initially, saying that one intended to vote might very well increase the embarrassment of admitting later to the same organization that one did not vote. For the census data 7.4 percent of the voting-age population lied about voting in 1988, while for the National Election Studies data, 10 percent of that population lied. Both the increase in nonvoters and the decrease in liars for the census data compared to the National Election Studies imply that the ratio of the latter to the former will be smaller for the census data.

If this peculiarity of the National Election Studies is the explanation for the difference between it and the census results, then the census results provide a more accurate estimate of the amount of lying in the National Opinion Research Center (NORC) data set we use. Just as in the census case, NORC only asks voters after the fact whether they voted, and voters cannot anticipate when they vote that they will be asked. In consequence, neither their vote nor their statement about whether they voted will be influenced by having previously been asked whether they expect to vote.

Harbaugh (1996) proposes an explanation for these results that is similar to our own. The incentive to vote, he believes, is the praise one can obtain from others. That is also the incentive for falsely claiming that one voted.

Even with the lies, statements about voter participation and charitable contributions can provide an alternative route to information. People do not have to observe actual behavior. They can place a limited amount of credence in people's assertions about their behavior. Lying about charity or voter participation can only have reputational value to the liar if others believe it has reputational value. That belief is sustainable only if the set of people, liars and nonliars, who say they voted or gave to charity are on average more trustworthy than the truth tellers who did not vote or give to charity. But even with this expansion of the relevant information, there will probably still be many cases where one's charitable contributions and voting participation are known at most to a very limited set of people.

Conscience and Reputation Variables

We, however, do not wish to confine our interest to the charity and voter participation of which people are aware. We test our reputation theory against data on all individual charity and all voter participation. How can a reputation theory be applicable to these broader categories? Reputations cannot be increased by anonymous behavior. We maintain, however, that the same variables that are relevant in determining known charity and voter participation can also affect anonymous versions of these activities, through their impact on conscience, the driving force behind anonymous good deeds.

We do not have the same confidence in this proposition that we have in the applicability of the reputation model for known good deeds. The simple self-interest model that works in the latter case does not work for conscience, by definition, and we are unaware of any systematic attempt to determine the properties of conscience. We either try to understand, at least to some extent, how conscience works or abandon all efforts to explain anonymous good deeds. An alternative is to simply ignore anonymous charity while purportedly predicting total charity, as does Posner (2000).

There are two dimensions to conscience: (1) the social rules that are internalized by a conscience, (2) the importance attached to the social rules or how good or bad a person feels if he does or does not follow those rules. There are two obvious processes that help determine how individuals will vary by those dimensions: positive and negative reinforcement and indoctrination.

For the first, the greater the cost one has suffered in violating a social rule or the greater the rewards one has experienced in following a social rule in the past, the greater the internalized desire to follow the social rules now. But these costs and returns will be higher the more one gained from reciprocity in the past. Conscience produces a lagged response to reputational variables. But for most of those variables we only know current values, which, however, are positively related to past values. In consequence, conscience, as well as reputation, will produce an empirical relationship between those current reputational variables and prosocial behavior.

This process would be quite likely to work for a specific social rule under specific circumstances. "Do not lie when one is likely to be caught." But we also expect it to be generalized, perhaps with less intensity, to lying in general or even to following social rules in general. To the extent that reinforcement produces this response of following social rules in general, we expect reputational variables to successfully predict behavior that conforms to the social rules, even under circumstances of limited information. Even when others do not know of one's behavior, reputational variables can explain prosocial rule behavior.

Wilson (1993) shows that psychopaths, who obviously have no conscience when it comes to the well-being of others, also have little concern with the future. As discussed in chapter 2, social rules encourage concern with the future as well as concern about others. That conscience about such disparate social rules vary together suggests that following social rules in one context increases the probability that one will follow other social rules.

The other determinant of conscience, indoctrination, is produced by either the behavior or language of one's parents and close associates. The more one's parents, say, follow the social rules and admonish one to follow those rules, the greater the conscience return to that person in so doing. One predictor of the importance of a conscience to a person is the frequency of such parental activity. Parents follow the social rules more frequently the greater their reputation return in so doing and the more important conscience to them. The latter in turn depends in part upon the behavior of their parents, and so forth.

There are several important consequences. First, a conscience is in part the result of parental reputational signaling in the past. Since, however, there is a positive relationship between parental and one's own characteristics, conscience leads to the same predictions about the impact of one's own characteristics on charitable contributions when parental characteristics are unspecified or incompletely specified.

Second, a conscience has a more general component to it than reputational signaling itself. When a parent follows a social rule, the child learns more than a particular social rule. She also learns that it is important to follow social rules. In consequence, the greater the reputational return to parents in following social rules where others can observe that behavior, the higher the probability that the child will observe not only that rule, but rules for which compliance is difficult to observe. In particular, we would predict that parents who have high reputational returns are more likely to have children who give to charity even when those gifts are not observed.

Third, this parental role in conscience provides a test of the effect of reputational variables on conscience. If conscience increases with parental reputational signaling, then charity and voting participation should increase with an increase in any parental reputational variable. As we see later, the model developed in this chapter implies that education is a reputational variable. In the voting participation regressions of chapter 4 we do find a positive relationship of voting participation to the only parental reputational variables for which there is data—father's and mother's education. (For the charity regressions parental variables are not available.)

Wilson (1993) provides supporting evidence of both the proposition that parents are crucial in producing consciences and that part of that production is nonspecific, that is, parents produce a general sense of duty in addition to targeting it to particular activities. Those who sheltered Jews against the Nazi's were close to parents who emphasized the importance of dependability, self-reliance, and caring for others, though the care they had in mind could not have been specifically sheltering Jews from the Holocaust.

That conscience usually applies to all the social rules has another important consequence. In this chapter we show that if charity is simply motivated by self-interest, it will pay others to treat charity as a signal for trustworthiness. But we also believe that charity motivated wholly or in part by conscience generates a sign to the same effect. Indeed, the possession of a conscience increases the willingness of others to reciprocate because they need not monitor the reciprocity as closely. A conscience increases the probability that a person will reciprocate even if one cannot find out whether they have done so.

A curious problem is produced because conscience motivated charity increases a person's trustworthiness more than does charity designed explicitly to so signal. Those who give for reputational reasons will want to disguise their reason for so doing. Hence, such people usually do not talk about their charity because talk would be reputation- rather than conscience-driven. At the same time reputational signalers will want others to know that they have contributed. The solution is for beneficiaries to do the publicity either by publishing a list of contributors or by selecting neighbors or coworkers as solicitors.

This limits considerably the amount of information coming to others from a person's own statements about his charity. We saw earlier that this was useful information. There seems to be no similar social restriction on people revealing that they voted. Indeed, that must be virtually the only way others find out about voting participation. Perhaps that is one of the reasons for this relative lack of modesty for voter participation. Blowing one's own horn is the only way it will be blown.

The Miller (1989) study of lies in voter participation provides a test of a sort for the relationship of reputational variables to conscience. The reputational return from voting and lying about voting are the same, assuming that the probability of the lie's being detected is virtually zero, as it is in surveys by strangers. The two behaviors differ in three respects: the cost of voting, the conscience returns from actually voting, and the conscience costs of lying. Holding the first cost constant, any increase in the conscience returns from voting and in the conscience costs of lying increases the probability of voting. If the proportion of actual votes to lies about votes increases with a variable, conscience increases with that variable. Miller finds that the proportion of those who actually voted to those who falsely claimed that they voted is increased by increases in education, which in turn is positively related to the returns to reputation. Hence, conscience increases with that reputational variable.

The problem with this test is that education could have effects on voting participation other than through reputation. That problem could be mitigated if this same test could be run on all of the reputational variables that we later identify. Consistent results for all of these variables would, then, be a convincing test. Unfortunately, we do not have the data for this more rigorous testing. What we have provided might be regarded more as an agenda for a test, rather than a test itself. Still the evidence is at least mildly encouraging.

Bernstein, Chadha, and Montjoy (2001) provide data that permit another test for the impact of reputational variables on conscience.[1] They compare regressions explaining respectively actual and self-reported voting participation by variables that are either directly or indirectly reputational variables. For most reputational variables one cannot predict the sign of that difference because of the conflict of two forces. On the one hand, the cost of lying increases with an increase in a reputational variable, since lying is a violation of the social rules. On the other hand, the reputational return from lying increases, since the returns from others believing that one has voted increase. There is, however, a set of reputational variables that should have no effect on the cost of lying: those variables that are specific to the reputation associated with voting participation but not related to reputational returns from other behavior including lying. Bernstein, Chadha, and Montjoy (2001) provide three such variables: (1) partisanship, whether one were a strong Democrat or Republican compared to being a weak partisan or independent, (2) contact, whether anybody has urged one to vote or not, (3) non–Deep South, the Deep South has been a region where there is and has been a lower percentage of closely contested general elections (lags play a significant role in the behavior about which we are concerned). All of these variables increase or decrease the reputational return from voting. They all affect the interest of one's associates in whether one voted or not. But there is no obvious reason why a partisan, for example, should have a greater cost of lying. Hence, all these variables should have a bigger coefficient for reported votes than for actual votes. And they do: (1) partisanship, .049; (2) contact, .103; (3) non–Deep South, .175.

Since the reputational cost of lying operates in the direction opposite from the reputational returns from doing so, reputational variables that affect the cost of lying as well as the returns from doing so should have either smaller differences in coefficients for reported and actual voting than the three coefficients just discussed or even negative differences between those coefficients. Bernstein, Chadha, and Montjoy (2001) provide four such variables: (1) education, since those with greater education discount the future less, and this discount rate is an important determinant of reputational returns; (2) church attendance, since as discussed later, number of friends increases with church attendance; (3) nonblacks; (4) non-Hispanics, since Bernstein, Chadha, and Montjoy do not include in their analysis important reputational variables such as income and occupation that are negatively correlated with both blacks and Hispanics.[2] All of these variables do, indeed, have smaller differences measured algebraically than do any of the three previous variables: (1) education, .039; (2) church attendance, .011; (3) nonblack, −.175; (4) non-Hispanic, −.071. The probability of all of these coefficients being smaller than the three previous coefficients by chance is .028. So it does appear that the conscience costs of lying are significantly affected by reputational variables that are not focused on a single activity such as voting participation. This is some evidence that reputational variables do increase the role of conscience.

Reputation seeking and conscience have more in common than the role of reputational variables in explaining their respective intensities. On both counts one follows the social rules. On both counts one is not *directly* concerned with the consequences to others. The relevant consequences of one's actions are the consequences to oneself—one's reputation for, or one's self-assessment of, trustworthiness. To keep things simple in the theory that follows, we ignore conscience and focus exclusively on the direct reputational returns to prosocial rule behavior. But one must remember that that theory works empirically as well as it does because conscience yields similar predictions. Even our empirical use of conscience is limited—largely confined to our discussions of lying behavior and lagged variables.

A Comparison of Approaches

We assume that a person gives to charity to signal that he is trustworthy. Ours is not the first analysis to focus on the signaling characteristics of charity. Glazer and Konrad (1996) developed a signaling theory of charity, where a person's income is that which is signaled. They present substantial evidence for signaling, but none for income's referent role beyond the rather uninteresting positive correlation of charity and income. Income's referent role is questionable for the bulk of charity. For charity with localized collectors the people who know one's charity will know one's standard kinds of conspicuous consumption, such as house values, that are much more highly correlated with income than the specific charitable contributions of which they are aware. If charity signals, it has to signal something for which more conspicuous, cheaper alternatives are not available. Trustworthiness qualifies as such a referent.

Most people give to more than one charity, and, in consequence, there will be few who know all of a person's charitable contributions. The relationship of a family's total charity to its income is far from perfect. The relationship of a specific contribution to that income will be orders of magnitude less. That is not a problem if trustworthiness is the referent. People are interested not in a person's general trustworthiness, but in how much she can be trusted in a relationship with them. A specific charity provides information to specific people no matter how small the relationship between that specific charity and the total.

There is a common view that charity is responsive to social pressure (Morgan 1977). The analysis of signaling has advantages over a more general social pressure model. (1) Signaling explains why people care enough to change their behavior toward you if you give to charity. (2) Our signaling model has more testable implications than an unspecified social pressure model.

Define trustworthiness as the probability that a person will reciprocate a favor. As we shall see, this probability is increased by the person's previously doing a favor. Why should a person resort to charity to signal trustworthiness when he could do so by directly doing another person a favor? There are two reasons why charity will *sometimes* be the preferred signal. (1) Charity often signals trustworthiness to a larger group of people than does a favor for a single person because the latter could be motivated by a special relationship not relevant to others. (2) Doing favors for somebody is not always a viable option. People want favors when they want them and from whom they want them. Receiving a favor has a cost in the form of either having to reciprocate or developing a reputation as a moocher. In contrast, charity places no obligations on the person receiving the information about one's trustworthiness. Hence charity is always an available option to increase one's trustworthiness.

Reciprocity

Given our hypothesis, one cannot understand charity unless one understands its referent: trustworthiness in reciprocal relationships. Nearly all human interactions involve some degree of trust. Even transactions in perfectly competitive markets provide opportunities for fraud and opportunism, and economists have begun to recognize that trust is important in such relationships. Trust is especially important in nonmarket transactions with a time dimension. John might need Ivan's help today, but Ivan might want John's help tomorrow. To get any return from his favor Ivan must trust John.

Why should Ivan help John in the first place? Doing somebody a favor both increases the probability that (1) he will do you a favor and (2) that others will do so. Now, we focus on only the first by assuming that nobody else knows about the favor. We look at the second in the charity case, since it is the basis of returns to that activity.

We develop a mathematical model of reciprocity in appendix 1. The essence of the model and its conclusions are straightforward. The most crucial characteristic of the reciprocity we examine is nonsimultaneity.

Favors are given in one period with the hope, but not the guarantee, that they will be reciprocated in the next period. The game is started by somebody asking another person chosen at random for a favor. People know the relevant characteristics of the distribution of others, but they do not know individual characteristics.

Though reciprocity is a relationship between two players, we assume that each player has many potential partners, so that no player will continue dealing with another player if he expects to do better by choosing another potential partner at random. This assumption accords with reality, and it vastly simplifies the analysis. Maximizing behavior when one is forced to deal either with a single potential partner or not deal at all is quite complicated. How many refusals to reciprocate on the part of a potential partner should lead one to refuse to do a favor oneself?

An individual can choose between several alternative "trustworthiness categories" listed from the lowest to the highest. (There are some other options that we do not include because they never will be chosen.) He can be a nonplayer, that is, he neither asks for nor does a favor. He can be a moocher, that is, he asks for a favor, but he never does a favor either in reciprocation or otherwise. He can be a reciprocator, that is, he reciprocates favors done by others but will not do a favor for somebody who has not previously done him one. Finally, he can be a favor initiator, one who both reciprocates favors done by others and is willing to do favors to those who have not previously done him a favor.

In terms of our model, these choices do not depend upon variation in moral superiority person to person. (Our model ignores the role of conscience.) Which category a person chooses depends both on individual characteristics and these same characteristics for the group upon whom he is depending for favors. These characteristics are the gain from receiving a favor (g), the cost of giving a favor (c), and the rate of time preference (r). The relevance of the first two characteristics for individual decisions is obvious. The rate of time preference is important because of the nonsimultaneity between favors received and favors given. One is more likely to give a favor now in the hopes of receiving a favor later the less one discounts the future.

These characteristics for the group are also important to the individual because his decision to do somebody a favor depends upon the probability of that favor being reciprocated. That probability in turn is a function of the individual characteristics that determine whether somebody will be a moocher or not.

There is an obvious result, but one upon which all our other results depend. Suppose Ivan does John a favor and asks John to reciprocate the favor in the next period, but John refuses. John is a moocher. If John were to ask Ivan for a favor in the subsequent period, Ivan would refuse not because Ivan is indignant, though indignant he well might be. The individual characteristics that made John a moocher in the previous period would be likely to make him a moocher in subsequent periods. Ivan can do better than depend upon John for future favors. He can ask at random for a favor and have a higher probability of receiving one.

John, of course, knows better than to ask Ivan for a favor. He will ask somebody else. Since in our model his reputation except to Ivan is unsullied, John has as good a chance of receiving a favor as anybody else asking a new person for a favor.

But there still is a cost to being a moocher. It is this cost that leads some self-interested people not to mooch. No special virtue is required to be trustworthy. John has a lower probability of a favorable response from others than John would have had with Ivan if John had previously reciprocated Ivan's favor. In the latter case, Ivan would with certainty continue granting favors to John, assuming that Ivan's characteristics had not changed in the meantime. Ivan was willing to do John a favor when he was not sure whether John was a moocher or not. He must certainly be willing to do him a favor now that he has detected that John does not mooch. Once a reciprocity partnership has been established, it persists.

This same pattern of behavior also explains why somebody might be a favor initiator rather than simply a reciprocator in spite of the higher costs of the former. The higher costs are obvious. The favor initiator is taking a greater chance that he is doing a favor to a moocher. The reciprocator, in contrast, knows with whom he is dealing. He can do a favor with confidence that it will be reciprocated. But that lower cost means that there will be some people who are reciprocators in addition to those who are favor initiators. A favor initiator will have his favor reciprocated if his potential partner is either a favor initiator or a reciprocator. A reciprocator will get a favor only if he is lucky enough to ask a favor initiator. In consequence, the probability of getting a favor is higher for a favor initiator than a reciprocator before a partnership has been established. After a partnership has been formed, it makes no difference whether a person was initially a favor initiator or a reciprocator.

To see the essential result from our model, allow individual gains from a favor (g) to vary among individuals and treat the cost of giving a favor (c) and the rate of time preference (r) as constant for the group. High-g individuals will be favor initiators; the next highest g's will characterize reciprocators; the g of moochers will be lower but positive; and people will be nonplayers if their g is less than o. An individual in deciding her strategy compares the discounted value of costs and gains. But since costs per favor and discount rates are constant, individuals are only differentiated by gains per favor. Since the returns to being in a higher "trustworthiness" category are increases in the probability of receiving a favor, those individuals with more to gain per favor will choose a higher "trustworthiness" category, holding constant the other parameters. Under similar circumstances those with lower costs and with lower discount rates will also choose higher "trustworthiness" categories.

Charity: Theory

Suppose there were a way to advertise at some cost that a person was either a favor initiator or a reciprocator. Favor initiators and reciprocators gain more from reciprocity than do moochers. Hence, they can afford to engage in more costly advertising than can moochers to convince others that they are what they say they are. This kind of advertising is available: charity. In other words, the level of charity can be used as a signal of one's trustworthiness. As has been well established in the literature (Spence 1973), for example, people can signal even when they are not aware that they are so doing. All that is required in our case is that charity givers are aware that people are more willing to be reciprocity partners with them the more they contribute to charity and that others are aware that they get better reciprocity partners from charity givers than from others. In other words people only have to be aware of the returns to them that are a function of their own behavior. In our case the results will be exactly the same whether people know what governs others' responses or not.[3]

Favors to John are not the only way that Ivan's reputation can increase to John, though we define Ivan's reputation to John as John's assessment of the probability that Ivan will behave to benefit John in response to John's helping Ivan. Anything that Ivan does that increases this probability increases his reputation to John. In appendix 2 we show that charity has that effect on one's reputation.

There are two possible signaling equilibria. We look at only one of these: where others believe that charity of a given amount C is being used as a signal for trustworthiness. We then show in our simple model that that belief is confirmed only for the appropriate C. The other equilibrium is where nobody believes that charity is a signal. Under those circumstances nobody has an incentive to use it as such. There is no equilibrium where some believe that charity signals and some do not so believe. One or another of those two groups must be wrong.

Why should the belief in charity as a signal arise in the first place? There is a natural evolution that could generate this belief. Start with the simple reciprocity that was previously analyzed. Now introduce others observing these reciprocities. It is reasonable to suppose that these others would prefer to do a favor for somebody who has done a favor to a third person compared to somebody who has been a moocher. The mathematics of the appendices bear that supposition out. Hence, being a favor initiator or a reciprocator has reputational returns beyond the returns in any particular relationship.

For two reasons, these reputational returns are higher the lower the probability that favors will be reciprocated within a given relationship. First, within the specific relationship a favor giver requires a higher gain from reciprocity in order to compensate for the greater risk of mooching from others. This greater gain makes him a more likely reciprocator to others. Second, the lower the direct expected gain from reciprocity, the greater the reputational gain must be to justify favor initiating. As we shall see, the greater the reputational gains one gets, the more reliable a person will be as a reciprocity partner to others. If one adopts a strategy of favor initiating with those who almost necessarily will not return it and who everybody knows are almost necessarily unable to do so, one can maximize one's reputational returns from favor initiating. Favors to the destitute are manifestations of such a strategy, and such favors are the primordial form of charity, which is nothing but favor giving where lack of reciprocating returns is a certainty.

Apart from this natural evolution from reciprocity to charity, there is another reason why we expect to see the signaling equilibrium with positive charity in contrast to a signaling equilibrium where charity is zero because others do not believe that charity signals trustworthiness. Charity contributes to group survival. We shall argue in detail in chapter 6 that redistribution of income to the poor increases group survival. Charity is one way to get that redistribution. Furthermore, as we shall immediately see, charity as a signal separates reciprocators from moochers. In consequence, people will be more likely to initiate favors. More reciprocation can take place with a resulting increase in group survival.

In appendix 2 we develop the charity model. We assume that people who are asked to give favors know with certainty the amount of charity that the would-be favor recipient or initiator has contributed. We also assume that individuals vary only in one of the three characteristics entering their decisions, their gain per favor, g, their costs per favor, c, or their discount rate, r.

Under those circumstances there is a unique amount of charity, C, that will just separate moochers from everybody else if others believe that that charity so separates. That charity level will be what the moocher can gain from reciprocity if people thought he was a reciprocator before he showed his true colors by not reciprocating. No moocher has an incentive to hide his true colors at C. Since the moocher gains nothing from a lower price, he gives nothing to charity.

However, reciprocators and favor initiators do have an incentive to pay C so that they will not be considered moochers. This is where the results of the previous section come in. Both favor-initiators and reciprocators gain more from reciprocation than do moochers, so they are willing to pay a higher price than moochers to gain access to reciprocity; that higher price is C. C will, indeed, be required to participate in reciprocity. Nobody will do a favor to somebody they are sure is a moocher. Since all other favor initiators and reciprocators pay C, a would-be reciprocator will not be selected unless he pays C to charity.

In this charity model the probability of a person's reciprocating a favor when he receives one initially from a favor initiator is dramatically different from that probability given simple reciprocity. Since the favor initiator will only give favors to favor initiators or reciprocators given charity, he is certain that his favor will be reciprocated. That probability is now 1, the same probability that a reciprocator faces of having his favor reciprocated by a favor initiator in the subsequent period. Since bygones are bygones, reciprocators act as if they were favor initiators when it is their turn to give a favor. This means that the minimum gain required to be a favor initiator will be the same as the minimum gain required to be a reciprocator, as verified by the equations in appendix 2. All reciprocators will also be favor initiators.

The amount of charity, C, given by each reciprocator or favor initiator is independent of the mix of favor initiators, reciprocators, nonplayers, and moochers in the group. In the reciprocity model previously discussed individual behavior depends very much on that mix. The reason for this difference is easy to see. In reciprocity that mix enters into determining two key probabilities: the probability of receiving a favor if one asks and the probability of having a favor that one gives reciprocated. In the simple charity model, one only asks favors from favor initiators or reciprocators and one only gives favors to that set. Hence moochers and nonplayers are irrelevant. Since all reciprocators are favor initiators in the simple charity model, that distinction is also irrelevant. The only group characteristic that enters into individual decisions is the proportion of partnerless favor initiators compared to the total number of favor initiators. (In our model the only favor initiators who will respond favorably to a request for a favor are those who do not already have a partner.) That proportion does not depend upon the "trustworthiness" mix of the group. In the steady state it is determined simply by the rate of entry and exit out of the group.

While the charity per reciprocator does not depend on the "trustworthiness" mix, total charitable contributions from the group do. These total contributions will be C times the number of favor initiators or reciprocators in the group. Group charitable contributions should increase proportionately to an increase in the proportion of favor initiators or reciprocators in the group. We expect that anything that increases the mean gain from a favor, or reduces the costs of granting a favor, or reduces the rate of time preference should increase the proportion of favor initiators or reciprocators. In consequence, it should increase the amount of charitable contributions from a group.

There is one serious problem with the simple charity model whose results we have summarized. That model works whether individuals vary by gains per favor, costs per favor, or rates of time preference as long as only one of those characteristics varies. When individuals within a group vary by two or more of these characteristics, the charity model becomes quite complicated. For one thing, as we show in appendix 2, there is no level of charity such that all reciprocators will pay and no moochers will do so. Because the appropriate model is much more complicated, we will continue to work with the simple charity model. However, we will not use any of the implications obviously dependent upon charity acting as a perfect screen.

These models of reciprocity and charity can be applied with slight modifications to the case of trust in the employer-employee relationship given imperfect monitoring of the employee's behavior. The employee can do the employer a favor by behaving in a responsible manner, that is, how he would behave if he were perfectly monitored, even though he is not fully compensated for that behavior initially. The employer can do the employee a favor by fully compensating him for trusted behavior before he demonstrates his trustworthiness.

There are several differences between this case and the simple reciprocity model. In the latter case the behavioral choices are discrete and successful partners want favors at different times. In contrast, both compensation and the trustworthy employee behavior are continuous rather than periodic events. We can approximate by converting this continuous case to a discontinuous case with a single period equal to the expected time required to determine whether the employee has or has not been trustworthy. Another difference: in the simple reciprocity model two potential partners want favors at different times, so it is clear who will give the favor first. In the employer-employee case both would like to be the first recipient of the favor. Which comes first, the compensation or the behavior, will be determined by the magnitude of two conflicting processes.[4] Whichever dominates, the firm has an incentive to hire trustworthy employees, and, hence, to screen by their charitable contributions. In this case, the source of worker variation unknown to the firm will be variation in their time preferences, since both the gains and costs facing prospective workers for the same job is the same, for they would all face the same compensation package and temptations. There is evidence that human resource managers do, indeed, try to determine the trustworthiness of their employees, and to do so seek to determine their "service orientation" and their orientation toward "social behavior" (Murphy and Luther 1997)

Charity: Tests

Throughout this book we test our theory with regressions. Sometimes the theory produces a unique testable prediction. Sometimes, however, an additional specification is required to generate a prediction. Obviously, confidence in the latter tests depends upon confidence in the specifications. We try whenever possible to defend the specifications on the grounds of either reasonableness or with relevant evidence beyond our own regression results. Occasionally, neither defense is totally convincing, and so no real test of the theory results in these cases. But even here, finding the specifications that would make theory consistent with evidence provides an opportunity for future tests of the theory.

As in much of economic research, the variables we use are determined by data availability rather than variables that precisely measure our theoretical constructs. Often, this means that there are alternative explanations of the variables' behavior. When possible we examine alternative hypotheses. Also, the large number of quite different tests throughout this book make it unlikely that our results can be explained by these alternative hypotheses.

At the beginning of this chapter we used lying about charity as an important bit of evidence in favor of our reputational theory of charity. But lying creates problems with our tests of that theory. Our survey data combines actual contributions to charity and lies about those contributions. This is a common problem in nearly all studies of charitable donations. For the most part they are based on either survey data or income tax data. Lying problems exist for income tax returns as well as surveys.

Still, we cannot deny that lying about charity does pollute our data. Reputational needs can cause one to lie about giving as well as actually giving. However, we would expect the latter to be more sensitive to reputation than the former. The costs of lying also go up with a concern with reputation, as do the conscience returns from actually contributing. In consequence, we would expect lies about charity to be less sensitive to reputation variables than actual behavior. Therefore, it would be hard to attribute all of the connection between reputational variables and self-reported charity to lies. Still, we cannot deny that lying about charity does pollute our data. Reputational needs can cause one to lie about giving as well as actually giving.

There are two sets of testable implications that can be derived from the model of charity signaling trust: (1) those from signaling in general, and (2) those specific to the reciprocity model. In the latter we focus on time preference. The greater the rate of time preference for a group, the less charitable contributions from that group. We look at several variables related to the rate of time preference: occupation, education, and assets. Those occupations with steeper age-earnings profiles select individuals with lower time preferences, since more of their returns are delayed. Those with more education are also selected in part by low rates of time preferences. High assets mean that a person is more likely to be a lender, who faces lower interest rates at the margin. Assets, of course, are part of the budget constraint, but this does not explain the volunteer labor, asset relationship.

Now, examine the implications of signaling in general. One of the most important properties of most charity is the small number of people who know about any given charitable contribution. A requirement for signaling through a given charitable contribution is that a potential reciprocity partner will be aware of the contribution. On that account charitable contributions should increase with increases in the number of people whom a person knows well enough for them to be aware of his contributions. But people whom one knows that well might already have had enough dealings with the person to have some idea about his trustworthiness. Why do they need a charity signal? Furthermore, people who know lots of other people are more likely to have enough reciprocity partners. Why do they need to signal? The answers to both questions are similar.

Even if one is sure that a person is not a moocher for a low-cost reciprocity, one might be uncertain for more expensive interchanges. Even if one has a partner for low-cost reciprocities, there is interest in convincing that partner and others that one can be trusted in high-cost reciprocities. There is no reason to suspect that most people are more interested in convincing strangers that they are trustworthy rather than acquaintances and partners. In any case, most charity can only be used as a signal for people whom one already knows. So it would not be surprising if the more people one knows, the more one contributes to charity. But the process discussed in the previous paragraph could conceivably generate the opposite sign.

We can rule out, however, another process that could produce a negative relationship between number of associates' variables and charity. Suppose that, indeed, people were more trustworthy the higher the value of a variable positively related to number of associates, say church attendance. Then church attendance can itself be used as a signal that a person is trustworthy. Seemingly, this signal could be used as a substitute for charity. As a result, charity would be negatively related to church attendance.

But that is not the way it works. Suppose that everybody knows others' church attendance. Then charity only signals trustworthiness conditional on church attendance. Whether people with higher church attendance use more charity in their signaling boils down to exactly the same issue as that already addressed without considering church attendance as a substitute signal. Will the possible diminishing returns to signaling trustworthiness be sufficiently compensated by the fact that one's fellow congregants know more about whether one has given to some charities? No new issue is raised by church attendance as a substitute signal. Of course, the more imperfect knowledge of others' church attendance, the less church attendance will serve as a substitute signal for charity.

Even though there is some uncertainty about the sign of the relationship between number of associates and charity, we are still able to get one unambiguous prediction. There are several variables positively related to the number of close associates. They should have similar directional effects on charity.

The proxies we use for number of close associates are church attendance, how long one has lived in a neighborhood, home ownership, marital status, and income. (1) Church attendance: Obviously, the social life of a community is often built around the church. (2) Similarly, one knows more people in a neighborhood, who are more likely to know one's charitable contributions, the longer one has been in a neighborhood. (3) A homeowner anticipates that he will be in a neighborhood longer, and, hence, makes more effort to make neighborhood friends. Homeowners also have a greater incentive to join civic associations related to maintaining property values for the neighborhood. (4) Married people have more associations than do singles, since associations are being developed by at least two people rather than one. (5) The number of associations increases with income and assets, as does the money value of the favors exchanged. For virtually all of these variables there is some evidence that they are, indeed, positively related to number of associates.[5]

We also believe that age should be positively related to charitable contributions, though through a somewhat more complicated process. The average slope of the age-friendship relationship is not significant.[6] The important feature of aging, however, is the increasing difficulty of acquiring new friends, except in certain retirement communities. This considerably increases the return to convincing one's current friends that one is trustworthy. This cost of additional sampling probably helps explain the charity effect of many of the variables discussed above: migration, marriage, and home ownership in particular. For our purposes, it makes no difference whether the charity effect of these variables is attributable to number of close associates or to the costs of acquiring new associates.

Using data from the *National Study of Philanthropy* (Morgan 1977), we look at four charity dependent variables: (1) Following Boskin and Feldstein (1978): the logarithm of (total money and property family contributions to charity plus $10); (2) the logarithm of (these contributions to the church or church-sponsored activities plus $10); (3) the logarithm of (nonchurch contributions plus $10); (4) the logarithm of (hours of voluntary labor in the year plus 10 hours) for the head.[7] In all these regressions we use as our price variable whether a person itemizes his tax deductions.[8]

The primary bias generated by the exclusion of the rest of the price variable will be on the coefficient of the income variable, since the marginal tax rate is dominantly a function of income. The income coefficient will be biased upward by this exclusion. But since income is in the regression, this generates no obvious bias in the *regression coefficient* for the other variables positively correlated with income. Most of the other biases on the other variables will be dependent on the difference between income and taxable income. For example, the more business or mortgage interest deductions one can take, the lower taxable income relative to actual income, and the less the marginal tax rate. This will tend to create a downward bias in the home ownership regression coefficient and reduce the effect of occupation on charitable contributions. Similarly, the lower tax rates for married couples, holding family income constant, will tend to bias downward the marriage regression coefficient.

The regression results in table 3.1 show that those occupations with the greatest age-earnings slopes, such as professional, managerial, and skilled workers, have coefficients that are positive and statistically significant.[9] The greatest coefficient for such occupations is for managers for whom trust is particularly important. The largest charity coefficient of all occupations belongs to the self-employed, for which age-wage slopes are inappropriate. (The self-employed either do not receive wages or the wage is arbitrary.) But trust can be particularly important in the client relationships many of them possess.

The pattern of these results is similar for two components of charity: charity through the church and other charitable contributions, but there are some interesting differences. The age-earnings slope provides a better predictor of charity by occupation for nonchurch contributions than it does for church contributions. Usually, work associates, in contrast to friends, are more aware of other contributions than church contributions. The opposite would be true for friends. A possible exception is the self-employed, for whom fellow church members are potential customers. It is not surprising that the self-employed comprise the only high-trust occupational group for whom the coefficient for church contributions is greater than the coefficient for other contributions. The lower discount rates that help determine whether one chooses a high-trust occupation would increase charitable contributions both in the work and the social environment. However, the greater gains from trust that characterize the occupations themselves are returns peculiar to work.

The occupational pattern of volunteer labor is even more closely related to the occupational pattern of age-earnings slopes. All of the high-slope occupations have greater coefficients and greater t values in that regression.[10] However, the self-employed have a virtually zero

TABLE 3.1. Charity Regressions

	Char.	Char.	Char.	Church	Non.	Vol.	Slope
Int.	−4.28	−2.88	−3.24	−1.81	−2.37	.742	
t	−6.72	−4.06	−4.51	−2.76	−3.98	1.49	
Inco.	.431	.345	.343	.245	.331	.027	
t	7.79	5.90	5.90	4.56	6.77	.616	
Asset	.063	.062	.062	.052	.052	.021	
t	6.71	6.40	6.42	5.90	6.42	2.82	
Item.		.744	.749	.610	.561		
t		6.84	6.90	6.05	6.15		
Att.	.032	.036	.031	.036	.013	.014	
t	16.82	15.72	15.45	19.49	7.83	9.02	
Neib.	.051	.081	.080	.107	.018	.023	
t	1.26	1.94	1.90	2.76	.518	.722	
Home	.351	.148	.147	.187	.100	.069	
t	3.18	1.20	1.19	1.65	.962	.787	
Marr.	.443	.392	.395	.337	.306	.017	
t	4.07	3.35	3.38	3.12	3.13	.199	
Age	.069	.047	.050	.036	.036	.030	
t	3.88	2.35	2.47	1.96	2.12	2.15	
Age^2	−.0005	−.0003	−.0003	−.0003	−.0002	−.0004	
t	−2.93	−1.51	−1.60	−1.32	−1.29	−2.38	
Educ.	.096	.056	.054	.045	.058	.047	
t	5.69	2.69	2.63	2.35	3.31	3.58	
NILF	−.323	−.230	−.211	−.138	−.112	.330	
t	−1.73	−1.20	−1.15	−.880	−.449	2.93	
Pro.	.243	.274	.266	.153	.390	.496	146.4
t	2.07	1.93	1.82	1.13	3.44	4.67	
Mgr.	.434	.440	.450	.350	.535	.535	166.3
t	2.50	2.86	2.87	2.40	4.32	4.60	
Self	.665	.701	.677	.735	.546	.017	
t	2.83	2.78	2.65	3.10	2.73	.236	
Cler.	.152	.083	.086	.156	.032	.419	114.5
t	1.36	.650	.610	1.13	.598	3.74	
Skill.	.259	.208	.213	.220	.116	.238	85.8
t	2.02	1.44	1.42	1.56	1.23	2.22	
Oper.	−.117	−.123	−.116	−.061	−.182	−.034	65.3
t	−.422	−.443	−.417	−.237	−.784	−.157	
Lab.	.028	.125	.137	.046	.185	.062	64.2
t	.096	.430	.470	.170	.755	.276	
Farm	−.118	−.079	−.061	.079	−.344	−.419	61.2
t	−.317	−.209	−.161	.228	−1.06	−1.43	
Race	.058	.173	.170	.100	.011	.141	
t	.385	1.00	.989	.628	.079	1.18	
Jew	.298	.258	.225	.105	.433	−.118	
t	1.38	1.17	1.02	.522	2.36	−.683	
Cath.	−.319	−.305	−.309	−.329	−.061	−.434	
t	−3.33	−3.04	−3.09	−3.57	−.723	−5.73	
View			.156				
t			2.55				

TABLE 3.1. *Continued*

	Char.	Char.	Char.	Church	Non.	Vol.	Slope
Numb.						.111	
t						4.00	
R^2	.45	.44	.45	.44	.38	.17	
N	1,400	1,247	1,247	1,247	1,247	1,374	

Char. = log(total contributions + $10); Church = log(contributions to church + $10); Non. = log(nonchurch contributions + $10); Vol. = log(hours of volunteer labor + 10); Slope = age-earnings slope of the 1969 earnings of white males with 12 years of school who worked 50–52 weeks that year (U.S. Census 1973) (we took the difference in mean earnings for those 55–64 years old and those 18–24 years old and divided by 38.5).

Independent variables are as follows: Int. = intercept; Inco. = log(family income) assigning 1 to 0 income (this transformation is also made for all independent variables in log form); Asset = log(total assets); Item. = dummy variable with 1 = if a person itemized deductions on his or her federal income tax; Att. = number of times per year respondent attended church; Neib. = log(number of years residing in neighborhood); Home = dummy variable with 1 if homeowner; Marr. = dummy variable with 1 = married; Age = age in years; Age² = age squared; Educ. = number of years of school; NILF = dummy with 1 if not in labor force; Pro. = dummy with 1 if professional occupation; Mgr.= dummy with 1 if manager; Self = dummy with 1 if self-employed; Cler. = dummy with 1 if clerical or sales occupation; Skill. = dummy with 1 if skilled worker or foreman; Oper. = dummy with 1 if an operator; Lab. = dummy with 1 if laborer or service worker; Farm = dummy with 1 if farmer; Race = dummy with 1 if white; Jew = dummy with 1 if Jewish; Cath = dummy with 1 if Catholic; View = answers to the question: "Do you think a person is likely to give more if the amount he gives is made public?" (if "Yes," then 3; if "No," then 1; if equivocal answers 2); Numb. = number of children under 18 in household; R^2 = multiple correlation coefficient squared; N = sample size. With regard to occupation, for the regression coefficients the occupation of comparison is miscellaneous occupations. The t values compare the occupation with the weighted average of low slope occupations—operators, laborers, farmers, and miscellaneous occupations for all higher slope occupations—with the weights given by their respective proportions in the sample. For low slope occupations the t values use miscellaneous occupations only as the occupation of comparison.

coefficient in the volunteer labor regression, probably because the value of their time is greater.[11] The greater visibility of volunteer labor explains the greater impact of occupation on volunteer labor than on contributions. More people are likely to know about a person's volunteer labor than about the usual monetary contribution. Hence, volunteer labor is likely to act as a better signal.

Education, our other low-interest proxy, behaves the same way as occupations. It has a significantly positive coefficient in all regressions, and its elasticities are greater in the volunteer labor regression (though not its coefficients) and are greater for nonchurch contributions than for church contributions.

Consider the variables that are related to the number of close associates who would know of one's charitable contributions: time lived in the neighborhood, home ownership, income, marital status, church attendance, and age. All of these variables have significant coefficients in most of the contributions' regressions, and most have significantly positive coefficients in all the regressions.

The church attendance coefficients are particularly worthy of note. Of all variables it has the largest t values in all the contributions regressions including nonchurch contributions. That one often has nonchurch associations with the people one meets in church may help explain the positive effect for nonchurch charity. An alternative hypothesis is that expected afterlife returns or some other source of church-generated "trustworthiness" motivates both kinds of contributions. However, one would expect people to believe that contributions through the church to be so much more effective for that purpose that nonchurch contributions might very well be reduced given this better substitute. Later, we examine evidence that allows one to distinguish between these two hypotheses.

The greater visibility of volunteer labor has the consequence that close associations become less important in determining charity because there will be more strangers that know of the volunteer labor. As a result the church, home ownership, and the time in the neighborhood coefficients are smaller in the volunteer labor regression.[12]

The regression results also suggest that a person's charity is affected by the group to which he belongs, holding constant individual characteristics. If the probability that a person is trustworthy is a continuous function of his charitable contributions, his relative contributions will be important in determining whether he becomes a partner. *He* is chosen rather than others. Hence, the amount of the charity of others in his group will be important in determining the amount of one's own charity.[13] There is evidence for this group effect. We find a negative effect of Catholics in all regressions and a positive effect of Jews in some regressions.[14]

Social Capital

This chapter's results are analogous to Glaeser et al.'s (1999) results that focus on social capital rather than charity. The similarity of these results should come as no surprise. Glaeser et al.'s definition of social capital is the cumulative investment in trustworthiness. In our analysis charity is an investment in trustworthiness. Those that have an incentive to increase their social capital should find it in their interest to contribute to charity. In consequence, the variables that are significant in determining "trustworthiness" in Glaeser's regressions also tend to be significant with the same signs in the charity regressions when those variables are available in both data sets. "Trustworthiness," like charity, increases with education, income, church attendance, and marriage. These results lend some support to the idea that charity signals trustworthiness.

Glaeser et al. use two different variables as their measures of "trustworthiness" and "trust": (1) number of nonprofessional organizations to which respondents belong; (2) answers to the question, "Generally speaking would you say that most people can be trusted or that you can't be too careful?" a measure that they call "GSS Trust" (where *GSS* stands for the General Social Survey from which their trust question comes). A rationale for the first measure is that trustworthiness increases with community involvement. The more people one knows, the greater the reputational costs of nontrustworthy behavior. The second measure appears to be a measure only of trust rather than trustworthiness, but, of course, it would be difficult to get reliable answers to questions about one's own trustworthiness. There is a good reason for expecting the trust question to also measure trustworthiness. The most obvious evidence that one has of the anticipated behavior of others is one's own behavior in similar circumstances. In addition, we would expect trust to be a function of the ratio of successful reciprocity relationships one has had to the unsuccessful ones. That ratio is, in part, a function of one's own trustworthiness characteristics.

Glaeser et al., then, show that this second measure of trust actually works in predicting trustworthiness in a trustworthiness experiment. The biggest effect of this variable is on others' behavior toward one, rather than one's own behavior: trustworthiness rather than trust. While the parties to this experiment do not know a person's answer to the trust question, the experiment has them meeting before the trust game is played. In consequence, they are able to make some assessment of the other's trustworthiness prior to the game, especially if they knew each other before the experiment started. Evidently, in this game the most important determinant of behavior is how others assess the trustworthiness of their partner in the experiment rather than their assessment of trust for people in general.

The peculiar nature of this GSS measure of trust does, however, generate some differences in the charity regressions and the trustworthiness regressions using that variable. Jews give more to charity but have less trust. Blacks have less trust but do not give less to charity. The obvious explanation is the one Glaeser et al. give. Minorities are less trusting of people in general because people in general are less likely to be members of the same minority group. (The coefficient for blacks is insignificant using the number of organizations variable, and Jews are not included in that regression.)

"Warm Glow" and Signaling

The Morgan (1977) data that are the basis for our regressions give some rough idea about the importance of signaling for charity in general. They ask: "Do you think a person is likely to give more if the amount he gives is made public?" Forty-five percent answered yes, while only 29 percent said no, with the rest giving equivocal answers. We construct a variable, "Views," in which a 3 is assigned to a "Yes," a 1 to a "No," and a 2 to other answers. Table 3.1 shows a significant positive impact of "views" on charitable contributions. Those who answer yes to this question believe that others are more responsive to social pressure probably because they themselves are more responsive. In consequence, they give more to charity than others. Glaeser et al. (1999) use a very similar argument when they use a variable that explicitly measures trust as a measure of trustworthiness. They, like we, find that such a measure works in the sense that it successfully predicts trustworthy behavior.

Of all the determinants of charity, the only ones that have a significant impact on "views" are church attendance and the dummy variable, "Jew," with positive t values of 3.18 and 2.00 respectively. The former result is evidence for the proposition that the crucial role of church attendance in determining both church and nonchurch charity is the greater associations with which it is related and the resulting greater social pressure for contributions rather than altruism or concerns with an afterlife. Jews may be more aware of social pressure because they are tighter knit due to their minority status.

The Beneficiaries of Charity

Charitable contributions benefit somebody other than the contributor. Altruism, the standard explanation, is not required. That is fortunate because altruism does not explain donor behavior. While contributing to charity is costly to the individual, the choice of beneficiary costs the individual nothing. That does not mean that the individual is indifferent between beneficiaries. He wants to distribute his charity to maximize its effectiveness as a signal. He is particularly interested in signaling to his group that he is trustworthy to members of his group. As developed in chapter 5, one way to signal this preference for particular people is to imitate their behavior. Charity choice can be used to signal whom one wants as partners in reciprocity by imitating their choices. But others are doing the same thing. As chapter 5 shows, this mutual imitation multiplies the impact of any exogenous determinant of choice common to the group. Group survival implies that this determinant is some benefit shared by others, even if these benefits are small. Targeting charity so that a particular group approves is a way of demonstrating trustworthiness toward that group. That group will be more enthusiastic the greater the benefits to the group from the charity. Charity to the poor, cancer research, funds for the church organ all fit that bill.[15] No altruism is required to produce this effect of creating external benefits; just a concern with what others think.

One would predict, therefore, that the greater the group benefits from an activity, the greater the expected charitable contributions to that activity. Government expenditures that reduce the external benefit to private contributions for an activity should partially crowd out these private contributions. But government contributions should have no impact (holding real income constant) on the signaling needs that motivate charitable contributions in general. Total charity should not be affected by government expenditures when total charity is broadly conceived. There can be some impact on measured charity, however. Total charity includes the loss in total income generated by engaging in all prosocial activities and not engaging in antisocial activities. As government activity reduces the external benefits from measured charity compared to other activities like voting or other community activities, there can be some crowding out of measured charity, but it should be less than the crowding out of the particular charities most closely related to government actions.

The Price of Charity

It has been standard procedure in the empirical studies of charity to estimate the price elasticity of charity by looking at the response of charitable contributions to changes in income tax rates, since charity is deductible in determining taxable income. This procedure makes sense given the altruistic theory of charity. But the interpretation of the results is quite different given any signaling theory of charity. The charity that separates moochers from reciprocators is the charity that people pay, that is, the net cost to them of the contribution given the tax benefit. In consequence, total charitable *expenditures* should be invariant with respect to a tax rate, holding real income constant. To keep *expenditures* constant, *contributions* will have a price elasticity of 1, as far as the substitution effect is concerned.

This same prediction holds for the more general "warm glow" theory of charity. Warm glow is assumed to come from the sacrifices people make for the public good. Just as in the signaling case, these sacrifices are a function of the amount net of taxes that people pay rather than the amount the charity receives. Again, that leads to a prediction of a price elasticity of 1 when charity is measured by contributions rather than expenditures.

Clotfelter (1985) surveys price elasticity studies. He finds considerable variation in estimates. Most of those studies have elasticities close to 1. The major exceptions are the large price elasticities produced by studies based on the same data set we use—The National Study of Philanthropy. Elasticity estimates from these data are suspect.[16]

More recent, and, on the whole, better studies surveyed in Tiehan 2001 tend to find price elasticities less than 1, though Feenberg (1987) estimates this elasticity as 1.63. For example, Randolph (1995) finds a price elasticity of only 0.51 with a standard error of .06. However, Tiehan (2001) herself finds price elasticities varying between 0.94 and 1.15. Obviously, this wide range of estimates over all studies does not provide much confidence. At least, however, our predicted 1 is within that range.

All of these empirical articles on price elasticities have one thing in common: they are all simply empirical articles. The only theory they use is that of the negatively sloped demand curve. We provide a theory, which not only predicts a negative elasticity, but a precise value for that elasticity. Even if it turns out that that prediction is wrong, the prediction is a worthwhile exercise. It is an implication of the standard warm-glow theory of charity as well as our more specific signaling theory. If it doesn't work, that means something else is going on. We believe that "something else" cannot be simple altruism, since the theory and evidence against the operation of the latter is so strong. So finding that "something else" will require finding out why.

A Similar Analysis

The analysis that comes closest to ours is that of Posner (2000). He also treats charity as a signal of trustworthiness. His basic model differs in an important respect from ours. He uses a prisoner's dilemma model with cooperation and defection as the two options. Trust is required in this model because each player makes his move without knowing the move of the other party. We use a reciprocity model in which trust is required because one must do a favor without knowing whether the other party will reciprocate later. We believe that reciprocity is a more common pattern of the behavior related to charity than is simultaneous decision-making. Our model also assumes many potential partners while the typical prisoner's dilemma model does not. Not only is this assumption more realistic; it vastly simplifies the analysis by eliminating many strategic options. Our model produces a richer set of implications. Posner predicts, as do we, more signaling for those with lower discount rates. We predict also more signaling from those with greater gains and lower costs from reciprocity. These latter predictions are particularly important because these gains and costs from reciprocity vary with prospective partners in reciprocity. This variation plays a crucial role in the chapters that follow. We also investigate a whole range of empirical implications from signaling that Posner does not.

The most significant difference between Posner's work and ours is his contention that social norms in general are arbitrary. In the charity case, that implies that the beneficiaries of charity are arbitrary. Indeed, for signaling purposes it doesn't make much difference who receives the benefits. We maintain, however, that group selection does have an important role to play in determining those beneficiaries and many social norms as well. By and large the beneficiaries of charity can be explained by group selection, and group selection's role in signaling plays a crucial role in later chapters.

Because, however, group selection operates so slowly, there are also many charities that must be otherwise explained: for example, charity for animal hospitals. There are multiple equilibria associated with signaling unless constrained by something else like group selection. These multiple equilibria can have important implications in their own right, for example the instability of the role of ethnicity, an instability stressed by Kuran (1998).

While Posner provides no systematic data testing his signaling model, he provides a rich set of examples. Most of that evidence supports our position as well. The rest shows a lot of noise in social norms. But since some noise is consistent with patterns in social norms, that evidence is also consistent with our approach.

CHAPTER 4

Political Charity

In the last chapter we developed a reputational theory of charity, a theory about any prosocial behavior that has costs to the individual so engaged. Voter participation and commonly defined charity qualify as such behavior. The former has time costs and is regarded as having favorable social consequences. There is a positive externality from either being a voter or being the sort of person who would vote. The willingness to accept the legitimacy of democratic government policy with which one disagrees is an important component of social harmony, and one fostered by high voter participation. There is some evidence for this contention. In addition to self-serving "get out the vote" drives of political parties and their allies, there are frequent public service announcements from neutral sources such as the Advertising Council,[1] and some polities tax the act of not voting.

Because the participation occurs so infrequently, some might regard voter participation as a poor vessel for signaling reputation. But the resulting reduction in returns is matched by a similar reduction in costs. Many give infrequently to specific charities. A person cumulates a reputation for trustworthiness by many prosocial acts, one of which could well be voter participation.

There is a more serious objection to voter participation as a signaling device: the limited information that others have about whether an individual voted or not. There is very little direct observation of an individual by others whose good opinion matters to that individual. In the last chapter, we saw, however, that people can get information about voting participation from individuals stating that they voted. In spite of the substantial lying from those who so state, the probability that a person actually voted is increased by his saying that he voted. Even so, information is scarce.

A similar problem exists for charity. We hypothesized that our theory's successful predictions in that case were the result of a combination of actual reputational signals and conscience, and the latter we argued in the last chapter is positively related to reputational variables.

We use the same argument here, though it well might be that there is less information about voter participation than charity. There certainly is less information from direct observation, though the taboo on bragging about one's charity, discussed in chapter 3, does not hold with equal force for statements about voting. In any case, the a priori case for predicting voter participation through reputational variables is highly dependent on conscience being thus predictable.

The literature has long recognized some obvious features of voting behavior: (1) Any single person's vote has virtually no impact on an election; (2) people vote anyhow; and (3) the only way this seeming paradox can be resolved is by the existence of some private return to voting rather than a return from influencing the outcome of an election. The private return we propose is dominantly a conscience return with probably a little reputational signaling as well.

Who Is More Likely to Vote?

Reputation variables in part determine voting participation whether motivated directly by reputation or indirectly by conscience. Hence, the same variables that determine charitable contributions determine voting participation. In chapter 3 we made four predictions. Now, all we have to do is substitute the word *voting* for *charity*. (1) We predict that the more people one knows, the more likely he will be to vote. The more people one has known in the past, the more one will have developed a conscience. (2) Since the returns to trustworthy behavior are delayed returns—future reciprocity gains—those with lower rates of time preference have more to gain by signaling trustworthiness. As developed in chapter 3, that implies, that those with a lower rate of time preference in the past would have developed more of a conscience applicable to behavior about which others know little. Those with greater education and steeper age-earnings profiles will tend to have lower rates of time preference. (3) People with greater incomes or greater assets will also have lower rates of time preference. In addition they will tend to have greater reciprocity gains in dollar terms simply because they deal with greater-valued transactions. Because income levels have some stability over time, these groups will also have more to gain in the past from developing a conscience, which as a by-product leads to more frequent voting. However, the cost of voting—the value of time—also increases with an important component of income, wage income. (4) The income of people who are self-employed is particularly dependent on the reputational gains that can be generated by prosocial behavior. Hence, they should vote more frequently.

We test these propositions about voting with the *General Social Surveys, 1972–1996* (NORC 1996). The most serious problem with that data was discussed in chapter 3 in a different context. There is a substantial portion of lying nonvoters among those counted as voters. There is a reputational incentive to lie about voting as well as a reputational incentive to vote. Are regression results that show that reputational variables explain voting attributable to the liars rather than the voters? Bernstein, Chadha, and Montjoy (2001) showed that all seven of the variables we employed and that we can identify as reputational variables that were significant in a regression using self-reported votes were also significant with the same sign in a regression using actual votes, though the values of the coefficients differed in the two regressions.[2]

We explain VOTER (= 1 if respondent reported voting in the last presidential election; = 0 if not, but was eligible to vote) using a wide variety of relevant variables. The results are in table 4.1.[3]

Community Involvement

We first test the proposition that the probability of voting increases with the number of people one knows. This hypothesis implies that those who are more involved in the community will be more likely to vote. There are several variables in the NORC (1996) data set that are related to community involvement, though they have other possible meanings as well.

MEMNUM, the number of organizations to which one belongs, has a strong positive relationship to VOTER ($t = 8.87$). Community involvement affects VOTER in another way as well. The more frequently one attends church, the more involved one is in church activities. Since the church is such an important vehicle for socializing, frequent church attendees are also people with more acquaintances.[4] The relationship of ATTEND—the frequency of attendance at religious services—to VOTER is particularly large. Since several cross-products of ATTEND to other variables—various religious groups—were employed, we look at the value of the slope of ATTEND at the average values of the other variables included in the cross-products, $b = .0168$ ($t = 15.01$).

The alternative hypotheses about the effect of church attendance revolve around the content of the religious message. The more one attends church the more likely one is to confront either messages about piety or about social activism, with the mix depending upon the particular church one attends. One suspects that a message about social activism would increase the probability of voting more than a message about piety. Since the former is more relevant to voting, one would predict a tendency to vote among the less pious, qua pious, as opposed to more frequent church attendees.

The ATTEND effect occurs among Catholics and Protestants, but not Jews. Whether Protestants are Fundamentalists or mainline has no significant impact. We believe that any ATTEND effect among Jews is masked by the sect effect. Orthodox Jews are more likely to attend services than Reform or Conservative Jews. This masking can only occur if Orthodox Jews are less likely to vote than other Jews. Among Jews, then, there is some indirect evidence that Jewish piety reduces votes, or Jewish "do-gooding" increases votes. But there is no indication that the same holds for Christians. The coefficient of the cross-product of Fundamentalist with attendance is virtually zero.[5]

Another variable that has a community involvement component is age. It is common knowledge that the old vote more than other groups, and this relationship is not confined to the United States. Studies of the Netherlands (Jaarsma, van Winden, and Schram 1985) and Canada (Lapp 1999) come to the same conclusion. But to our knowledge, nobody has provided a satisfactory explanation. There are lower time costs to voting after retirement, but that does not explain why throughout the age distribution voting participation increases with age. In fact, the coefficient for age squared is significantly negative, with $b = .0001$ ($t = 16$). This result is just the opposite of what one would expect from the cost-of-time hypothesis.

The slope of the age-voting participation relationship at mean age and the means of other variables used in cross-products with age is equal to .0084 with $t = 35.74$, a t value far and away the largest of any associated with any other explanatory variable. This average slope implies enormous differences in voting probabilities for the young and the old. Over a span of fifty years the voting probability of the old would be .42 larger than the young. Given a mean reported voting probability of .704, this implies that the voting probability of the old is almost twice that of the young, holding other variables constant.

The signaling explanation for this result is the same as our explanation in the case of the positive age-charity relationship. The cost of acquiring new friends goes up with age, so the return to impressing old friends about one's trustworthiness increases.[6] However, there is a puz-

TABLE 4.1. OLS Regression for Voter Participation (t values in parentheses)

Variable	Regression		Variable	Regression	
Self-Interest			City		
FY	.0516	(8.01)	LCCIT	−.0250	(1.98)
FY2	.0004	(.23)	SCCIT	−.0288	(3.85)
SELF	.1538	(2.13)	SSURB	−.0228	(2.92)
GOVR	−.0205	(2.19)	LSURB	−.388	(2.50)
UNION	.0147	(2.82)	OURB	−.0460	(5.82)
			SCITY	.0054	(.82)
Personal Background and			MCITY	.0138	(1.62)
Political Party			SUBRB	.0062	(.61)
BUSA	.1106	(5.90)	LCITY	.0140	(1.54)
PED	.0035	(3.66)			
MED	.0026	(2.47)	Religion		
NEWS	.0892	(6.10)	MAIN	.0019	(.22)
REPUB	.0036	(2.49)	JEW	.0655	(1.80)
REPUB*BLACK	−.0433	(8.67)	CATHOLIC	.0190	(1.43)
REPUB*FY	−.0036	(2.56)	NOREL	.0300	(1.83)
STRONG	.0742	(26.42)	OTHREL	.0294	(1.11)
NCOLYR	.0747	(16.90)	ATTEND	.0035	(.66)
COLYR	.0547	(9.40)	JATT	−.0007	(.06)
MALE	.0084	(.96)	PATT	.0145	(3.11)
MARRIED	−.0053	(.35)	CATT	.0135	(2.79)
MALE*MARRIED	.0338	(3.24)	FUNDAT	.0004	(.38)
CHILD*MALE	−.0199	(1.15)	FYINCOME	.0988	(3.63)
NCHILD*MALE	−.0084	(1.21)	FMARRIED	−.0552	(1.03)
ADULTS	−.0183	(3.84)			
MALE*ADULTS	.0071	(1.02)			
CHILD	−.0045	(.39)			
NCHILD	.0034	(.77)			
BLACK	.1019	(8.21)			
Occupations and Industry			Community Involvement		
WRITER	.0296	(.94)	AGE	.0311	(18.43)
LAWYER	.0037	(.11)	AGE2	−.0002	(15.93)
CLERGY	.0053	(.14)	STATMIG	−.0295	(4.72)
CLERGYFU	.0368	(.91)	CONTMIG	−.0403	(6.26)
PRIEST	−.0347	(1.19)	AGECOLYR	−.0012	(13.25)
BLACCL	.0238	(.89)	AGENCOLYR	−.0005	(5.72)
PROF	.0429	(5.87)	MEMNUM	.0183	(8.87)
MGM	.0155	(1.87)			
CLERK	.0414	(6.67)	YEAR	−.0016	(4.24)
SALES	.0408	(5.15)	N	25,485	
ARMY	.0497	[3.04]	RSQUARE	.248	
GOV	-.0783	[1.53]	MEAN	.7095	
LOWTEACH	.0112	[.96]			
COLTEACH	.0280	[1.74]			

TABLE 4.1.—Continued

Variable	Regression		Variable	Regression	
Regional			Regions when 16		
NE	−.0215	(1.02)	16NE	.0395	(1.82)
MA	−.0630	(4.10)	16MA	.0200	(1.26)
ENC	−.0210	(1.53)	16ENC	.0193	(1.31)
WNC	−.0157	(.98)	16WNC	.0179	(1.09)
SA	−.0765	(5.41)	16SA	−.0003	(.02)
ESC	−.0916	(4.88)	16ESC	.0346	(1.84)
WSC	−.0597	(3.76)	16WSC	.0081	(.48)
M	−.0257	(1.60)	16M	.0281	(1.55)
SIGETHNIC	9				

Note: The key to abbreviations is as follows:

Self-Interest
FY = ln of family income relative to mean family income
FY2 = the square of FY
SELF = self employed equal 1
GOVR = recipients of government aid
UNION = union member or spouse of a union member equal 1

Personal Background and Political Party
BUSA = born in the U.S. equal 1
PED = father's education
MED = mother's education
NEWS = how frequently one reads newspapers
REPUB = party identification
* = cross product
STRONG = absolute value of difference between party identification and independent
NCOLYR = number of years of noncollege education
COLYR = number of years of college education
MALE = male equal 1
MARRIED = married equal 1
ADULTS = number of adults in the household
CHILD = child in family equal 1
NCHILD = number of children
BLACK = black equal 1

Region
NE = Northeast
MA = Mid-Atlantic
ENC = East North Central
WNC = West North Centrla
SA = South Atlantic
ESC = East South Central
WSC = West South Central
MT = Mountain

Occupation and Industry
WRITER = writer or journalist equal 1
LAWYER = lawyer equal 1
CLERGY = clergy equal 1
CLERGYFU = cross product of clergy and fundamentalist
PRIEST = Catholic clergy equal 1
BLACCL = black clergy equal 1
PROF = professional equal 1
MGM = management equal 1
CLERK = clerk equal 1
SALES = salesmen equal 1
ARMY = armed forces or police equal 1
GOV = employed by government except armed forces, police or education equal 1
LOWTEACH = noncollege teacher equal 1
COLTEACH= college teacher equal 1

Regions when 16
Resided in 1 of 8 regions when age 16

City
LCCIT = large central city equal 1
SCCIT = small central city equal 1
SSURB = suburb of small central city equal 1
LSURB = suburb of large central city equal 1
OURB = other urban equal 1
SCITY = in small city when 16 equal 1
MCITY = in medium city when 16 equal 1
SUBRB = in suburb when 16 equal 1
LCITY = in large city when 16 equal 1

Religion
MAIN = nonfundamentalist Protestant equal 1
JEW = Jew equal 1
CATHOLIC = Catholic equal 1
NOREL = no religion equal 1
OTHREL = minor religions equal 1

272## 64   *Signaling Goodness*

TABLE 4.1.—*Continued*

ATTEND = frequency of church attendance	AGECOLYR = interaction of age and number of years of college education
JATT = cross product of Jew and ATTEND	
PATT = cross product of Protestant and ATTEND	AGENCOLYR = interaction of age and number of years of noncollege education
CATT = cross product of Catholic and ATTEND	
FUNDAT = cross product of fundamentalist and ATTEND	MEMNUM = number of organizations to which one belongs
FYINCOME = average relative family income of members of one's church	YEAR = year of observation
	N = sample size
FMARRIED = proportion of married people in one's church	RSQUARE multiple correlation coefficient squared
	MEAN = Mean voter participation
Community Involvement	
AGE = age	SIGETHNIC: There are dummy variables for each of 38 ethnic groups specified in Nelson 1994, and this refers to the number of such that were significant at the 5% level or better.
AGE2 = age squared	
STATMIG = within state migrant equal 1	
CONTMIG = interstate migrant equal 1	

zle that we do not solve. The age-voting relationship is extremely large relative to that relationship for charity, and we suspect the information about voting participation is less than information about charitable contributions.

One alternative hypothesis is that the age-voting relationship is really a cohort effect. There has been a consistent decline in voting participation over time in the United States. If voting participation were habitual, older people would, then, be more likely to have the voting habit. But this cannot explain most of the relationship.[7] Furthermore, the time trends that generate a cohort effect are mostly attributable to the decline in community involvement over time through increased television watching and a decline in the importance of the extended family.

An alternative hypothesis for the age-vote relationship cannot be so easily dismissed. People acquire political information with age, as do their friends. That information could well increase political interest as well as the political interest of their associates. It makes more sense for them to signal their goodness by voting compared to alternative charities. However, as seen in chapter 3, nonvoting charitable contributions increase with age. Clearly, political interest cannot explain both aging's effect on voting and on charity. There is more telling evidence that information has, at best, only a partial role in the age-vote relationship. We have a much better measure of political interest than age: STRONG—the absolute value of the difference between a person's party identification and the party identification of an independent, where party identification is measured on a seven-value scale with strong Democrat scaled at 0, strong Republican at 6, and independent at 3. STRONG is, indeed, strongly related to voting. However, its t value of 26.43 is still substantially less than the t value for the age-voting slope.

There is another variable related to information and political interest: whether the respondent ever reads a newspaper. It is significantly related to VOTER: b = .089 (t = 6.10). But, again, the effect is far weaker than the age effect. These results confirm that political interest can only partially explain the age-voting relationship.

Migration is another variable related to community involvement. Migration reduces the number of associates where one presently lives and the power of the extended family and any familial pressure to be "good." Our prediction that migrants vote less frequently is confirmed for both intrastate and interstate migration. For the former the slope is –.0295 (t = –4.72); for the latter this slope is –.0404 (t = –6.26).[8]

One also expects marriage to have a community involvement component. A couple tends to have more associates than a single person. In the charity case, where charity is measured as charity per family, marriage increased charitable contributions substantially. In the volunteer labor case, where it is measured as volunteer labor per person, marriage has no significant impact. In the voting case, where again it is votes per person, marriage significantly increases the voting frequency of men, but it has no significant impact on the voting frequency of women. In the voting regression the coefficient of the cross-product of marriage (1 if married) and gender (1 if male) is .0337 (t = 3.23), while the coefficient on the marriage variable is insignificant: –.005 (t = –.352). The latter coefficient measures the effect of marriage on women given the cross-product term in the same regression. (Gender has no impact on the voting behavior of single persons.) This differential gender effect of marriage on voting could be attributable to the relative specialization of married women in child- and home-related activities, where reputation is less relevant.[9] Glaeser, Laibson, and Sacerdote (2000) provide some support. They show that males have more community involvement than females in the sense that the former belong to more organizations. So at least this type of community involvement is gender specific.

Another variable related to community involvement is city size. The smaller the city, the more likely people will be involved with each other. Our study yields mixed results with respect to this variable. Living in a rural area increases the probability of voting relative to each of the other city size categories, but there are no other significant city size effects.

On balance, the results of this section correspond closely with the results for private charity (chap. 3). The same community involvement variables that play an important role there play an important role in determining voting, even though the alternative hypotheses that might also explain these phenomena are quite different. Voting and charity also share the same major disappointment. City size results are not convincing in either case.[10]

Income

Just as in the case of age, it is all too well known that voting frequency increases with income, and our results confirm the obvious.[11] In the voting regression the slope of the logarithm of relative family income at the average value of relevant other variables is .0419 ($t = 9.66$).

In contrast to the age case, though, there is a standard explanation for this result: simple self-interest. "Higher income people have more to lose or gain in dollar terms by the political process, and, hence, they are more likely to vote." But that explanation is not convincing. The costs of voting, private costs, also go up with income because these costs are primarily time costs. In contrast, the outcome returns that increase with income are public returns and will be miniscule to the individual because of the free-rider problem. In chapter 5 we will see that the small self-interest effect when shared by a person's associates can get multiplied into a big effect, so that self-interest variables play a significant role in explaining voter positions. However, in this case this simple multiplication will produce a negative relationship between voting and income, which will be magnified through the imitative process.

To explain the positive effect of income on voting we must find a source of private returns to voting that increases with it. The conscience and reputational returns to voting might very well fill that bill. Reputational returns increase with income because one knows more people the larger one's income, and the value of what is exchanged in reciprocal relations is also likely to increase with income.[12] Since income is a reputational variable, increases in income will tend to strengthen conscience. We, again, do not know a priori whether that is sufficient to outweigh the increase in costs associated with income, but it is possible. The simple self-interest story is not because of the free-rider problem.

If the private returns increase with income, then imitation can multiply that positive effect. One of our variables shows that effect at work. Holding individual income constant, the likelihood of voting increases as the income of one's church associates increases. The vote-FINCOME slope is .099 ($t = 3.62$), where FINCOME is defined as the estimated average relative family income of the members of the narrowly defined church denomination of the respondent, where that income is estimated by the income of those in the NORC sample.[13]

When costs of voting do not increase with a variable, but benefits do—even when those benefits are public benefits—the imitative process will be sufficient to produce a discernable positive effect on voting. Being a member of a union or having a spouse that is a member (DUNY) increases the probability of voting: $b = .015$ ($t = 2.82$). Other self-interest variables fare less well. If one is a government employee other than a teacher, policeman, fireman, or member of the armed forces, one's probability of voting declines insignificantly: $b = -.028$ ($t = -1.53$). For protective government workers the b is significantly positive: $b = .050$ ($t = 3.04$), and for noncollege teachers $b = .011$ ($t = 0.96$).[14]

In addition, there is a dramatic case where self-interest does not work. Welfare recipients form one of the groups most affected by government policy. They also have one of the lowest time costs of voting. However, being a welfare recipient, holding other variables constant including income, lowers the probability of voting: $b = -.020$ ($t = -2.18$).

But this result is predicted by our model. Those on welfare have one of the smallest reputational returns from prosocial behavior, since their income is not dependent on what others think and they have relatively few associates. An explanation in more popular language: welfare recipients are alienated from society, and, hence, see no need to perform any voluntary social duties. Both explanations are community involvement stories. The latter goes from emotion to voting response. The former goes from returns to response. One suspects that if the former were not true, people would learn that the emotional response did not pay and revise it accordingly.

Partisanship

Concern with reputation not only affects one's total investment in reputation, but the way in which that investment is distributed. One is more likely to vote the more likely others find out that one does. Conversations about politics, which can lead to questions about whether one voted, are more likely to occur among the most partisan. A person is also more likely to be driven to vote by conscience the more important she and her friends believe the outcome of the election to be, even though she recognizes the impotence of a single vote in determining election outcomes. Her sense of duty is determined largely by what her group regards as her duty. Partisanship should increase this sense of importance of election outcomes and, hence, increase the probability of voting. Indeed, earlier in this chapter we saw that a measure of partisanship—STRONG—strongly increases the probability of voting with a t value of 26.43. Next to age it is the most significant determinant of voting participation.

Expressive Voting

The behavior of STRONG seemingly contradicts the expressive voting hypothesis of Brennan and Buchanan (1984). They maintain that voters with extreme views will "cheer" less and hence vote less because they identify less with candidates, who because of electoral pressures are forced toward the center. In chapter 5 we will criticize that proposition. In this chapter we can examine relevant evidence. The STRONG variable is not an ideal variable to test expressive voting. However moderate candidates are, they are usually either strongly Republican or Democratic.

Instead, however, of using party identification to identify extreme positions, we can use people's self-classification by liberal and conservative categories. There are seven categories from strong liberal through moderate to strong conservative. In a regression where STRONG is not included we use dummy variables for all these categories except moderate, which is the control group. In the voting participation regression we observe the following regression coefficients (with t values in parenthesis): strong liberal, .057 (3.05); medium liberal, .051 (5.66); leaning liberal, .035 (4.27); leaning conservative, .033 (4.38); medium conservative, .031 (3.78); strong conservative, .017 (1.02). Since the average self-classification for those voting Republican or Democrat was 3.65 and 4.53 respectively, the candidates were appealing to someone with a score between 4 and these values. That is, we expect candidates to position themselves somewhere between the position best suited to win in the primary (3.65 and 4.53 respectively) and the position best suited to win in the general election (4). Brennan and Hamlin would predict the coefficients should be significantly smaller for the strong relative to the moderate relative to the weak. They are not. None of the differences in regression coefficients between these categories is significant. There is no evidence to support their form of the expressive voting hypothesis. The only significant result is that moderates vote less than other categories for the obvious reason that they and their friends are less interested in politics than are the other categories.[15]

The Self-Employed

Probably no group has a greater stake in its reputation than the self-employed. This group includes many professionals like doctors and lawyers whose reputations are the essence of their business and entrepreneurs whose trustworthiness is of particular concern to customers. It is no wonder, then, that the self-employed vote more frequently than others, just as they contribute more to charity. In the voting regression the dummy variable for self-employment has a $b = .015$ ($t = 2.14$). There is, however, an alternative self-interest explanation for this result. The self-employed are probably affected more by government policy than other groups. They, certainly, can see the effect more easily than others, since they are often directly affected by policies that affect others only indirectly. This simple self-interest story when magnified by the imitation effect could produce the higher voting probability of the self-employed.

Education

In the United States the voting-education relationship is quite substantially positive with larger t values than that for the income slope even though we divide the educational effect into two components. The slope of the less than college education variable taken at the means of relevant other variables is .031 ($t = 12.43$). For college education this slope is .019 ($t = 9.87$).

There are three obvious processes that could produce a positive relationship between education and voting. (1) The educated have lower rates of time preference than others, and, hence are willing to invest more in their reputation. (2) The educated have more political information than others, and, hence, greater interest. We have already discussed the impact of information and interest on voting. (3) The educated have had a longer exposure to those proclaiming the virtues of voting—the socialization effect. The conscience of voters is a function of the investment that others make in developing that conscience. Larger investments are made in the case of the more educated.

There is some evidence suggesting that the third hypothesis has at least some power. The impact of both college and noncollege education on voting declines with age. For the cross-product of age and non-college education, b is $-.00062$ ($t = -5.40$); b for the cross-product of age and college education is $-.0012$ ($t = -12.09$). This decline in the effect of education on voting occurs in an environment where the continual exposure of the more educated to higher-income people would tend to increase their voting propensities. It does appear that education has an indoctrinating effect on civic virtues that dissipates substantially over time. (In the case of college education the positive education effect is completely gone by the age of sixty-two.)

The education of both one's father and one's mother increases the probability of a person's voting. The regression coefficient for father's education is $.0035$ ($t = 3.65$), and for mother's education it is $.0026$ ($t = 2.47$). This could be attributed to either the indoctrinating effect of parents in creating a conscience or the relationship between one's current associates and parental associates.

Occupations

Our theory leads to two predictions about the effect of broad occupational categories on voting. (1) Those occupations with steeper age-earnings profiles have a greater incentive to vote. Low rates of time preference increase the gains to reciprocity, and hence the gains to reputation-enhancing behavior. (2) Members of occupations who associate more with people with higher incomes and education should vote more because of the importance of imitation in determining their votes.

What we find is that all broad white-collar occupations vote more frequently than do all of the blue-collar occupations. Three of these white-collar occupations have about the same voting propensities. Managers vote less frequently than the others, so this evidence does not support the first hypothesis about the relationship of age-earnings slopes and voting, and it provides only mixed support for the imitation hypothesis. White-collar workers associate more with each other than with blue-collar workers. The lifestyles of the two groups are somewhat different. However, it is likely that high-income professionals will do more associating with lower-income professionals than they do with clerks with the same lower income. We expect, for example, high-income doctors to associate more with low-income doctors, if such there be, and low-income lawyers than with low-income shipping clerks. Yet holding individual incomes and education constant, professionals do not vote more frequently than clerks. This conflicts with the predictions of the second hypothesis that those who associate more with higher income and education groups should vote more frequently.

Ethnicity

We expect a respondent's ethnicity to have a significant effect on his probability of voting. A person tends to associate with members of his ethnic group, and he imitates the behavior of those associates. These associations could be more or less intense because of variation in geographic concentration, language, and other barriers to assimilation. Indeed, the coefficients of many of the ethnic group dummies are significant, far more than can be attributable to chance. There are nine ethnic dummies out of thirty-eight that are significant at the 5 percent level. Testing the hypothesis that this result is attributable to chance, $t = 5.29$.

There is a more interesting hypothesis about ethnicity. Those ethnic groups whose members' characteristics increase voting probabilities, should vote more, even taking into account the effect of those characteristics on individual voting. We found a significant positive effect on voting of the proportion of the ethnic group born in the United States. However, we did not find a significant relationship to voting for the ethnic group's education, income, or political partisanship, all variables that on the individual level have a substantial impact on voting.[16]

There is some evidence that supports either the role of the average education or income of an ethnic group in increasing voting participation. In spite of appearances to the contrary, the main low-income, low-education group, DRAN, has lower voting participation than whites in general.[17]

Our results in general strongly support the role of reputational variables in determining voting participation, we believe dominantly through the operation of conscience. Alternative hypotheses, like voting out of narrow self-interest or because of identification with candidates, fare less well.

CHAPTER 5

Political Positions and Imitative Behavior

What determines people's political positions?[1] Two hypotheses have dominated the literature. On the whole, economists have emphasized self-interest (Stigler 1971; Peltzman 1980). But some (for example, Kau and Rubin 1979, 1982; Kalt and Zupan 1984) maintain that political positions are influenced by ideology. These economists base their ideology hypothesis in part on altruism (Kalt and Zupan 1984).

Both of these hypotheses have the same fundamental flaw. They both focus on the consequences of the policies that people advocate. In the Stigler and Peltzman models a person votes and advocates those policies that maximize his real income. We call this narrow self-interest. In the standard altruism models one is interested in voting to maximize some weighted average of the real income of oneself and others.

The problem with these hypotheses is the well-known free-rider problem. An individual's vote or advocacy usually has a miniscule impact on the outcome of any election. Therefore, for most people there are extremely small expected returns to advocating any policy through the impact of that policy on the advocate. While this observation has frequently been made by those exploring the determinants of whether one votes, only a few have seen its possible importance in determining how one votes or what one advocates (Kalt and Zupan 1984; Brennan and Buchanan 1984; Schuessler 2000). If the expected returns of the policy consequences of advocacy are so small, other returns from advocacy—the private returns—will dominate in determining behavior if such returns exist.

So what? Brennan and Buchanan (1984) argue that these private returns make it difficult to formulate predictions about the political process, since there are myriad sources for these returns. Not surprisingly, empirically oriented political economists have not accepted this invitation to close shop, especially since the standard self-interest model sometimes successfully predicts political behavior. But focusing on private returns need not lead to the abyss, nor to a rejection of the empirical successes of the narrow self-interest theory. Concentrating on the dominant private returns allows one to construct a testable model with some implications similar to, and some quite different from, the narrow self-interest model.

The key point of this chapter is that political behavior can generate private benefits by helping people fit in with desired friends and associates. Political positions are then chosen not because these positions are the desired outcome for voters, but rather because one wants to associate with certain people and they have certain positions. People imitate others in choosing political positions. To put it in terms used by Brennan and Buchanan, people cheer for causes that others important to them are cheering for. The interaction between positions chosen for this reason and positions chosen for income-maximizing reasons, then, leads to many interesting testable implications.

The narrow self-interest model also fails empirically in some major ways. Across the globe some of the biggest political clashes are between ethnic or religious groups rather than economic groups. For example, poor Protestants in Northern Ireland tended to support the Unionist cause in spite of the higher average income of Protestants. The imitation hypothesis easily explains this phenomenon.

The classic work of Berelson, Lazarsfeld, and McPhee (1954) provides a prima facie case for imitation in political positions. They find that a person's political position was closely related to the political position of family, coworkers, and friends. Of course, this could be attributable to the fact that a person shares common characteristics with these groups, and Berelson et al. did not use appropriate statistical tools to control for this effect. However, in their results the effect of associates is very much larger than the effect of common characteristics. In consequence, if such tools had been used, one would not expect the common-characteristic effect to eliminate the imitation effect.

Conceivably, their results could be explained by people choosing associates for their political views rather than vice versa. However, it is hard to see how the former could exist without the latter. If people choose associates for their political views, it pays people to develop political views that will get them chosen by those whom they prefer. Berelson et al. provide direct evidence of this revision of political views in response to the views of friends. They find that where a voter's friends had the same party preferences as he did initially, he was much less likely to change his preference than when the party preferences were different (5 percent of 416 voters in contrast to 9 percent of 69 voters). In spite of the few voters changing preferences, the difference is statistically significant ($t = 2.34$). Furthermore, this change in positions cannot be attributable to changes in characteristics, so imitation seems the sole explanation for that result.

Imitation also seems responsible for "bandwagon" effects: one's own position is a function of one's perceptions of the position of others in general. One is more interested in imitating friends, but one is also concerned with general attitudes. For example, Marsh (1984) showed that an average person's position on abortion was affected by being told differing stories on the trends in public opinion about that issue.

Many have claimed that imitation is a fundamental trait of human behavior, for example, Lumsden and Wilson (1981), Berelson (1964), Moschis and Moore (1979). Not only is it a trait common to all cultures, but one shared with many of our animal forebears. This suggests that at least the predisposition to imitate is an innate human characteristic. Economists, however, have done little with this idea. One exception, Becker (1971), has modeled the effect of imitative behavior on demand elasticities. The most compelling evidence for imitation as a general social phenomenon is the persistence of variation in customs across cultures like greeting rituals where that variation is not explicable by differences in economic conditions. How else could the customs be transmitted from one generation to another except by imitation, or "memes" (Dawkins 1989), the social equivalent of genes?

One of the reasons people imitate each other is to take advantage of their information. Some people know more than others. It makes sense for the latter to imitate the behavior of the former. In particular, it generally pays the young to imitate the old. Even among those with equal information, it often pays to imitate the group, since the group knows more than any one individual in that group.

The obvious other reason for imitation, of political positions in particular, is that people want others to imitate them. Why should a person care that he is imitated? And why should another person care that he cares? There is a payoff to reciprocal relations with others. That reciprocity often requires trust. We saw in the chapter 3 how one could signal trust by charity. But a person is interested not only in how trustworthy another person is in general, but how trustworthy that other would be toward him in particular. One way of providing that information is to imitate the behavior of the people with whom one is most interested in reciprocal relations.

As already discussed, it pays to have a reciprocity partner that most wants to be your reciprocity partner. Under those circumstances the partner is most likely to reciprocate any favor. That a person signals that he wants to be your partner makes you want to be his partner. The imitation signal is "almost" self-confirming. When a person imitates your behavior, he is not imitating somebody else's behavior. Assuming that both know of his behavior, it is believable that the person most wants to be a partner with the person that he imitates.

We expect this signaling model to successfully predict behavior even when signalers are unaware that they are conforming to the views of their desired associates. All that is required is that people, in fact, engage in this conforming behavior and that others care whether they conform to their views, even though they, too, might not know why they care.

"What constitutes good public policy?" is not an easily answered question. About the only relevant information that most people have in forming their beliefs is what others say. One gets de facto signaling as long as the relevant others are those with whom they wish to associate. Trial and error can lead to this signaling. Following this strategy, both the signaler and the recipient of the signal are rewarded by a better set of friends.

Asch (1963) provided evidence of the role of others in forming one's beliefs under circumstances where that role was clearly not optimal for truth seeking. A substantially larger number of people denied the evidence before their eyes—large differences in the length of lines on a piece of paper—when all others denied such evidence in their presence than when none so denied it (32 percent compared to 1 percent). The Asch case differs from political positions in one important respect. Virtually everybody had the relevant evidence to determine the relative length of lines. In contrast, very few have the evidence to determine which political position is "correct" or how to even begin to define "correctness." For most the only available option is to depend on the views of others to determine their political position. When in doubt, believe as others do.

But there is one important similarity between the two cases. In neither case did people receive a significant explicit reward for a "right" answer. In the Asch case there were no monetary rewards for correct answers. In the political position case one's political position has virtually no impact on policies actually adopted. In both cases, then, there is little incentive to use other than the roughest rule of thumb in determining positions, especially when, as in the political position case, that rule of thumb generates larger returns to the individual in the form of friendships and approval than would rules more appropriate for truth-seeking purposes.

In contrast to conscious maximizing behavior, such trial and error is guaranteed to produce only a local maximum (Elster 1984), and our signaling theory refers to a global maximum.[2] It is not surprising, therefore, that reality does not always agree with this simple theory. In particular, a person's beliefs are also a function of the beliefs of those with whom she wished to associate in the past.

That this behavior could arise is understandable. People have a conscience that involves the incorporation of the beliefs of others into their own beliefs. By its very nature a conscience is at least somewhat backward looking, since it has been formed by past associations. There was no selective pressure to make it more forward oriented. In the distant past, when preferences were being formed by selection, there was little social mobility and little migration other than group migration. Under those circumstances, present and past associates were virtually identical, except for births and deaths. Even now, there will be a close association between the beliefs of past associates and present associates, in part because a person tends to choose present associates from those who conform to his past beliefs. But there is currently enough social mobility and individual migration that lagged beliefs will play an important role in what follows.

The alternative imitation hypothesis is that people adopt the political positions of the more knowledgeable rather than those with which they most wish to associate. But surely, imitation for knowledge cannot be important for political positions. The low private payoff to more informed political positions implies little incentive for more knowledgeable voting (Downs 1957). Even for private behavior that does have costs, the young, particularly adolescents, often imitate each other, with whom they wish to associate, rather than more knowledgeable elders.

The most compelling case for imitation as either signaling or de facto signaling, as opposed to imitation for information, is that people really care about whether one imitates their political positions. That is a care that is hard to understand if one were simply providing information to others by one's behavior. This concern with other's political views makes much more sense if conformity is construed as a mark of friendship. Conservatives are not welcomed with open arms by many liberals and vice versa, as the typical university environment attests. But the belief that conformity is a mark of friendship is only self-sustaining if, in fact, it is such a mark.

The Multiplicity of Political Positions

Because political positions are determined in part by reputational motivations, the same person can have different political positions for different occasions: voting, talking to friends, talking to pollsters, and talking to a wider audience (Kuran 1995). These activities can differ either because reputation's importance differs among them or because the people according the reputation can differ. Each of these activities can have an effect on political policies. Political economists studying democracies have tended to stress the impact of voting because it ultimately determines whether politicians are elected or not. But the other activities are important in democracies as well. Polls help shape policy between elections by giving politicians a sense of the issues that ultimately determine votes, and public declarations of policy help influence the votes of others and the behavior of government officials. In the absence of democracy, voting no longer counts, but publicly expressed opinions still might.

Strictly speaking, our reputational theory is inapplicable to voting itself, since one cannot enhance one's reputation with anyone by a secret vote. Indeed, we do not test our theory with actual voting data, but use polling information instead. However, we believe that our general results also apply to voting in a somewhat attenuated form. As discussed in earlier chapters, there is a conscience cost of lying. Under usual conditions this provides an incentive to vote similarly to one's public statements about one's political position. In the no-lying scenario, one's public statements and one's voting are jointly determined. One's public statements will be influenced by the returns to voting particular positions, and one's voting will be influenced by the returns to making particular public statements.

No doubt there can also be a return from voting differently from the way one talks. If one has friends who verbally support different candidates, there is a return to verbally supporting the candidate of the friend with whom one is talking. Obviously, though, one cannot vote both ways. One must lie to at least one set of friends if one talks to both about candidates. Similarly, there is some incentive to lie to pollsters if one expects pollsters to have different views than one's friends.

In this kind of lying there is a fairly high probability of detection if the audiences communicate. The higher this probability, the greater the cost of lying. There is evidence for lying when the probability of detection is small. For example, Reese et al. (1986) found that answers to ethnically sensitive political and social questions depended significantly on the ethnicity of interviewers as well as the ethnicity of respondents. The difference for interviewers was in the direction of trying to please both sets of interviewers. This is evidence that public statements about political positions are, indeed, influenced by the political positions of others.

Of course, the approved political position of employers or governments would also have a greater impact on self-reported votes, and the impact could be greater than on actual secret votes. For the United States this latter concern is not very important for most people because governments are usually not in a position to retaliate for "bad" voting, and employers are faced with roughly competitive labor markets. Such concerns certainly could be present in other political contexts.

Another source of lying in statements about political positions or voting is conscience. Conscience-determined political positions are largely produced by the approved political positions of past associates because conscience is largely the internalization of those views. The approved political positions of a person's past can be different from the approved political positions of current associates. One might want to give greater weight to the former in voting than in discussions with current colleagues and friends. Even if a person lies about a vote determined by conscience, his vote will be affected by the views of others— past associates in this case rather than current associates.

There remains one other possible return to lying about how one voted. Desirous of the best of both worlds, people could talk about their votes to maximize their reputation while voting to maximize their narrow self-interest. However, for this process to operate, the returns from maximizing narrow self-interest must be greater than the costs of lying. In a large group setting, however, the obvious gain to voting one's narrow self-interest is exceedingly small, and there are substantial costs to lying. So people's votes and public pronouncements would be alike as far as narrow self-interest is concerned.

Kuran (1995) takes a different position. He posits an expressive utility return to voting that has two properties: (1) it is increased by voting to promote one's self-interest over and above the direct self-interest returns of so doing, and (2) it is not very sensitive to the magnitude of the direct self-interest that one promotes by one's vote. In consequence, despite the free-rider problem, there can still be a substantial expressive utility return to voting one's self-interest.

Even if Kuran is correct, voting would still be affected by what others think, as long as some voters find the cost of lying greater than the returns to expressive utility. Two conditions are required for there to be no connection between voting and what others think. First, there must be a "considerable" amount of lying if, as our evidence later shows, verbal political positions are dominated by what others think. Unfortunately, however, we do not know enough to specify more precisely what "considerable" means.[3] Second, lying must be motivated by the expressive utility return from voting, since the other reasons for lying still produce voting determined by what others think.

Given the secret ballot, the only evidence about lying about how one voted comes from the difference between actual election results and polling information about those results. However, that difference is only an imperfect measure of the amount of lying. On the one hand, that difference could be attributable to causes other than lies about political positions. Polls are from a sample of voters, some of whom might lie about their own probability of voting. In consequence, some of the difference could be attributed to sampling variability and sampling bias. In addition, if there is a time gap between polls and voting, some people could change their minds. These problems are minimized with exit polls, in which only actual voters are queried immediately after they vote.

On the other hand, the difference between polling results and actual votes could understate the amount of lying. This difference would not catch lies about voting Democratic, say, if they were counterbalanced by lies about voting Republican. Only the difference between the number of those lies would show up in the difference in polls and actual votes. However, lying should be dominantly one-sided. To make their predictions more accurate, reputable polling organizations encourage their pollsters to question as neutrally as they can. As a result, polling respondents are unaware of the political proclivities of particular interviewers.[4] In consequence, they can only respond to what they assume is the average position of interviewers. If, for example, they believed that that average position was pro-Democrat, only Republican voters would lie to hide their Republican vote.

Of course, voters could have different beliefs about the average position of interviewers. If that difference creates some incentive for both Republicans and Democrats to lie, the beliefs are not likely to stray very far from the belief in a 50 percent split among interviewers, especially when party affiliations are roughly equal. Given the cost of lying, it is unlikely that a Republican would lie that he voted Democratic when there is a probability close to .5 that his interviewer would also be a Republican.

For presidential elections in the United States the difference between polls and election results is quite small. In the sixteen presidential elections beginning with 1940 the average difference between the Gallup Poll just before the election and actual election results was only 2 percent (Gallup 1999).

However, Kuran (1995) cites elections where there were disagreements between polling and election results. Racial issues were central to Kuran's two examples from the United States. Many lied because they thought interviewers would not approve of their alleged "racist" attitudes. In the New York City mayoralty race of 1989 between the white, Rudolph Giuliani, and the black, David Dinkins, the differences between pre-election polls and election results were from 12 percent to 16 percent, while the differences between election results and exit polls were 4 percent to 8 percent (Kuran 1995). In the 1990 Louisiana senatorial race featuring David Duke, of Ku Klux Klan fame, the difference between pre-election polls and election returns was 19 percent. Kuran provides no exit poll results, but, as discussed earlier, one expects the amount of lying thus revealed to be less than that implied by pre-election polls.

Lying for reputational reasons is likely to make verbal political positions that contain those lies more responsive to reputational variables than voting behavior. However, we do not know exactly how much lying is required for all of the verbal reputational effect to be attributable to lying. As discussed in note 3, we only have a fuzzy idea of the value of a key term required to make that determination: the percentage of voters who would vote the same way whether they were motivated by self-interest or reputation. We do not know whether 19 percent is sufficiently large or not, but it is unlikely that 2 percent is big enough. In the latter case the value of that key term must be 96 percent or more.

The presidential elections to which the latter number is relevant are important in themselves. Even if the percentage of lies estimated for them are completely unrepresentative of other elections, one would conclude that some important elections are affected by reputational variables, if polling data indicates that they are so affected. But we would expect the lying results for these elections to be closer to the typical election than the Kuran results. Kuran's purpose was to show that there existed elections where substantial lying occurred. In pursuit of that objective there was no need to randomly select elections. Rather, he chose those elections that he believed were dominated by lying. While presidential elections are not randomly selected elections either, the selection of those elections was determined solely by readily available data. As far as we know, there is no particular reason why presidential elections should exhibit less lying than most other elections.

Furthermore, it is not clear that the lying in Kuran's case was generated by self-interested voting. There is an alternative explanation. There is a well-established media bias in favor of most liberal causes, including more aid for blacks (Lichter, Rothman, and Lichter 1986, for example).[5] In the absence of other information to the contrary, people's best estimate of average attitudes toward race is likely to be these attitudes displayed by the media. They would, then, expect the average pollster to also have these attitudes. But, because of the bias, these attitudes will be systematically more problack than those possessed by the average friend. But since one values friends more than pollsters, one's vote is more likely to imitate the former. This creates an incentive to lie to pollsters in political campaigns that focus on black issues.

We would expect less of this lying in presidential elections because people have better information about the relevant general attitudes than what the press tells them. Most would know that the electorate is roughly evenly split between Democrats and Republicans. Their best guess is that pollsters would have a somewhat similar split. Though they might like to please pollsters by their responses, they would not know how to do so. This same process is applicable to most of the other elections that pit a Democrat against a Republican. In consequence, our result of little lying in presidential elections seems applicable to most other general elections as well.

The evidence hardly compels in determining whether Kuran's self-expression variable has an impact on voting. There might very well be some difference between voting and public political positions attributable to the greater role of self-interest in the former. However, we expect no massive difference in the usual case. Since in the next two chapters we make a strong case for the important role of reputational variables in determining public political positions, that similarity of voting and public positions in the usual case implies that voting, too, will be affected by reputational variables, albeit indirectly and possibly with somewhat different values relative to the various regression coefficients.

The Model

To deal systematically with political positions it is necessary to quantify them. If there were but a single issue, such as total welfare expenditures, the issue itself would generate a simple metric. But with multiple issues there are multiple dimensions. For our purposes, however, there is no harm in simplifying by working with a single dimension. (In any case, Poole and Romer [1985] provide evidence that the choices we will be analyzing are consistent empirically with a unidimensional approach.) We pretend, along with Peltzman (1980), that there is but a single issue: nondefense government expenditures with fixed proportions among its components and its financing. The political position of any person i, P_i, is measured by the amount of those expenditures that he advocates. S_i is defined as the amount of those expenditures that maximize his own self-interest. When examining alternative hypotheses, however, we look at some of the more obvious consequences of a multidimensional P_i and S_i.

Assume that (1) utility is a declining function of the difference between one's political position and someone else's, and (2) utility is also a declining function of the difference between the political position one adopts and one's income-maximizing political position. We assume that utility for the ith person takes the following explicit form:

$$U_i = c_i \sum w_{ij}(-(P_i - P_j)^2) \, h_i(P_i - S_i)^2, \tag{1}$$

where w_{ij} is the weight that i gives to imitating j's political behavior with $\sum w_{ij} = 1$, c_i = the weight i gives to the weighted average of the squared differences between i's position and that of others, and h_i is the weight i gives the difference between his position and his own self-interested position.

Maximizing U_i with respect to P_i,

$$(1 + b_i)P_i = \sum w_{ij}P_j + b_i S_i, \tag{2}$$

where $b_i = h_i/c_i$, so his position will depend upon both the positions of others and his own self-interested position.

To get an explicit solution for the P_i, consider a simple case. Assume that b_i is the same for all i. Suppose that there are only two groups with n_1 people having $S_1 = 0$ and n_2 having $S_2 = x$. Assume further that all those in a group have the same w_{ij}.

Then, equation (2) becomes

$$(1 + b)P_1 = (n_1 - 1)w_{11}P_1 + n_2 w_{12}P_2,$$
$$(1 + b)P_2 = (n_2 - 1)w_{22}P_2 + n_1 w_{21}P_1 + bx. \tag{3}$$

Given that the sum of the weights equals 1, the solution is

$$P_1 = xn_2w_{12} / (b + n_2w_{12} + n_1w_{21}),$$
$$P_2 = x(b + n_2w_{12}) / (b + n_2w_{12} + n_1w_{21}). \tag{4}$$

If $w_{ij} > 0$ and $j \neq i$, $0 < P_1 < P_2 < x$. $P_1 < P_2$ is consistent with a simple narrow self-interest model. Those in each group take positions closer to the self-interested positions of each group. But the other part of the inequalities—a shift of political positions toward the mean—is not. It does not require preposterous assumptions about the parameters of equation (4) to obtain a substantial impact of the political position of others on one's own political position. One needs simply a low b, the weight of narrow self-interest relative to imitation.

Suppose, for example, that $n_1 = n_2 = 5$, $b = .01$, $x = 1$, and $w_{ii} = 10w_{ij}$ $j \neq i$. (One observes association patterns by income consistent with a low w_{ij} relative to w_{ii}.) Then $P_1 = .478$ and $P_2 = .522$, much closer to the mean political position than to their respective self-interest political positions (0 and 1). Even if $w_{ii} = 100w_{ij}$, $j \neq i$, and all other conditions remain the same, $P_1 = .356$ and $P_2 = .644$.

While it appears likely that voter imitation is a powerful determinant of political positions, imitation is uninteresting as a predictor of behavior by itself. A voter imitates other voters, but at the same time they are imitating him. The political positions of others are endogenous variables. Imitation's seeming emptiness is probably why an imitation model has not been emphasized in the voting literature. But there are exogenous variables in the system: the narrow self-interest of the participants. The resulting model, however, differs from a simple narrow self-interest model. The political positions of others affect the final results by making one's political decision a function indirectly of the narrow self-interest of others as well as one's own narrow self-interest. The existence of narrow self-interests as exogenous variables is crucial not only to political behavior but social behavior in general. In our simple model without narrow self-interest the reduced form would be indeterminate. Even in the more general model developed in the next chapter, variation in narrow self-interest is required to produce variation in political positions.

Imitation Theory

We believe the imitative component of this model is attributable to people signaling the group with which they most want to be friends. However, there is a problem with that attribution that must be addressed. The economist's usual way of predicting behavior is by finding an equilibrium solution, that is, a solution in which none of the participants has an incentive to change his own behavior. When a person signals, he is trying to influence the beliefs of others about his future behavior toward them. A signaling equilibrium, then, has two components: (1) the behavior of the signaler, and (2) the beliefs of the receivers of that signal. A signaling equilibrium requires that the signaler has no incentive to change his behavior given the beliefs of others, and that there is no reason for others to change their beliefs given the signaler's behavior. The latter condition will be satisfied when the actual behavior of the signaler is consistent with the beliefs that others have about his behavior.

Now, suppose that a signaler is behaving in terms of equation (2) and that others know the weight that the signaler places on the self-interest term relative to the imitation term $(b_i / (1 + b_i))$. Equation (2) can be a signaling equilibrium if the return to choosing a political position closer to one's narrow self-interest is sufficiently small because of the free-rider problem. Suppose, for example, that in terms of the units of our imitation model, trillions of dollars of nondefense government expenditures say, his narrow self-interest position is 20 and that of the friends he most desires is 10 and $b = .01$. His resulting political position is 10.1. However, his friends realize that that 10.1 means the friends he most wants have a political position of 10, not 10.1. The signaler has made no sacrifice of friendship by adopting a political position that reflects somewhat his narrow self-interest. Indeed, if the signaler chose a political position of 10, he would be signaling that the friends he most wants have an average political position of 9.9. Since the friends he most wants have a political position of 10, he is worse off in terms of his friendship by strictly imitating their behavior than by almost imitating them.

The signaler would be even better off in terms of his narrow self-interest if he had a higher value of b_i as long as others realized that he had a higher value. No matter what political position he adopts, they would know that his most desired friends had a political position of 10 and he would gain a miniscule amount by voting more in line with his narrow self-interest. But suppose that others believed his b_i equals .01. Then he cannot arbitrarily increase his b_i without considerable loss in desired friendships. Indeed, he will have no incentive to choose a b_i greater than .01 by even a small amount if, as we have assumed, the return to doing so is less than the cost of the resulting loss in friendship.[6]

This logic generates multiple equilibria. Whatever b_i others believe the signaler to be using is the b_i the signaler will use as long as the signaler knows what others believe. (This is a different meaning to b_i than given in the simple utility-maximizing model of equation (2).) History rather than signaling theory determines the actual b_i. We expect, however, the signaler to give a substantial weight to imitation $((1 - b_i) / (1 + b_i))$. Imitation is the natural way to signal one's friendship, a way that operates in many contexts besides political choice.

Furthermore, a substantial weight to imitation is required for political choice to be a viable signaling device. The greater b_i, the greater the effect of signalers' perceptions of their own narrow self-interest on their behavior. But receivers of those signals will often know neither the self-interest of the signaler nor the signaler's perception of that self-interest. Nor will receivers be sure what b_i signalers are using. Given these information problems, signaling will only work if it can be applied in a simple way where the predominant component of the signal is the imitation component.

The more interesting question is why there should be a narrow self-interest component in the signal at all. We think the answer is "mistakes."[7] In a small-group setting, it pays individuals to give some weight to their narrow self-interest in their choices. It would not be surprising if individuals would do some of the same, at least initially, when making political choices in a large-group setting. But contrary to most processes, such "mistakes" are not eliminated over time because they are costly. As long as others expect such "mistakes," that expectation is built into how others interpret the signaler's behavior. The average level of the "mistakes" signalers have made determines the b_i receivers expect. It, therefore, pays signalers to make this average level of "mistakes" in the future.

The emphasis in this chapter is on the imitation effect both because of its importance and because of its neglect in the literature. However, we also save narrow self-interest from the theoretical inadequacies of the standard economic model. The free-rider problem destroys narrow self-interest as a motivation for how one votes. But with signaling, people might very well give some weight to narrow self-interest in voting because others believe that they are doing so.[8]

Implications: Self-Interested Behavior

The imitation model shares a common implication with narrow self-interest. Those who have a self-interest in supporting greater government expenditures will do so more than those who do not. From equation (4),

$$P_2 - P_1 = bx / (b + n_2 w_{12} + n_1 w_{21}) > 0. \tag{5}$$

From the definitions of x, $S_2 - S_1 = x > 0$. Hence, the differences in political positions conform to the differences in self-interested positions. Since both this prediction and the kind of results discussed in this section have appeared in the literature, neither is great news nor a distinctive feature of our model. There are two reasons for discussing these findings at this point. First, doing so provides a simple way to introduce variables that play an important role in subsequent tests. Second, it is not unimportant that these roughly familiar results can be predicted from a model that does not rest on the shaky foundations of narrow self-interest in a large group setting.

To test for self-interested behavior it is necessary to have an empirical measure of political positions and to specify independently of voting behavior what constitutes the self-interest of particular voters. Since Peltzman (1984, 1985), Kau and Rubin (1982), and Enelow and Hinich (1984) found Republicans supporting less government redistribution, one can use the Republicanism of voters as a measure of their opposition to such programs. Along with observations from 15,125 individuals on other variables over the period 1972–86, NORC (1986) provides data with seven levels of that variable: strong, moderate, and weak levels of support for Republicans and Democrats, respectively, and independents. The most obvious way to scale this variable is strong Democrat = 0; not very strong Democrat = 1; independent close to Democrats = 2; independent close to neither party = 3; independent close to Republicans = 4; not very strong Republican = 5 strong Republican = 6. We call this measure *RN*.

While obvious, this scaling is also somewhat arbitrary. Party identification is of interest because it can help predict the behavior of voters. If the difference between strong Democrat and not very strong Democrat has half the impact on electoral decisions of the difference between not very strong Democrat and independent close to Democrats, that difference should be scaled by half as much. We devised another scaling, called *R,* based on that principle.[9]

Following the lead of many economists, we measure self-interest monetarily. Using such a measure, Peltzman (1985) provides evidence that the losses from redistribution rise with income. Even though there are other components of self-interest, there is no reason to believe that their existence would invalidate the relationship between income and losses from redistribution.

The job of determining other gainers and losers from redistribution is more difficult. Fortunately, a careful specification is not required for the implications we examine here. Nearly all our tests use just the income variable. We roughly guess at other gainers from redistribution: those receiving government aid; those in industries that expand as a result of government redistribution (education, public administration, health and hospitals); those not employed full-time, the unemployed (on the assumption that they are more likely to be unemployed now or in the future and receive government aid); and those who are not self-employed (on the assumption that the business taxes that the self-employed pay are not all immediately collected from others through higher prices). In addition, we include union membership, since union interests have been served by those advocating bigger government expenditures, though we provide no explanation for that alliance.

The first column of table 5.1 tests self-interested behavior using regression results with the Republicanism of individual voters, measured by R, as the dependent variable. The coefficients of income and the other self-interest variables conform significantly to the predictions of both the narrow self-interest and the imitation models. The self-employed identify with the Republican Party. Those that are not fully employed, employed in "government industries," and those who are unionized identify with the Democrats.

Implications: Group Effects

Call groups for which w_{ii} in equation (3) is greater than $w_{ij} i \neq j$ *association groups.* The imitation model predicts that individuals in association groups will vote in terms of the income of their group as well as their own individual incomes. With more high-income members in one's group, one has more of an incentive to imitate high-income behavior.[10]

To put this implication to work, one has to identify association groups. We claim that ethnic and religious groups are association groups in the United States. Both ethnicity and religiosity are salient characteristics in the United States determining associations whether or not there is some intrinsic requirement that they do so. As one can confirm by data on marriage patterns, actual probabilities of association are greater within ethnic and religious groups than between them. There should be a close relationship between these actual patterns of

TABLE 5.1. Regression Results and Related Data (*t* values in parentheses)[a]

Independent Variables[b]	Republican		Income		1909 Wages
			Dependent Variables[c]		
Self-Interest					
Income	.0240	(8.30)			
Self-employed	.0273	(5.03)			
Full-time employee	.0024	(.58)			
Government aid	−.0225	(−4.63)			
Industries					
College	−.0442	(−3.49)			
Other education	−.0196	(−2.89)			
Public administration	−.0129	(−2.18)			
Hospitals	−.0146	(−2.16)			
Union	−.0338	(−9.02)			
Regions[d]					
NE	.0364	(3.54)	.1669	(5.34)	
MA	.0511	(7.09)	.1036	(4.73)	
ENC	.0213	(3.16)	.0474	(2.32)	
WNC	.0071	(.82)	.0270	(1.02)	
SA	−.0148	(−2.06)	−.0399	(−1.85)	
ESC	−.0320	(−3.41)	−.0522	(−1.85)	
WSC	−.0358	(−4.30)	.0233	(.93)	
MT	.0206	(2.01)	−.0075	(−.23)	
City					
Large standard metropolitan area (SMA): central city	−.0548	(−6.78)	.0751	(3.07)	
Large SMA: suburb	−.0003	(−.05)	.3698	(15.71)	
Other SMA: central city	−.0371	(−5.42)	.0586	(2.84)	
Other SMA: suburb	−.0069	(−.97)	.2569	(11.94)	
Other urban	−.0127	(−2.30)	.0844	(5.04)	
Ethnic					
Africans	−.1231	(−14.60)	−.1572	(−6.16)	
Chinese	.1104	(2.30)	.2725	(1.87)	
Japanese	.0092	(.20)	.1002	(.70)	
Philippine	.0085	(.20)	.1690	(1.28)	
Indian	−.0054	(−.09)	.0472	(.27)	
Arab	−.0272	(−.38)	−.0727	(−.34)	8.12
Greek	.0942	(1.87)	.3166	(2.07)	8.41
Yugoslav	−.0309	(−.97)	.0609	(.63)	11.69
Spanish	−.0082	(−.35)	−.0514	(−.73)	10.51
Portugese	−.1102	(−2.72)	.1702	(1.38)	8.10
Hungarian	−.0568	(−2.52)	.1283	(1.87)	11.65
Russian	−.0262	(−1.40)	.2081	(3.66)	11.01
Lithuanian	.0280	(.88)	−.0729	(−.75)	11.03

TABLE 5.1.— *Continued*

Independent Variables[b]	Dependent Variables[c]				
	Republican		Income		1909 Wages
Rumanian	−.0173	(−.35)	−.2462	(−1.64)	10.90
Mexican	−.0268	(−1.90)	−.2660	(−6.21)	
Irish	−.0019	(−.27)	.1453	(6.73)	13.01
German	.0046	(7.45)	.1232	(6.50)	13.63
English	.0528	(7.74)	.2352	(11.53)	14.13
Scottish	.0560	(4.54)	.2367	(6.34)	15.24
Danish	.0407	(1.86)	.2680	(4.03)	14.32
Finnish	−.0502	(−2.30)	.0162	(.24)	13.27
Italian	−.0087	(−.89)	.0501	(1.67)	10.29
French	.0545	(3.97)	.1578	(3.78)	12.92
Belgian	−.0606	(−1.42)	.1776	(1.37)	11.01
Austrian	.0083	(.36)	.0959	(1.38)	11.93
Czechoslovakian	−.0155	(−.92)	.0167	(.32)	12.01
Dutch	.0630	(3.97)	.1416	(2.93)	12.04
Norwegian	.0517	(3.55)	.1969	(4.44)	15.28
Swede	.0327	(2.13)	.1090	(2.33)	15.36
Pole	−.0201	(−1.67)	.0727	(1.99)	11.06
West Indian	−.1069	(−3.71)	−.0971	(−1.11)	
Puerto Rican	−.0223	(−1.01)	−.3836	(−5.48)	
South, Central American	−.0057	(−.18)	−.0324	(−.34)	
Native Americans	−.0142	(−1.25)	−.1022	(−2.94)	
French Canadian	−.0039	(−.21)	.1142	(2.01)	10.62
Other Canadian	.0283	(1.21)	.1758	(2.47)	14.15
Swiss	.0561	(1.94)	.1238	(1.41)	12.61
"American"	−.0790	(−6.56)	−.1532	(−4.18)	
Religions					
None	−.0215	(−2.62)	.0363	(1.61)	
None—average[d]	−.0364	(−4.89)			
Catholic	−.0267	(−2.94)	.0263	(1.70)	
Catholic—average[d]	−.0656	(−12.96)			
Jewish	−.0799	(−3.47)	.4466	(10.08)	
Attendance: Protestant	.0036	(4.00)			
Attendance: Catholic	−.0052	(−3.61)			
Attendance: Jewish	−.0095	(−1.47)			
Age	−.0062	(−9.44)	.0584	(30.90)	
Age^2	.00006	(8.23)	−.0007	(−34.45)	
Age slope[e]	−.0012	(−9.41)			
Education	.0033	(4.07)			
Father's education	.0031	(4.57)			
Mother's education	.0015	(2.05)			
Sex	.0038	(.95)			
Year	.0015	(3.46)			
Intercept	.2444	(6.42)	−.3580	(−.17)	
R^2	.1254		.1668		

TABLE 5.1.— *Continued*

Source: National Opinion Research Center (1986); Higgs (1971).

[a]Sample size: 15,125.

[b]Independent variables are defined as follows: Income = family income in a year divided by mean family income in that year. Quadratic, cubic and log income function were also tried. The squared and cubic terms were not significant and the log income terms worked no better than income. Self-employed dummy = 1 if person or spouse self employed. Full- time employee dummy = 1 if person was a full time employee. Government aid dummy = 1 if person or spouse received government aid in the last five years. Regions: Pacific is the region of comparison (NE = Northeast; MA = Mid-Atlantic; ENC = East North Central; WNC = West North Central; SA = South Atlantic; ESC = East South Central; WSC = West South Central; MT = Mountain). City: Rural is the city category of comparison. Ethnic: Ethnicity unspecified is the ethnic group of comparison. Religions: Other religions, mainly Protestant, is the religion of comparison. Attendance = Number of days attended church per year. The attendance variables are attendance times the appropriate religious dummy. Education = Year of school. A squared education term was also tried, but not found to be significant. Sex = 1 if male. Year = year of interview.

[c]Dependent variables are defined as follows. Republican = Republican Party identification, scaled by the 1976 presidential election. (For details see Nelson 1994.) The results are robust with respect to the scaling procedure. Income = family income defined in footnote b of this table. 1909 wages = Observed past income. See note 17 for chapter 5.

[d]The averages are not additional variables. They are the coefficient of the given religious variables taken at the mean level of church attendance for that group compared to the omitted group (Protestants) taken at the mean level of church attendance for that group.

[e]Slopes are also not additional variables. Instead, they are combinations of the appropriate independent variables that yield slopes at the mean value of that independent variable.

association and the *w* for two reasons. First, actual associations are determined in part by the preferences measured by the *w*. Second, the very fact of association tends to produce a higher *w*. It pays to give greater weight to the political position of those with whom one might associate than to the position of others.[11]

One can test the hypothesis that is the focus of this section: that people in high-income groups will have high *R*, holding constant their own income. The ethnic dummies in the Republicanism equation of the first column in table 5.1 provide a measure of the ethnic group's role in determining the political positions of individuals holding their own income and other individual characteristics constant. They are a measure up to an additive constant of the political position of the group that is not explained by individuals responding to their own individual characteristics other than ethnicity. This allows one to determine the indirect effects of those characteristics on the behavior of those with which they associate. For purposes of calculating these dummies, one wants to control for all the important individual characteristics that could influence an individual's vote. Hence, there is a rather large list of variables in the first column of table 5.1. One can relate these dummies to the average relative family income in the sample by ethnic group—the second column in table 5.1.[12] The imitation model predicts that the regression coefficients of the ethnic dummies in the Republicanism equation (B) should be positively related to the value of these dummies in the income equation (I). Indeed, they are for a sample of thirty-seven ethnic groups.

$$B = .0041 + .1260 \ I. \tag{6}$$
$$(-.537) \ (2.79) \qquad (t \text{ statistics in parentheses})$$

There are at least two alternative explanations for the relationship of these ethnic variables that flow from the narrow self-interest theory. First, the primary system insures that the party that specializes in the interests of low-income voters qua low-income voters will tend to be the advocate of their other interests. To succeed in a primary a candidate must appeal to the majority of his own party. For example, Democrats push black interests as well as the interests of those with low income because blacks constitute a larger proportion of Democratic voters than voters in general.

Probably the most important manifestation of that process is the lead of the Democratic Party in affirmative action and some kinds of civil rights legislation. A relatively few ethnic groups are purportedly beneficiaries of that legislation: blacks, Native Americans, American Hispanics, and Orientals.[13] There is some question about whether those benefits are restricted to elites and whether on net Orientals benefited at all. However, it is likely that many within these groups believe they are beneficiaries, but it is unlikely that all believed themselves to be equal beneficiaries. Under these circumstances the best way to control for the possible affirmative action beneficiaries is to eliminate them from the sample.[14] Then,

$$B = .0075 + .159 \ I. \tag{7}$$
$$(-.69) \ (2.37)$$

A version of the altruism hypothesis also generates a relationship between group income and voting behavior. If, as Adam Smith (1976) believed, people give greater weight to the well-being of other people the more contact they have with them, they will vote in terms of group income as well as individual income. But this specification of the altruism model comes from a rather special theory of altruism, and it is based on observed behavior that is easily explained by the imitation model, used also by Smith.

Implications: Lags

The last section's result is not an overwhelmingly convincing verification of the imitation hypothesis, if one believes either the narrow self-interest or the altruistic model to be a viable alternative. There are specifications of those hypotheses that could lead to the same results. But the story is changed considerably when one talks about voting behavior as a function of group income sixty years in the past. All of the alternative hypotheses—self-interest and altruism alike—require group income to measure either the self-interested position of the group or the permanent income of the individuals in the group. Group income of sixty years ago will not serve as such a measure, especially when present group income is also included in the regression.

In contrast, long lags make sense in the imitation model, though are not required by it. Reasonable specifications of the imitation model generate long lags. Convert equation (4) to a set of simultaneous difference equations. Assume that people know the political position that maximizes their immediate narrow self-interest, but that they discover with a lag the political position of others.

$$(1 + b)P_{1t} = (n_1 - 1)w_{11}P_{1(t-1)} + n_2 w_{12}P_{2(t-1)},$$
$$(1 + b)P_{2t} = (n_2 - 1)w_{22}P_{2(t-1)} + n_2 w_{21}P_{1(t-1)} + bx. \qquad (8)$$

Look at the case where a person associates exclusively with a dominantly high-income group. Assume, for example, that within the group $n_1 = 2, n_2 = 8, w_{ii} = 10w_{ij}$ $j \neq i, b = .01, x = 1$. But suppose that group was formerly a low-income group ($n_1 = 8$ and $n_2 = 2$). It takes seventy-three periods for both low-income and high-income members of that group to move their political positions halfway between their equilibrium low group income position and their equilibrium high group position.[15] Equation (8) helps explain custom. A lag in people's perceptions of the views of others produces a slow response of their own views to changes in the self-interest of the group.

While this is just an example, equation (8) implies in general that lags will be shorter the larger b with no lags if $b = 1$. When there is a significant private gain to a behavior, b will be much greater. In consequence, we expect b to be smaller for voting and for mores formation than for activities related to the production process.[16]

Therefore, we expect greater lags in this voting case than in the usual economic problem. Since we do not know precisely how long a lag to expect, the imitation model itself does not provide any precise guide to its length. Our choice of the lag period is, therefore, dictated by other considerations. We want to choose a time period sufficiently long that lags generated within the alternative hypotheses are unlikely to be observed, and that present and past group income are clearly distinguishable, and we must work within data constraints. The voting behavior observed is for 1972–86. The past year income chosen is for 1909. Our test will be of the imitation model with lags of sixty-three to seventy-seven years against the hypotheses of narrow self-interest, altruism, or the imitation model with much shorter lags.

We test the lag hypothesis using ethnic groups. We use as an imperfect measure of their past income the weekly wages of the foreign-born in 1909 by ethnic groups, as shown in the third column of table 5.1.[17] Call these wages *PI*. Since there were no data for any of the affirmative action beneficiaries, we, of necessity, control for affirmative action by eliminating those groups. We get marginally significant results of *PI* on ethnic Republicanism.[18]

However, there is even more convincing evidence that some combination of past and present income helps determine Republicanism among groups. One obvious reason why the results were only moderately informative above is that the data forced use of 1909 income. Supposedly, the whole stream of past income is relevant with unknown weights. Present and 1909 income will not serve as adequate proxies for other years if the time path of income varies by ethnic groups. Furthermore, the appropriate weights for each year can vary by ethnic groups depending upon their own stream of immigration to the United States. This problem can pose insuperable difficulties in determining the precise role of past and present income separately.

But the problem can be overcome if one is simply interested in determining whether or not there is a combined effect of the two. Take, for example, the case of ethnic groups each of whose income relative to average income has remained constant over time. Then, one need not know the lag structure in order to estimate the combined effect of past and present income on political positions. While one cannot find any such groups, one can find groups whose relative income positions exhibit some stability over time. We ran a very simple test using this principle. We sorted ethnic groups by whether they had higher or lower than the median values of *I* and *PI* respectively. We then compared the mean of *B*, the ethnic dummy coefficients in the Republicanism equation, for those groups with high values of both *I* and *PI* with the mean of *B* for those groups with low values of both.

As shown in table 5.2, the difference between the two means was

.054, t = 5.54. With 14 degrees of freedom this is extremely significant. Furthermore, the data provide additional justification for this testing procedure. The categories of ethnic groups with unstable income—either low values of I and high values of PI or vice versa—should have more in-group variation in B attributable to variation in the lag structure of income paths than the categories of ethnic groups with stable income—either high or low values of I and PI. Indeed, this is the case. The ratio of the average value of the variance of the former to the average value of the variance of the latter is 9.92, significant at the .001 level. So a way of organizing data to determine if there is a combined effect of long past and present income can be used to show that both present and long past income are relevant in determining current political positions.

TABLE 5.2.   Republicanism of Ethnic Groups Classified by Present and Past Income

High I, High PI		Low I, Low PI	
Irish	−.002	Yugoslav	−.031
English	.053	Spanish	−.008
Scottish	.056	Lithuanian	.028
Danish	.041	Arab	−.027
French	.055	Italian	−.009
Dutch	.063	Rumanian	−.017
Norwegian	.052	Pole	−.020
Other Canadian	.028	French Canadian	−.004
Mean	.043	Mean	−.011
σ	.0192	σ	.0172

High I, Low PI		Low I, High PI	
Greek	.094	German	.047
Portuguese	−.110	Finnish	−.052
Hungarian	−.057	Swedish	.033
Russian	−.026	Czech	−.016
Belgian	−.061		
Mean	−.032	Mean	.003
σ	.0685	σ	.0394

Note: Republicanism regression coefficients are from table 5.1.

I = family income per family; PI = past family income per family; both as defined in Table 5.1. High and low determined by direction of deviation from their respective medians.

There is also evidence of lags of a different sort. Not only does the self-interest position of a group change over time, but an individual can change groups over time, though this is less true for ethnicity than other group identifiers. Past, as well as present, associations should have an impact on an individual's political position. This would be especially true of political positions that are generated by conscience: internalized social norms. An important part of that "social capital" is past associates. We find that both father's and mother's education have a significant positive effect on a person's Republicanism with coefficients of .0031 and .0015 respectively. The respective t values are 4.57 and 2.05. Of course, fathers and mothers are often still alive, so that some of this result can be explained by current association with parents. However, the order of magnitude of these results suggest that more is going on. The slope for father's education is virtually identical to the slope for the individual himself (.0033).

Similar results are obtained in chapter 8. Long past associations affect current political positions. City size and regions when the respondent was sixteen often play as big a role in explaining political positions as does current city size and region.

Expressive Voting

Others have rejected the narrow self-interest theory of voting for the same reason we did: the free-rider problem. They also have sought some private return to voting. Schuessler (2000) believes voting to be a search for "identity." Brennan and Hamlin (1998) maintain that that private return lies in the joy of actively cheering on one candidate or another. Voting is like rooting for one football team or another.

We believe that there is merit to this position, though it is ad hoc. There is often a fervor associated with voting, just as soccer fans often riot at the drop of a ball. But these "cheering" and "identity" theories don't get very far unless one has some idea about what the cheering and identification are all about.

Brennan and Hamlin posit that one cheers more for candidates whose political position is closer to one's own. Voting for a candidate is just a form of cheering, where the compensation for the costs of voting is the fun of cheering. This resolves the free-rider problem associated with voting, but does not explain how individual political positions are determined. Hence, their theory as developed is consistent with any theory about the determinants of political positions, but seems to have a natural fit with our theory of imitation.

Often we adopt behavioral rules that are sustainable because they achieve goals of which we are unaware. Cheering seems to be one such case. Cheering works because one's desired friends are cheering for the same candidate or team. Cheering is an emotional form of imitation. We believe that the implications of cheering are the same as the implications of imitation.

Brennan and Hamlin, however, believe cheering has implications that it does not have. They assume that one cheers because one identifies with a candidate, rather than cheering because one identifies with one's fellow cheerers. But look at team sports. In cheering Michael Jordan, Chicago Bull fans never questioned his Chicago roots. All that was important was that the Chicago Bulls were the *Chicago* Bulls. Few Chicago fans still cheer for him when his current team, the Washington Wizards, play the Bulls.

While Brennan and Hamlin are more interested in voting than sports fan behavior, their mistaken view about cheerer identification also leads to mistakes in predicting voting patterns. They believe that people are more likely to vote if they identify with the candidate. Since electoral success generally requires moderate candidates, they believe that extremists are less likely to vote than are moderates. As we saw in chapter 4, this can be rejected empirically.

Conclusion

The imitation model is better both theoretically and empirically than either the standard narrow self-interest or altruism models of voter behavior. In contrast to the other theories, the imitation model appropriately focuses on private returns to private actions rather than public returns. Empirically, the observed impacts of present and past group income on voting behavior are inconsistent with any version of narrow self-interest except imitation for information. That version of narrow self-interest has two problems: (1) the large group problem endemic to any narrow self-interest model of voting behavior; (2) a failure to explain why people vary their political position as the position of those to whom they talk varies.

The main empirical conclusion is that associations matter profoundly in determining voting patterns. Ethnic and religious groups, not including the beneficiaries of affirmative action, explain 32 percent of the explained variance of Republicanism, while the self-interest variables of table 5.1 and education (partially a measure of permanent income) explain only 20 percent. (This latter number exaggerates the role of narrow self-interest, since many of the self-interest variables and education have another important role examined in the next chapter.) Imitation theory helps explain what the narrow self-interest model (except imitation for information) cannot explain—the large proportion of conflicts generated by ethnic and religious differences.

CHAPTER 6

Goodness

In the last chapter we saw how people adopt political positions to signal to others that they want to be their friends or to be involved in reciprocal relationships with them. We saw that it is credible that the signaler will be more trustworthy toward those whose political position he imitates than toward others. But a person can also use political positions to signal in two other ways.

First, one can signal trustworthiness to some members of one's group by an alternative to imitation. One can be either a practitioner, enforcer, or advocate of group morality. All of these activities involve a cost, though the cost is somewhat different for each. For the practitioners the price is obvious—not getting the private returns from violating those mores. Enforcers who use ostracism pay the cost of avoiding relationships that could be of benefit to them. Public advocacy of group morality has obvious time and money costs. But there are two other costs. First, advocacy of morality raises the cost to the advocate of his violating the morality. He would not only be guilty of the sin itself, but of hypocrisy, in effect lying about his behavior by publicly opposing such behavior. Second, advocacy of group morality reduces the advocate's relations with violators of that morality.

These two costs generate a dual signal from morality advocacy. One of these signals is similar to charity signaling. Instead, however, of paying a money cost to indicate trustworthiness, morality advocates pay a conditional cost—a greater cost if they violate group morality and are exposed. This greater cost would be justified only if it revealed to others that the moralizers were more trustworthy. In addition, moralizers are more likely to practice group morality. Such practice is a signal that moralizers place a high value on reciprocal relations. But moralizers also signal that they do not wish to have reciprocal relations with violators of the social rules. This makes them more trustworthy to members of the group who do not violate the rules. We call this dual signaling *morality signaling.*

It is clear from the foregoing that morality signaling increases the trustworthiness of the signaler to his fellow moralizers. Both of the signals produced by morality advocacy generate that result. For others the two signals send conflicting messages. The part of the signal that is analogous to charity makes the signaler more trustworthy to everybody. But the part that is a condemnation of immorality makes the morality signaler less trustworthy to the immoral. Which of these messages dominates probably depends upon the nature of the reciprocal relations involved. For close friendships morality signalers are unlikely to make good partners with the immoral. If, however, the relations are less intimate, such as the relations between employer and employee, the greater generalized trustworthiness of the morality signalers would tend to dominate.

Second, there is a signal of quite a different character, and the one on which this chapter focuses. A person can use political positions to signal general trustworthiness as opposed to trustworthiness within one's narrowly defined group. We call this *goodness* signaling.

The thesis of this chapter is that goodness is asymmetric for an important set of issues: redistribution to the poor, and environmental and educational expenditures. That is, one signals goodness by advocating more government expenditures in these areas, but signals its opposite by advocating less expenditures. Furthermore, for these issues there is no morality signaling generated by advocating less expenditures. Though virtually unexplored in the literature—Sowell (1995) is a rare exception—rough versions of our idea are popular. The "do-gooder" label is often assigned to liberals by their foes, usually with a touch of derision. It is interesting that even conservatives recognize that many liberals are signaling goodness by way of political positions that the conservatives find objectionable. When it comes to name calling, "do-gooders" is one of the more benign ways to denigrate a foe.

The processes producing asymmetry for these issues will be examined later. So too will be the process producing what we call "two-sided" goodness—issues where goodness signalers take the opposite position from morality signalers. Before we do this, however, we want to model the political decision process with asymmetric goodness. It will be easier to understand asymmetric goodness knowing what it involves.

Political Positions as Signals

The model we employ is simply an extension of the imitation model developed in the last chapter. The mathematics are in appendix 3. An individual adopts a political position to maximize utility derived from three sources: (1) narrow self-interest—the gain to his self-interest in having his self-interest realized; (2) the signaling returns from imitating his friends; (3) the returns from signaling—goodness.

Two features of this decision process should be noted. (1) As previously explained, narrow self-interest returns should be small because of the free-rider problem. (2) The political positions of others are endogenous variables determined by the same process determining the original individual's political position. Others get a return from imitating the original individual's political position. The big impact of imitation on the reduced form is to make a person's political position a function of the narrow self-interest of others and their preferences for goodness.

In consequence, it does not take a very big goodness effect for the goodness of oneself and others to play an important role in determining political positions. The only rival to goodness in determining equilibrium outcomes is narrow self-interest with its small returns. Furthermore, even if one does not signal goodness, one's political position is not goodness free. It is affected by the goodness of the others imitated.

The gain to a person signaling goodness by way of political positions is that some others find that person more trustworthy. For the signaling to differentiate people there must be some cost, or everybody would have an incentive to so signal. For standard charity the costs are obvious: the money or time costs of the charity. Our model of voting behavior reveals the implicit costs of goodness. To buy more goodness, one buys less of the other two components determining political positions. Because of the free-rider problem, people get little return from public political positions motivated by narrow self-interest. Hence, the major cost of goodness will be the possible loss of valued friends.

That cost will produce a signal of generalized trustworthiness because those who use the signal wish more relations with people in general at the expense of relations with their closest associates. That wish by itself makes the "do-gooder" more likely to be a good reciprocator in general at the cost of being a poorer reciprocator for his closest associates. For example, a high-income person advocating more redistribution to the poor would be rightly seen as more trustworthy in dealing with the poor and the middle-class, but less trustworthy by the rich. He would be less likely to do a favor for his fellow rich just because they were rich, and more likely to ignore income in determining whether he would do a favor for others.

Two signals seem to be generated from one's political position: (1)

with whom one wishes to associate, and (2) how much one wishes to specialize in one's associates. Therefore, some ambiguity in the signal would seem to be created. It will often pay the signaler to use some key word, like *compassion,* along with his political position to indicate that the deviation from his most wanted friends' political position is attributable to goodness rather than a desire for a different set of friends. Though this can mitigate the signalers' costs, it will not eliminate them, because his desired friends will still believe that he is willing to sacrifice their interests in favor of more general social interests.

Long-Run Equilibrium in Mores

For both charity and goodness "good" causes are determined by what social rules—mores—define as good causes. For standard charity it is irrelevant to the individual's survival which cause gets his dollars, holding constant the signaling efficiency of a cause. Similarly, an individual's survival is not affected by the cause he chooses to display his "goodness," holding constant, again, the signaling efficiency of the cause. The causes selected will be those that mores promote as "good" causes.

But how are mores determined? First, we try to answer that question for long-run equilibrium. However, it is unlikely that long-run solutions will be sufficient because an important determinant of long-run equilibrium—group selection—operates so slowly.

The first requirement for the persistence of a social rule is that it can be enforced at least to some extent. In this section we want to focus on the formulation of social rules rather than their enforcement. For simplicity, we shall assume that the social rules with which we deal are enforceable. For a wide range of social rules that assumption is not preposterous. In primitive societies enforcement often came through ostracism. As discussed in the section "Reciprocity and Other Social Pressure" in chapter 2, the conditions of primitive society made that a particularly effective enforcement mechanism. In modern societies the police power of the state has taken over much of that enforcement role.

Primitive and modern society also differ in the way social rules are developed. In contrast to primitive societies, modern societies determine more social rules by laws that in turn are constructed by some formal government mechanism. The long-run equilibrium most relevant for purposes of predicting even contemporary behavior is probably the long-run equilibrium associated with hunter-gatherer societies, since those were the societies that existed throughout most of man's history. However, at the level of generality at which we are working, it doesn't matter whether we are dealing with primitive or modern society. The informal development of social rules in the former can be thought of as an analogue to voting. While it is more usual to think of social rules just as givens, they originated somehow. The past will play an important role in determining both voting and the informal choice of social rules. But the past decision process should be like the present. As seen in the last chapter, imitation produces long lags in both voting choices and the choice of social rules. In long-run equilibrium past decisions will be the same as present decisions. So social rules are determined by some weighted average of what individuals want the social rules to be, whether we are dealing with primitive or modern society.

In determining long-run equilibrium in social rules in any society two processes are at work. The first is either voting or an analogue to voting. The appropriate model of that process is the same as the model we previously used. There are, again, three components in the utility that individual's maximize: narrow self-interest, imitation, and goodness or moralizing.

The second process is group selection. Competition between societies makes some social rules grow in coverage relative to others as long as there is variation in those social rules. Narrow self-interest by itself is insufficient in that competition. We shall detail later in this chapter the differences between decisions based on narrow self-interest and on maximizing group survival. But the winning social rules require the right amount of goodness and moralizing.[1] That is why they enter into the voting process in the first place. Group selection not only determines the amount of this signaling; it determines its contents: what issues will be used for signaling and which side of each issue signalers will take.

From Externality Correction to Goodness

As stated before, the process by which mores maximize group survival must be consistent with the maximization of individual survival as well. That not only requires equilibrium in the sense that once the maximizing mores are in place there is nothing within the system to make the mores change, but also that the equilibrium is attainable from likely starting positions.

Begin with a goodness-free society: only present and past imitation and narrow self-interest are involved in determining the "votes" for the mores. In terms of the last chapter, the imitation component of one's political position—in this case one's position about the mores—is determined by minimizing a weighted average of some function of the difference between one's own political position and two other terms: the political positions of all associates whether close or distant and the political position that maximizes one's own narrow self-interest. In that chapter the weights a person used were determined by the relative importance of the associates to that person. And, indeed, there is something natural about such weights. However, such a weighting pattern is not required. All that is required is that a person use the weights that other people believe he is using.

Look at a special case of imitation that is likely to operate. People have frequent interactions with a limited set of friends and occasional interactions with a lot of people. In this situation we can break their signaling into two components: they imitate their friends to signal trustworthiness toward them, and they signal goodness to signal trustworthiness to everybody else.

Since these components can be in conflict, the weights people give to these respective groups is important. Suppose that people start with the natural weights defined above with others believing that those are the weights. Will those be the equilibrium weights? Not if societies vary in the weighting pattern both used and believed to be used. Specifically, look at the weights given to poor distant associates and to rich distant associates. There is an external benefit to redistribution from rich to poor generated primarily by the positive but diminishing marginal value of income in increasing prosocial behavior and decreasing antisocial behavior. This external benefit in redistribution to the poor, generates a narrow self-interest return to the nonpoor in such redistribution.[2] Clearly, people would have to guess at this effect, and one would expect different societies to make different guesses.

Compare three societies: one that guesses that the impact of this externality is somewhat lower than it really is; one that guesses right; and one that exaggerates the impact somewhat. There are two forces affecting the fate of these guesses. The first is any tendency of wrong guesses to be later corrected—utility maximization. The second is group survival, which in this context is the only survival that counts.[3] If externalities were the only impact of income distribution on group survival, group survival would work exactly like mistake correction. But externalities are not the whole story of group survival, as we shall shortly see. Presuming that at the margin an extra dollar transferred from rich to poor adds to total survival, we would expect societies with more redistribution to grow relative to societies with less.[4]

Both information and survival eliminate the guess that underestimates externalities. But these forces conflict in determining the winner between the overestimate and the right guess, as long as the overestimate leads to redistribution equal to the group survival maximum or less.

The expected amount of redistribution could fall somewhere in between the externality correction optimum and the group survival maximum depending on the rate at which mistakes in the former are adjusted compared to the rate of change produced by group survival. We know that group selection moves slowly. But mistake correction also occurs at a snail's pace. The necessary information is hard to come by, and individuals have little incentive to either find the information or act on it if they do.

The most interesting feature, however, of mistake correction is that it too is influenced by survival. The expected redistribution is somewhere in the range between an externality correction optimum and a group survival maximum. Hence, a society can push the solution toward survival maximization by minimizing the rate of mistake correction in judgments about externalities.

Society has a simple device that does exactly that at no survival costs to the individuals who use it: emotional reactions about redistribution. These are what Loewenstein (2000) has called "visceral factors" that propel behavior in directions that differ from those dictated by careful weighing of long-term costs and benefits. Instead of calling for greater externality correction, plead for greater compassion. In both cases individuals would be signaling their goodness, so which plea would be employed is a matter of indifference to individual decision-makers. But the "compassion for the poor" cry is less prone to correction. The origins of such a soul-searching cry in externality correction are so disguised that it can hardly be criticized for overdoing a job that it doesn't seem designed to do. In consequence, a society that gets emotional about redistribution to the poor is likely to grow relative to a society that does not. The equilibrium amount of redistribution would be closer to a group survival maximum.

(Many social scientists [for example, Frank 1988] have rationalized emotions in terms of individual survival. We use instead a group survival argument. But the logic of the two approaches is the same when group survival does not conflict with individual survival.)

It is conceivable that the disguise for externality correction is so thorough that redistribution in long-run equilibrium would be exactly equal to its group survival maximum. It is also possible that it will be less than that because some mistake correction goes on in spite of that disguise. For simplicity, in the rest of this book we assume that long-run equilibrium is at the group survival maximum. But all that is important for our purposes is that group survival maximization is a component of long-run equilibrium. For example, we would expect asymmetric goodness in the case of redistribution to the poor. One signals goodness by advocating more redistribution to the poor, not by advocating less of this redistribution.

To make the argument tangible we have focused on a particular issue involving group selection, but the same analysis can be used for any group selection process that also involves externalities, and all seem to do so.[5] The foregoing suggests that that relationship is not accidental. Because the appropriate amount of externality correction is so hard to estimate, externality correction is an obvious source of mistakes in utility maximization. Some source of mistakes that lead to different social decisions is required for survival processes to have an impact.

Group selection, then, is crucial in determining how much goodness in political positions is required to signal generalized trustworthiness. But the reverse is true as well. Goodness signaling is required to produce mores that maximize group survival out of individual behavior that is interested solely in individual survival.

Long-Run Equilibrium in a Democracy

What will long-run equilibrium entail given a democratic government? The voting process determining political positions is similar to the analogous voting process determining the mores. Of course, because "voting" about the mores does not involve a secret ballot, public pressure is likely to be more important in mores formation than in voting. Conscience is likely to be more important in voting than in the mores. Moreover, there also can be a difference in the weights each individual has in determining final decisions. However, one gets the same result in long-run equilibrium whether goodness is defined by an equilibrium political outcome or by equilibrium social rules. The details of the voting processes are irrelevant. In both cases goodness is determined by that which leads to political decisions that when applied lead to outcomes that maximize group survival.

To determine the equilibrium goals of goodness, we must determine differences between voting decisions without goodness and survival-maximizing decisions. For the latter we will focus on the survival of the group making the decisions: roughly the number of long-run descendants.[6] This statement ignores the full impact of intersociety competition. Social rules maximize the number of people in the long run following those rules. Acculturation and conquest are other ways to extend these numbers. But for present purposes we simply focus on increasing the descendants of those following the rules.

There are two big differences between voting outcomes without goodness and policies that maximize group survival. First, what individuals want is different than that which maximizes their survival. What individuals want would determine their nongoodness voting decisions, while what maximizes their survival would be a component in the maximization of group survival. Second, the weights given to individuals in determining group survival are different than the weights determining voting outcomes.

In chapter 2 we saw that individuals maximize expected utility over their lifetimes. Concern with their children's welfare is built in to their own utility, but not built in enough to maximize the survival of their genes. Instead, social rules take up the slack, forcing people to invest more in their children than they would do just from altruism directed toward their children.[7] To achieve that result "do-gooders" advocate greater expenditures for child care in the form of education, day care, child nutrition, child safety, and so forth.

Consider redistribution. Others have discussed the externalities in redistributing income.

1. Insurance (Bishop, Formby, and Smith 1991; Overbye 1995). Risk-averse individuals would prefer a more equal distribution of income to a less equal distribution, so they run less risk of large declines in their income in the future.
2. Social cohesion and stability (Piven 1971; Hirshleifer 1994). Crime and riots are quite possibly a function of the degree of income inequality. But these externalities do not require goodness signaling for their correction, since utility-maximizing voters can do the job.

However, maximizing group survival requires maximizing the expected number of a group's long-run descendants, ignoring intersociety effects. The marginal survival return of a dollar to a poor person is substantially higher than this marginal return to a rich person. The impact of dollars on mortality rates in particular diminishes with increases in income. To maximize group survival ignoring externalities, redistribution should occur until this positive effect is balanced by the negative effect due to the deadweight losses associated with redistribution.

Deviations from Equilibrium I

Current mores are unlikely to correspond perfectly with long-run equilibrium mores because of the substantial difference in the hunter-gatherer world and our own. Group selection moves quite slowly in comparison to the rate of environmental change. Conceivably, a society could develop context-dependent mores: mores that specify behavior conditional on the environment. Cosmides and Tooby (1992) argue that the mind is adapted to handle reciprocal relations independent of their content. But that does not generate completely flexible social rules. There is no individual return to adjusting the goals of signaling in response to environmental change, since those goals are produced by group survival rather than individual survival. We expect some environmental changes that are not fully anticipated by mores. There was no survival return in the past in anticipating future environments such as the industrial revolution.

Instead, there is a simpler, though less efficient adjustment of the mores to environmental change: there is some flexibility in the mores. The social rules permit some changes in the social rules. But these changes in the social rules will only be roughly related to group selection over any time period too short for group selection to operate.

Economists have always been more confident in analyzing equilibrium than deviations from equilibrium, and that is true for us too. But the equilibrium generated by group survival takes such a long time to be realized that deviations from equilibrium are likely to be particularly important determinants of "goodness." While our discussion of the long-run equilibrium mores should hold for any society, our discussion of deviations from equilibrium is much more society-specific. We focus on the United States. Without the pressure of group selection, there is much more room for variation in social rules country to country. Nevertheless, we believe that certain patterns in these mores grew quite naturally from the equilibrium mores.

A standard source of deviations from equilibrium is lags. In chapter 5 we discuss why there are long lags in the signaling process of voters and present evidence for those lags.

Widespread government involvement in aid to the poor and externality correction is largely a twentieth-century phenomenon. Achieving survival maximization without an active government requires a much bigger goodness effect built into mores than achieving it by way of government. Moral pressure has to be large enough to overcome the free-rider problem associated with voluntary contributions. Not only would the required moral pressure need to be greater, but the issues requiring goodness to achieve survival maximization would differ. One function of charity is to fund activities with external benefits like health research or environmental amenities. Some people bear the cost, while others share the benefit. But people now vote to fund these expenditures. People vote for others and themselves to share the costs of externality correction just as they share the benefits of that correction. Goodness pressure is no longer necessarily required to correct for externalities qua externalities when that correction comes through government action.[8]

However, we would not expect an immediate full adjustment in the "good" causes. Once a convention gets established that determines how one signals goodness, that convention will die slowly. It would not be surprising if notions of goodness that developed in a world of little government still had some force in a big-government world.

There is one big difference between this deviation from equilibrium and the long-run equilibrium solution in determining the goals of goodness. Externality correction is an important goal of charity, but it would not be a goal of goodness in long-run equilibrium, because voters would engage in the appropriate amount of that correction without goodness advocacy.

In addition this lag would reinforce some of the long-run results. The externalities in helping the poor provide another reason for "do-gooders" to advocate more redistribution. We expect government to already correct for this externality. But given lags in goodness advocacy, we would expect "do-gooders" to imperfectly adjust to this new reality.

Deviations from Equilibrium II

There is another possible discrepancy between goodness signaling and group survival: the emotional content of goodness signaling. As discussed earlier, that emotion got self-interested individuals to choose social rules that maximized group survival in the past. But those emotions may not produce the same result in a changed environment.

One of the emotions that has contributed to group survival in the past is compassion. We have seen that compassion for the poor produces the redistribution that increases group size. Compassion for children who obviously require care helps generate social rules that would produce the survival maximum amount of child care in long-run equilibrium.

But the objects of compassion seemingly are not sufficiently specified to ensure that that emotion always contributes to group survival. Even within the environmental variation faced by hunter-gatherers, there was need for variation in social rules about sharing. Big-game hunting was an important determinant of sharing rules (Wright 1994), and its relative importance varied considerably among groups. At the same time, the costs of such flexibility were limited at this period in man's history critical to the formation of preferences. The group that was targeted for compassion was clearly defined—the tribe. Under those circumstances, there was little survival benefit to specifying the emotion further because there were few occasions for those emotions to go astray.

But now our society consists of groups potentially defined in many ways. Generalized compassion no longer is guaranteed to contribute to group survival. Who, then, will be the objects of compassion? There must be some convincing basis for a claim to either pity or helplessness, some analogue to the case of the poor or children. Typical objects of compassion are groups whose average real incomes are low who obtain group preferences even for members whose real incomes are high. Ethnic groups who have been mistreated in a society even though their average income is high might also induce compassion. Misinformation can also induce misplaced compassion. Union members can be viewed as Davids battling business Goliaths even though economic theory suggests that union gains are at the expense of poorer nonunion workers. Would the substantial prounion sympathies among nonunion workers continue to exist if they were aware that union gains were at the expense of their poorer compatriots?

Nor do we claim that compassion provides the sole basis for governmental redistribution. The rent-seeking behavior of special interest groups has been well documented (for example, Stigler 1971; Krueger 1974). However, most of the success of these groups depends upon stealth, the lack of general public awareness of their gains. And just as in the union case, whenever possible these groups try a compassion argument. "Pity the poor farmer." "Pity the worker whose jobs are protected by tariffs." Stigler showed that when the government distributed quotas, smaller firms obtained a larger share of those quotas than their output would have justified. Though the compassion argument is loose, the evidence suggests that at least as far as redistribution through government taxes and expenditures is concerned, that redistribution is on net toward the poor and away from the rich (Browning and Johnson 1984).

But this variety of compassion claims must not always have convinced, or compassion would have developed immunity from such claims by the survival process. A complete theory of goodness signaling would predict the time stream of such successful claims, but such theorizing is well beyond the confines of this book. We are content to note the current successful claimants for compassion in the United States, all of whom have some characteristic that will trigger that emotion.

Long-Term versus Ephemeral Goodness

Some may find the preceding discussion of the goals of goodness unsatisfactory. We claim that all of them originated to maximize group survival. But certain compassion-driven goals have the opposite effect. Hence, there is no simple relationship between goodness and group survival.

There are, however, some ways of testing our theory linking the goals of goodness to group survival. First of all, we maintain that the compassion-driven goals of goodness that are contrary to group survival have a common property. They coexist with goals that do contribute to group survival and have the opposite impact on political choices—goals produced by morality signaling. In contrast, all the goals of goodness without conflicting morality signaling contributed to group survival, at least at the time that these preferences were being formed.

We have also alluded to a second difference between goals that contribute to group survival and those that do not. The former have been around for a long time. In contrast, those goals contrary to group survival of necessity could not have stood the long-term test of time. It is instructive to examine the evidence, if only briefly.

First, look at the redistribution of income toward the poor. As we have seen, this policy is required by group survival in hunter-gatherer societies, so it has been around for a long time. It appears that this goal is opposed by the principle of taking responsibility for one's own actions. We claim, however, that this latter "goal" is simply self-interest at work in the voting process. The disincentives associated with any other rule create substantial deadweight losses. Anthropologists have frequently noted food sharing among primitive tribes. Posner (1980) and Wright (2000) explain this voluntary food sharing by the absence of government and the insurance motivations previously discussed. Such an externality of food sharing certainly contributes to group survival in the absence of government. We contend that the amount of food sharing is greater than the amount demanded by simple externality correction because of food sharing's other impacts on survival.

The most obvious cases of food sharing seem to occur for big game. It is obvious why big game is shared. It is too much for a single family to eat before it spoils. The hunting may also require large-scale cooperation, but the sharing usually goes beyond the cooperating group. What is less obvious is why any male would bother to hunt for big game rather than hunt for smaller game, when his expected meat consumption, as opposed to meat production, is greater in the latter case. The anthropologists' answer is that the big-game hunter parleys his greater food sharing either directly or indirectly into more sexual favors: directly by trading choice cuts of meat for sex, indirectly by demonstrating skills and obtaining prestige that ultimately leads to more or better sexual partners (Ridley 1997).

This could very well be a straightforward case of sexual selection where each partner is directly better off in terms of survival as a result of the pairing. At least among the Ache, a hunter-gatherer people in South America, the children that are the product of sex with big-game hunters have a better chance of surviving either because their genes are better or because they get special treatment (Wright 1994).

Alternatively, a more subtle kind of sexual selection emphasized by Fisher (1915) in a more general context would be required. The mate of the big-game hunter might have had even more surviving children in another partnership given her superior genes. But suppose females in general prefer big-game hunters. Then the male children of big-game hunters are more likely to successfully mate as long as they are more likely to be big-game hunters themselves through either training advantages or inherited roles.[9]

Sharing, then, seems to have been a very early feature of man's development. The payoff to that sharing appears to be enhanced reputation, which has an evolutionary return of more or better sexual partners. It is not clear, however, at least in the most primitive of sharing arrangements like big-game hunting, that the enhanced reputation of sharers is closely related to an increased reputation for greater trustworthiness. Sharing the big game is no evidence of trustworthiness in other relationships, since the hunter has no alternative but to share. However, the hunter often does not reserve for himself or his family the very best cut of meats (Ridley 1997). This sacrifice only makes sense in terms of an increased reputation for trustworthiness. Furthermore, those who choose to specialize in big-game hunting might do so because they have more to gain from relationships with others. These are, indeed, the most trustworthy.

Greater opportunities for signals for trustworthiness occur for charitable contributions in an agricultural society. Long-term storage of foods is feasible and money has been invented. Under those circumstances sharing does imply real sacrifices that can signal greater trustworthiness. There is evidence of charitable giving among the Jews of the biblical era (Domb 1980) and in the Greek city-states (Constantelos 1991). There was also a system of public relief in Athens (Constantelos 1991).

Child Care

We have seen that group selection demands social rules that generate more child care than would be produced by utility-maximizing individuals absent social rules. The latter give less weight to the future than is appropriate for the survival of their own genes. Here, too, we find social rules in the distant past as well as in the present that encourage child care, and we find no opposing goodness or morality goal.

The most important social institution increasing child care is the family. It insures in the traditional monogamous family that two parents will be participants in child support and rearing. The family is required because at least some males find it in their interest to have sex without the accompanying parental responsibilities. Women would be better off, as would their children, if they could enter into a long-term contract: "No sex without shared child care." Marriage is such a contract, which used to be enforced by assorted social costs of breaking the contract.

The availability of marriage makes women better off and men worse off, ignoring the future of their genes. In primitive societies, which are not notably feminist, that redistribution of income could hardly explain social enforcement of marriage. What does explain marriage is that children would be better off given this long-term contract.

However, the problem of the predatory male thus solved would be a possible problem even if both men and women were totally future oriented in their decisions. It might pay males, even in terms of genetic survival, to have multiple sexual partners (Wright 1994). The children of such males lose child care, but there will be more of them. Such men gain quantity of children at the expense of quality.

There is, however, a feature of the marriage institution in most past societies that cannot be explained if both men and women were totally future oriented: the moral opprobrium associated with having children out of wedlock. The fallen women is not simply a figment of Victorian novels. Such opprobrium, obviously, cannot withstand a high proportion of violations, as is the case in the contemporary United States. In the absence of rape, sex involves the voluntary choices of both man and woman. Hence, the genes of a totally future-oriented woman would be better off with whatever sexual choices she makes. Why should the community object if she chooses to be a single mother? There are two possible reasons. First, the community might have to subsidize the subsequent child care. Second, it might object to the reduced quality of the child. In either case the community is interested in child care beyond externality correction. Similarly, the community often places obstacles to divorce by mutual consent. The obvious explanation is community concern with the fate of the children that are involved.

We do not expect serious survival errors in parental decisions about food and shelter for the child given that the child is still dependent on the parents. There is maternal food sharing with the young for all primates. The appropriate behavior in this regard would be part of built-in preferences. What distinguishes man from his forebears is the longer time period of child dependency and the more complex training required. We would expect parents to give less than survival-maximizing weights to child welfare in both of these decisions. We would, therefore, anticipate some social intervention to set the weights aright for those societies that survive.

One solution to the less than all-encompassing interests of the parents in their children is to make the child finance his education. Hence, the development of the apprenticeship system. But that system only worked when the trainer was the employer, so the child could pay for his earlier training by providing later work at less than its marginal product. More general training, in particular for training in reading and arithmetic, often was provided by the community or charitable organizations, especially after commercial developments in the fourteenth century made such training more useful (Adamson 1930). There is, then, a long history of community involvement in child care in western Europe.

One way the society increased child care was to increase the payoff to individuals in producing higher-quality children. The community encouraged children to take care of their parents in their old age. "Honor thy father and thy mother" is the only one of the Ten Commandments of a nontheologic nature that encourages, rather than proscribes, a behavior (a "do" rather than a "do not"). We interpret this command to mean in part, "Help your parents in their old age." This behavior makes no sense from a survival point of view if individuals were maximizing their own genetic survival. Directly, it makes no survival sense under any circumstances, since the aged contribute nothing to future generations. Indirectly, it makes lots of survival sense, given man's dominant concern with his own well-being. If one expects one's children to provide social security, one will provide better child care to increase the probability that the child will be in a position to help them later.[10] Care for the aged seems to be an ancient social rule and one that currently faces no opposing rule of goodness or morality.

Health

Helping the sick and injured is another mark of goodness that appears to be a feature of primitive as well as modern societies. This feature of goodness also has no opposing goodness or morality signal. To some extent caring for the sick and injured in primitive societies requires no encouragement from social rules. Self-interested behavior of individuals would produce some health care from others who would be interested in their own future health care. This is simply reciprocity in operation. However, individuals discount the future and are uncertain about the probability that the present sick will be in any position to help those that help them. As a result, reciprocity without general reputational gain will tend to provide less health care than people want. In consequence, there is a greater external benefit to greater health care than would emerge from simple reciprocity. This external return generates mores that make advocating more health care a signal for goodness. In primitive societies this external return occurred without any state. The optimal level of health care required goodness signaling.

The Environment

As we saw earlier, group survival requires some social restraints on individual behavior because of both externality correction and the overly high discount rates used by individuals in their decisions. Both concerns would make environmentalism a "good" cause. But the record of social response to environmental problems is, as far as we can see, spotty. Property rights internalize some of the externalities, those consequences of one's actions confined to the property over which one has been given rights. But those property rights will not protect against overly high discounting of the future. Nor will they protect against consequences that go beyond the property in question.

As a result, there have been many ecological disasters attributable to man's actions. One such case is the extinction of large mammals such as the wooly mammoth in Eurasia, and of many species in North America after man's arrival (Diamond 1997). The extinct mammals seemed to have one common characteristic. Their range was wider than any tribe's territory, so that no one tribe could control their fate.

Even when a social group is large enough to effectively control some feature of the environment, it does not always succeed, as witnessed by deforestation in Ireland and the Easter Islands. On the other hand, there have been successful controls over the use of natural resources without individual property rights (Ostrom 2000).

There is one important difference between the environment and both redistribution to the poor and child care expenditures as far as group survival is concerned. Spoiling the environment need not have had much impact on group survival given the nomadic character of most hunter-gatherers. Even when they could not move, the worse the environment, the less it attracted competing groups. Failure to care for the environment, then, would result in fewer of the social group, but that group would not be obliterated by competing groups. There is, then, less survival pressure to come up with appropriate environmental decisions than the other decisions that we have looked at. In consequence, one would not expect environmentalism to be as dominant a part of the social fabric as child care and redistribution to the poor.

We suspect that the main attraction of environmentalism is derivative from other "good" causes: concern for health and concern for long-run consequences, especially those consequences that affect future generations. There is one way of distinguishing this derivative hypothesis from a direct group selection origin of environmentalism. Information could be important in the first case, but not in the second. In the first case, knowledge of the health and long-term consequences of environmental policy is necessary to determine that policy on the basis of those consequences. In the second case, group selection does not require that the participants know that a social rule works. It only requires that if the rule works, it survives. We have the sense that a crucial catalyst for the environmental movement has been information about the environmental consequences of pollution, information that came to the fore in the latter half of the twentieth century. Of all the "good" causes that might contribute to group survival, environmentalism appears to be of most recent origin.

Compassion for Poor Groups

The amorphous quality of "compassion" as a goal seemingly makes it applicable to groups other than the poor, as long as there is some sense in which the group is more unfortunate than others. One example: racial preferences without regard to individual income to minority groups whose members are on average poor. Such preferences make no sense in terms of the group survival rationalization of aid to the poor. Holding individual income constant, one would not expect the marginal survival returns of income to be greater for, say, blacks rather than whites. That is why Kuran (1995) finds an enormous private opposition to affirmative action. There is, however, a special externality rationale for special aid to poor minorities. There is a big imitation component of rioting and criminal activity. Members of isolated poor groups are more likely to harm others than members of richer groups, even holding individual income constant.

There is one problem, however, with governmental policy acting on the basis of this externality. Suppose that aid to a group increases with the antisocial behavior of that group. Then the group can increase that aid by engaging in antisocial behavior. This consequence of the attempt to correct for this externality may or may not outweigh the direct effects of externality correction.

Sowell (1990) provides cross-country evidence that either this externality or compassion toward poor groups did, indeed, influence government policy. He found several cases where redistribution was from rich majority groups to poor minority groups. He found no cases of redistribution from poor majorities to rich minorities when both participated equally in the electoral process.

In spite of the possible externality returns in aiding poor minority groups, this ethnic preference is of relatively recent origin. The reason is obvious. If it exists, the externality return only means that the richer group benefits somewhat from benefits to the poorer. It does not imply that that benefit is greater than the costs of having less income for themselves. When the poor minorities are not adequately represented in the electoral process, the richer majority will exploit them. This, too, seems to be supported by Sowell's results.

For either reasons of compassion or externality corrections, majorities and minorities alike consider aid to poor minorities a "good" cause, at least in the United States. But there is a conflicting cause for all, other than poor minorities: own-group preferences. Since this latter cause had survival value in the past, it has been around for a long time.

General Compassion

It, however, is apparently "good" to be "compassionate" toward groups when there is not even an externality rationale for doing so. The "good" support preferences for women, pacifism, criminal rights, and oppose discrimination against homosexuals, though, as we shall see, that support is greater publicly than privately. These positions can easily be explained by compassion. Women make less on the job because of home responsibilities. People die and are maimed in wars. Homosexuals are often mistreated. Being in prison or electrocuted is not considered fun. However, these compassions do not contribute to group survival.

Wars have had a big impact on group survival. Groups have been wiped out by their conquerors. But wars have more than just a genetic effect on group survival. The social institutions of the defeated are often destroyed even when the population is allowed to live.[11] The evidence of Diamond (1997) suggests that in very primitive societies losers in wars were wiped out except for nubile females. He asserts that only in fairly advanced societies were the losers allowed to live, usually as slaves. Pacifism was clearly not a winning strategy for group survival in the ancient world, when preferences were being formed. Simple prisoner's dilemma models suggest that it is not a winning strategy against tit-for-tat even now (Axelrod 1984), though many claim the issue to be more complicated than that. There is little evidence for pacifism in the ancient world, though there are some isolated cases, such as Aristophanes' *Lysistrata.*

On the face of it, homosexuality does not increase group survival, though some have argued that some degree of homosexuality is optimal to increase the amount of child care per child. That mores are usually opposed to homosexuality, however, suggests that group survival would be greater if the amount of homosexuality were less.[12]

Nor does compassion for criminals increase group survival. There is some evidence (Ehrlich 1975; Ehrlich and Liu 1999) that an increase in capital punishment reduces murders by more than the number of people executed. If so, group survival increases with more executions. It is also unclear whether the "humane" treatment of criminals promotes group survival. Torture is a more cost effective way of deterring crime than that imprisonment which would lead to the same amount of deterrence. At the very least, if group survival were one's sole goal, prisons should be made more unpleasant, especially since that is cheaper. Clearly, something other than group survival is motivating the compassion for criminals that make these options almost unthinkable.

Compassion focused on criminals rather than the victims saved is an example of a more general quirk in the operation of compassion. It is considered more important to help a given person than to provide that help to somebody yet unspecified.[13] While such a phenomenon now makes no sense from the point of view of group survival, it is explicable historically. The friendlier one is toward a person, the more one knows about him. During the period when preferences were being formed, one knew mostly only close associates. Special concern for them makes sense in terms of reciprocal compassion. Information media now make one know a lot about selective strangers. It is not surprising that people extend them the emotions developed for friends.

Women have a newfound role in the labor force produced by lower birth rates and labor-saving devices at home. However, women still bear the brunt of housework. As a result they have less prestigious jobs and are both overworked and underpaid (in some nonmarginal product sense; that is, males with which they associate make more). These grievances generate a women's movement where there is no comparable men's movement. These grievances and the women's movement making the population aware of these grievances have added compassion for women to the "do-gooders" arsenal of compassions. On its face, however, it would appear that feminism is not conducive to group survival. Feminism tends to reduce both the number of children and the amount of child care—the latter by encouraging women to work outside the home. Furthermore, there is no external benefit generated by preferences for women. Neither the insurance nor the social stability argument would generate special treatment for women. Few men change sex, nor are women more likely to riot than men.

The particular women's issue that we examine later in our statistical analysis is abortion. Compassion is two-sided in that case: compassion for women versus compassion for the unborn. But the compassion battle is only part of the story. Simple self-interest as distinguished from genetic self-interest leads to a proabortion position. In point of fact, the advocates of "family values" tend to oppose abortion, though it increases child care per child by reducing the number of unwanted children. But it could have indirect effects that operate in the opposite direction. By encouraging sexual activity outside of marriage, it reduces the number of marriages.

We have seen that all the compassions in this section are contrary to group survival. In consequence, we expect their importance to be a recent phenomenon. Pacifism is now marginally acceptable. In the past, wars, for example the Civil War, were unpopular among segments of the community, but not widely opposed like Vietnam. There have been pacifist plays in the past, but not the bevy of antiwar plays that began in World War I. Group survival in the past required the group to be willing to fight for its territory. Even now, patriotism vies with pacifism for emotional appeal. Similarly, women's rights vies with the group survival advantages, at least in the past, of the gender division of labor. Women did not even get the vote until the twentieth century. Concern for the well-being of criminals vies with the group survival advantages of strict law enforcement. It is not surprising that gallows day was a major source of entertainment in an earlier epoch.

Compassion for poor ethnic groups is also a recent phenomenon for a different reason. If it has external benefits, it has survival value for societies that are ethnically diverse. But for most of man's history societies were ethnically homogeneous. A strong sense of preferences for one's own ethnic group has survival value under those conditions, especially since one of the main forms of encounters with strangers was in war.

The material in this section supports the contention of Posner (2000) and Kuran (1995, 1998) that there are multiple signaling equilibria. Current goodness signaling in the United States is not uniquely predictable from group survival. However, the range of possible causes that could generate goodness signaling is not unlimited. Not all causes qualify on the grounds of either lags or compassion, seemingly the sources of deviations from group survival signaling.

Symmetries and Asymmetries in Goodness

When compassion conflicts with group survival, morality signaling generates opposite goals. Patriotism is contrary to pacifism. Similarly, some regard homosexuality as a sin worth fighting against. "Law and order" advocates oppose criminal rights. Advocates for family values engage in morality signaling in opposition to the feminists. For those issues goodness is two-sided.

But for those issues where compassion is not opposed to group survival, and is in some cases on the side of group survival, goodness is one-sided. These issues include the environment, the redistribution of income to the poor, and child development. It is clear how compassion contributes to survival maximization in these cases. Compassion is also relevant in defense of environmentalists. Pollution hurts the sickly, and compassion for animals is used by environmentalists, though that compassion is largely unrelated to the features of environmentalism that contribute to group survival.

Most of the interesting results we get are related to these cases of the asymmetric distribution of goodness. And these are also the cases in which economists have been most interested. When goodness is one-sided, its role in the political process is more easily detected.

CHAPTER 7

Activism

In this chapter we examine the behavior of activists. We define activists as those who use substantial amounts of time or money to influence public policy and who clearly proclaim their political position in so doing, but who have no obvious narrow self-interest gain from this behavior. Thus the definition excludes such individuals as lobbyists for price supports for agriculture and the organizations that pay their bills. The behavior of the latter cannot be predicted from the model that we use to predict our kind of activism.

Similarly, voting participation requires a different model, though voting also requires the expenditure of resources in political activity. Voting differs in two important ways from activism. First, given the secret ballot, voting need not disclose the political position of the voter. Given costs to lying, one can learn from others whether they voted without necessarily learning for whom they voted.[1] Second, as developed in chapter 4, there are positive externalities associated with voting. In consequence, voting participation, given its time cost, acts as a signal for trustworthiness just like more traditional charity, even though one might very well prefer lower voting participation among members of the opposition party.[2] Indeed, in chapter 4 we successfully predicted voting participation from our charity model.

Despite increasing information by publicizing grievances, the activism on which we focus does not seem to have net positive externalities, however. Usually those who strongly agree with the political position of the activist believe these external consequences are favorable and those who strongly disagree feel them unfavorable. But there are external costs to demonstrations that affect most people independently of their political position. Demonstrations are often disruptive, frequently involve illegal acts, and sometimes try to circumvent the democratic process.

People's views that there are negative externalities of demonstrations is revealed by the *General Social Surveys 1972–1996* (NORC 1996). A representative sample of the U.S. adult population was asked in 1985, 1990, and 1996 whether various forms of demonstrations should be allowed. While for some of these a clear majority (between 70 and 80 percent) agree they should be allowed, the form of the question itself is revealing. Respondents are asked whether demonstrations should be allowed, not whether demonstrations should be encouraged. The way the question is asked in that survey assumes that the activity has some costs to others.[3] Moreover, there are some forms of demonstrations that the majority of Americans believe should not, or probably should not, be allowed. Eighty-nine percent in that survey believe that demonstrators that occupy government offices should not or probably should not be allowed to do so. Sixty-eight percent believe that general strikes should not be allowed.

A similar kind of trade-off is manifested in the preaching or activist motivation for occupational choice. The preacher talks about issues of public concern, but he often uses public resources to provide an unbalanced examination of those issues when preaching extends beyond the specific occupation for which it is named. The preaching will be regarded as having negative externalities when the message is at variance with the views of those evaluating the externalities.

Those engaged in forms of activism with negative externalities or no externalities must get some return from their use of resources. Since in most cases there is no financial or even power return from these activities, the returns must be in terms of what the others who count think or would think about the activist's behavior if they but knew of it. Any favorable thoughts must be a function of the political position adopted rather than of the externalities of the activity itself.

One clearly expects a positive response to a particular form of activism for a particular cause from those similarly involved. Unless the activity itself has huge negative externalities, like bomb throwing, say, one expects a positive response from those sharing the cause even though they do not share the activity. But by the logic of the previous chapter, political positions are also determined by goodness and morality "signals," signals that are often in conflict. Activists should also engage in such signaling. In consequence, for asymmetric goodness, causes where morality signaling is inapplicable, we should expect much more activism for "good" causes rather than against them.

There is a reason why this goodness signaling will be particularly important in the kinds of activism we examine in this chapter: demonstrations and public declarations of political positions. These activities differ in an important respect from political discussions with friends; they have a wider audience. Goodness signals are distinguished by some concern with this wider audience, for they signal generalized trustworthiness at the expense of trustworthiness to any members of one's group that are not also involved in this goodness signaling.

Demonstrations

Our thesis is that people demonstrate for "good" causes, that people signal their goodness by loudly proclaiming their political position. This thesis has implications for both the causes about which people demonstrate and the characteristics of the people doing the demonstrating. For issues about redistribution and the environment goodness is dominantly on the side of those who want a greater role for government.

Demonstrations require not just "good" causes, but something about which to protest. The good cause must not have been fully achieved politically in the eyes of would-be demonstrators. In a world in which political decisions are determined primarily by majority rule, this need to protest will not be very important in determining which side does the demonstrating. One expects extremists on both sides to be more likely to demonstrate, because they are less likely to be satisfied with the kind of compromises generated by majority rule. These results are changed when policy is not the result of majority rule. Take, for instance, the Supreme Court decision *Roe v. Wade.* One expects more demonstrations from antiabortionists than proabortionists, because the proabortionists have less to protest about.

To investigate the nature of the causes that generate demonstrations, we looked at all demonstrations worldwide so listed in the archives of the *New York Times* for three months ending May 25, 1998. Table 7.1 lists these demonstrations by subject matter as we classify them. Undoubtedly, the particular issues that generate demonstrations vary over time, depending on what are the "hot" issues of the moment. However, there is no reason to suspect that the conclusions we draw from these results are particularly sensitive to the time period chosen.

The conclusion is that demonstrations are either about group interest or for "good" causes. In either case people demonstrate their trustworthiness to somebody by demonstrating. In the case of demonstrations for a group they establish their group loyalty. For our purposes the most interesting results are the fourteen demonstrations against either the free market or consequences of that market in operation in contrast to no demonstrations against government interference with the market. The antimarket demonstrations vary from protests against price increases to disagreements with free international trade. There are also four demonstrations demanding more environmental regulation and no demonstrations opposed to more of this regulation. (The four proenvironment demonstrations are in addition to the fourteen antimarket demonstrations.) In addition to the antimarket demonstrations there are also antigovernment demonstrations. But none of these latter demonstrations are against government regulation of markets. Rather, they are about dictatorship (classified as prodemocracy), police brutality, corruption, and governments' policies toward various ethnic groups (classified in the patriotism and ethnicity category). These results are strong evidence for the one-sided nature of "goodness" over economic and environmental issues.

There is another unsurprising result. There were eight demonstrations in support of student causes, and, of course, no demonstrations against student causes. This shows, at least in part, the impact of age on activism that loudly proclaims political positions. The older one is, the more associates one has acquired from one's nonpolitical activities. Some of these associates are likely to be offended by a friend's partici-

TABLE 7.1. Demonstrations in 1998 by Type[a]

Type	Number
Antimarket[b]	14
Pro-democracy	14
Antidemocracy[c]	2
Special interests[d]	6
Patriotism and ethnicity	18
Antiwar	3
Against corruption and police brutality	5
Pro–environment and animal rights	4
Student causes	8
Antiabortion	4
Pro-religion	2
Human rights[e]	1
Left wing politics[f]	1
Women's rights	1
Pro–drug and needle exchange	2

Source: Data from *New York Times* archives, May 25, 1998.
[a]For three months ending May 25, 1998.
[b]Against unemployment, poverty, and market induced price increases.
[c]For example, pro-Nazi demonstrations in Germany.
[d]For example, Italian farmers, New York cab drivers, California loggers.
[e]Against Chinese violations of human rights.
[f]Summary description too vague to classify more specifically.

pating in demonstrations. Young people, in contrast, start with a much cleaner slate. They can specialize in friends that have the same political views as they do and approve of demonstrations to support such views. This is particularly true of college students, many of whom live and associate frequently with only fellow college students.

Less importantly for our purposes, the demonstration data show more antiabortion demonstrations (four) than proabortion demonstrations (at most one, the women's right demonstration). As previously predicted, there are more pro-lifers unhappy with government policies than free choice advocates, and, hence, the greater number of the former demonstrating in spite of the fact that demonstrating for women's rights also signals "goodness."

The literature on demonstrations relevant for our purposes focuses on who is involved in demonstrations or who has a greater potential for demonstrations. (Researchers often focus on protest potential rather than protests themselves because the proportion of the population that actually engages in protests is so small.) Protest potential is determined by approval or disapproval of various kinds of protests. An example of such work is Marsh's (1977) study of Great Britain. He found that those under thirty had more protest potential than did those older than thirty. He also found that those who identified themselves as leftists had much more protest potential than did rightists. Though he found substantial differences between the two groups, the differences were nowhere as large as the discrepancies between antimarket and promarket demonstrations in our data. The ratios of protest potential by left versus right varied between 1.52 and 1.27, while our result showed a number of antimarket demonstrations and no promarket demonstrations.

There is an obvious explanation for this difference in results. Right-wingers are not simply promarket. They can be patriotic, anticrime, or antiabortion—"good" causes that generate demonstrations. In consequence, we would expect right-wingers to demonstrate more than those who are simply promarket. Evidently the difference in the number of antimarket demonstrations compared to promarket demonstrations is sufficient to produce more left-wing than right-wing demonstrations.

This section, then, provides evidence for asymmetric goodness with goodness being on the side of those who oppose market outcomes. That there are more antimarket than promarket demonstrations is a fairly obvious result. Its obvious validity only means that it has been consistently confirmed by everyday experiences. What is important is that there are no obvious alternative explanations to asymmetric goodness for this phenomenon.

Activists

There is one "occupation" peculiarly suited to preaching: the occupation of activist. One of the requirements of this occupation is that one is so classified by others. What does one do or not do to be so classified? First of all, one has to publicly declare or otherwise express a political position. But that is not a sufficient requirement. Those whose speech is financed by a business organization are usually classified by others as "business spokesperson."

Activists can be paid or unpaid. What distinguishes them in the public mind from "business spokespersons" is that either they or the contributors to the organization that finances them are not motivated by profits. (The leaders of such organizations, such as Jesse Jackson, can be well rewarded [Timmerman 2002].) However, the public believes that those who finance these organizations do not do so for profit. This is evidenced by the fact that when they are revealed to do so the revelation is considered scandalous (Timmerman 2002). Instead, there is a goodness motive. We predict that for issues where goodness is one-sided, more activists should be on the goodness side.

Levite (1996) presents some interesting relevant evidence. Looking at the *New York Times* from January 1994 to March 1995, he found reference to 289 liberal activists as opposed to 65 conservative activists. But the *New York Times* used an alternative way of describing some people involved in political activity: extremist. Levite found reference to 25 liberal extremists as opposed to 78 conservative extremists. He attributes the more frequent application of the pejorative label *extremist* to conservatives to the liberal bias of the media, the *New York Times* in particular. But whatever the name, there were 314 liberal activists or extremists and only 143 conservatives so titled. The ratio is more than two to one. The magnitude of these results is somewhat suspect as a measure of media bias. The *New York Times* has a more liberal editorial page than an average newspaper and displays more liberal bias in other respects as well. While evidence explored in chapter 9 supports a moderate media bias, it would be difficult to explain the large differentials found by Levite solely by this bias.[4]

We believe that there are two additional reasons why more liberals than conservatives are called "activists." (1) There are more of them, because one signals one's goodness more by liberal activism than conservative activism. (2) The very fact that one is more likely to signal one's goodness by liberal activism also implies that others, not just the media, would refer to the liberal activists with that kinder, gentler title. But there may be more conservatives labeled extremists because people think that conservative activists would just be signaling their group identification and not their goodness. Hence, the harsher designation, extremists, for them.

Lichter et al. provide more evidence about the media and activists. Look at table 7.2, where both the data and classifications are from their work. They look at the percentage of times a particular kind of source is cited as reliable by journalists versus being cited as reliable by businesspeople. For the issue "consumer protection" their list of reliable sources includes the Ralph Nader group, Consumers Union, and

TABLE 7.2.   Types of Sources Cited as Reliable (in percentages)

	Media	Business
Welfare Reform		
Liberals	75	17
Federal regulatory agencies	51	25
Federal officials	38	25
Conservatives	22	22
State and local agencies	16	30
Consumer Protection		
Ralph Nader/ Nader groups	63	33
Federal regulatory agencies	46	28
Consumer union	44	30
Other activist groups	41	26
State and local agencies	36	40
Business groups	22	49
Pollution and Environment		
Environmental activists	69	25
Activist federal agencies	68	56
Business groups	27	34
Liberal activists and officials	24	8
Other federal agencies	19	11
Nuclear Energy		
Antinuclear	55	—
Technical magazines	40	—
Federal regulatory agencies	39	—
Other government	37	—
Pro-nuclear	32	—

Source: Data from Lichter, Rothman, and Lichter (1986)

"Other Activist Groups." The latter "are nonprofit groups ranging from Consumer Federation of America and Common Cause to social activist groups like the American Civil Liberties Union and Americans for Democratic Action" (Lichter, Rothman, and Lichter 1986). These results confirm that these "Other Activist Groups" are dominantly liberal groups. Forty-one percent of journalists cite these sources as reliable, while only 26 percent of businesspeople do so.

For the issue "Pollution and the Environment" the only nongovernmental, nonbusiness reliable sources cited are "Environmental Activists" and "Liberal Activists and Officials." For "Welfare Reform" Lichter et al. list "Liberals" and "Conservatives" and business groups such as the Chamber of Commerce. Seventy-five percent of journalists cite some liberal sources as reliable, while only 22 percent cite some conservative sources as reliable.

There are two obvious explanations for these results that are not mutually exclusive. (1) The media mistrust conservative activists. (2) There are fewer nonbusiness conservative activists to be cited, or at least there are fewer that journalists have heard about. Lichter et al. find a wide disparity between the sources that businesspeople and the media regard as reliable, and that is what they emphasize: evidence that either the media mistrust conservatives or businesspeople mistrust liberals or some combination thereof.

But the evidence also supports the second hypothesis: there are fewer well-known conservative activists. Lichter et al. list sources regarded as reliable by either journalists or businesspeople. In that light the evidence is striking. It says that businesspeople know of no reliable sources outside of business that represent the conservative position on "Environment and Pollution." Businesspeople also know of few conservative reliable sources outside of business sources for "Consumer Protection," though Lichter's "Activist" classification is somewhat ambiguous. For "Welfare Reform" there also must be few conservative sources in spite of the overly inclusive definition of those sources for "Welfare Reform." Businesspeople cite some conservative sources as reliable with only slightly greater frequency than they cite some liberal sources (22 percent compared to 17 percent). Such similar percentages would probably not prevail if there were as many conservative activists as liberal activists.

Our explanation for these results is simple. Outside of business, the people who bankroll activists (perhaps themselves) want to be "good." Goodness is one-sided for the issues of welfare reform, consumer protection, and the environment.

The most serious alternative hypothesis that could possibly explain some of Lichter's results is the presence of business sources of information. Given such sources, there might be less need for nonbusiness activists. This explanation could possibly be relevant for "Consumer Protection" and for "Environment and Pollution," but not for "Welfare Reform." For the latter, business sources are not listed separately. The total number of conservative sources including business must be greater, not less, as a result of business provision of information. But even so there seem to be more liberal than conservative reliable sources.

Besides, one does not expect business sources of information to be close substitutes for other conservative sources. A serious problem with business-generated information is that, because business interest is often at loggerheads with public interest, it often is not credible. Who believes, for example, that the Tobacco Institute provides trustworthy information? Whatever the problems with activists' information—and we believe them to be serious, indeed—there is not an obvious problem of personal gain if the activists' policies are adopted. Conservative nonbusiness sources are more believable than business sources. If there were enough people who felt "good" about funding such sources, the existence of business sources would not be a major deterrent. On the other hand, even nonbusiness conservative sources will be regarded more skeptically than liberal sources, because people are more likely to assume a hidden agenda for the former. "Is this source being secretly funded by business?" Given that the "good" are generally liberal, something else is suspected to motivate conservative activists, namely, their narrow self-interest.

Philanthropy and Activism

Activism in general involves the use of both time and money resources predominantly, as we have seen, for "good" causes. In this section we focus on the use of monetary resources. Again, in the case of asymmetric goodness we predict that groups will devote more monetary resources for "good" causes than for the opposite side, ceteris paribus. The reason for the Latin qualifier is that the income of the contributors or of the unpaid activist can also play a role. Indeed, that is the most obvious variable determining activism by means of monetary expenditures. The data from NORC (1996) show that individual contributions to political parties are positively related to income. This, by itself, should increase the contributions going to "bad" activists, who tend to be pro–high income. If, then, one finds that, in fact, there are more "good" activists, that would be strong supporting evidence that asymmetric "goodness" is, indeed, one-sided.

Lenkowsky (1999) seemingly comes to such a such a conclusion. He finds that politically active groups on the left had revenue of nearly $4 billion in 1996 compared with $900 million for their competitors on the right. But, his underlying data—*The Left Guide* (Wilcox 1996) and *The Right Guide* (Wilcox 1997)—have serious problems for our purposes. The revenues of many labor unions are included, as are the revenues of the Chamber of Commerce. The motivations determining their behavior are clearly self-interested rather than "goodness" driven. Furthermore, many of the organizations included in these guides are multipurpose organizations—organizations that engage in both charitable activity and political activism. Counting all their expenditures as political activism vastly overstates the latter.

Fortunately, the underlying data is still useful. We can just count the number of goodness-motivated left- and right-wing organizations. Given this procedure, the charitable expenditures of an organization that is also politically active have no impact on the weight we give that organization. We count 1,283 left-wing activist organizations (not including unions), as compared to 1,108 right-wing organizations (not including the Chamber of Commerce), or nearly 16 percent more.[5] That difference is statistically significant: $t = 3.58$. That is some confirmation of the "goodness" associated with liberal political positions, especially given the political disposition of those most likely to establish philanthropic organizations—the rich. Of course, this difference in number of organizations is not nearly as dramatic as Lenkowsky's difference in total revenues.

We believe this difference in results arises in part because charitable philanthropies are more likely to become politically active for liberal causes than for conservative causes. Just like activists, philanthropic administration is a "do-gooder" occupation. In particular, these administrators are likely to advocate more government activity in the areas in which they specialize. Self-interest would have them operate differently if government activity crowded out charity. That self-interest, though, would be particularly unimportant if the philanthropy already had its funding—largely the case for the older, larger foundations. Age of the philanthropy would also be relevant in determining its political orientation, especially if the funding of the philanthropy is exclusively generated by preexisting endowments. The original administrators were selected by the founder, whose political bias would thereby have some impact on the organization. But the longer the organization continues, the greater the effect of the political orientation of potential administrators. Future members of the board are selected by present members of the board, including top administrators usually. This addition to the board of top administrators generation after generation makes the board take on progressively the political cast of top administrators.

There are three testable implications of this process. First, we would expect more charitable activity associated with liberal activist philanthropies than associated with conservative activist philanthropies. We observe two indirect indicators of this phenomenon. Lenkowsky reports that government grants to left-wing organizations were $500 million in 1996, while grants to right-wing organizations were only $19 million. The most obvious explanation for this result is that the government grants were focused on the charitable part of these organizations rather than on their activism. The largest single grant was to the Legal Services Corporation to provide legal services for the poor. While some of the difference in grants could conceivably be explained by a Democratic administration, a similar result cannot. Falk and Nolan (1994) report that in 1993, 78 percent of corporate donations to advocacy organizations went to left-wing organizations, and only 19 percent went to right-wing organizations. Corporations are not notable for their left-wing sympathies.

Second, the more likely a philanthropy is run by professional managers rather than the founders or their family, the more likely that philanthropy will engage in liberal rather than conservative activism. The larger the size of the philanthropy, the more likely it requires professional management. One would, therefore, predict a larger size for liberal activist organizations compared to conservative ones. We believe that this is a reason for the far greater differences observed by Lenkowsky in total revenue than in our observed differences in numbers between the two kinds of organizations. However, we cannot be sure because Lenkowsky includes some unions in his revenue estimates for left-wing organizations.

Third, we would expect any change in the degree of activism not associated with changes in the views of the founder or his heirs over the lifetime of the philanthropy to be toward more liberal or less conservative activism. We looked at the seven foundations that had greater than one billion dollars in assets according to *The Left Guide* (Wilcox 1996) and *The Right Guide* (Wilcox 1997). Four of them are currently liberal foundations that have become more liberally activist over time independently of changes in the political philosophy of the founding family: the Ford Foundation, the Robert Wood Johnson Foundation, the Rockefeller Foundation, and the Carnegie Corporation. One is now a liberal foundation that became more liberal at least in part because a son was more liberal than the founding father: the John D. MacArthur Foundation. One was a conservative foundation that grew less conservative over time in part because the son was less conservative than the founding father: the Pew Charitable Trust. One was a conservative foundation that grew more conservative through changes in the political position of the founder—the Lilly Foundation.[6]

These results have a larger purpose than simply explaining Lenkowsky's revenue data. They show that both contributors to political causes and philanthropic fund managers want to be "good" and that goodness is dominantly antimarket. This chapter in general provides evidence supporting this latter proposition. We show that there are more antimarket than promarket demonstrations. We show that both the media and business cite as reliable sources more antimarket than promarket activists, strongly suggesting that there are, in fact, more of the former.

CHAPTER 8

A Study of Political Positions

Hypotheses

In this chapter we test the theory developed in chapter 6 by focusing on three implications of that theory. First, the lower the cost of signaling "goodness," the more people will adopt "progoodness" political positions. This proposition cannot simply be derived from the downward-sloping demand curve because in our case there is a contrary force. When others know of an increase in the price to an individual if he adopts a given political position out of goodness, that individual signals more goodness by espousing such a position. So both the costs and the returns of signaling goodness increase with an increase in the price.

However, as shown in chapter 3, the amount of goodness signaled is the price of adopting a political position out of goodness times the political position itself (all, of course, measured in appropriate units). Assume the desired amount of goodness signaled is invariant with respect to price. That assumption corresponds to the standard assumption that utility is independent of price, holding real income constant. Then, to keep the goodness signaled constant, an increase in one of its components, price, must lead to a proportional decrease in its other component, political position. The price elasticity of demand for goodness signaling in political positions should be -1. The political positions associated with goodness should increase with a decrease in the price of goodness.

Another proposition has been developed in the previous chapter. People use more resources to loudly proclaim "good" than "bad" positions. This proposition not only applies to demonstrations and what is generally meant by political activism. It also applies to any occupational choice that is in part determined by the goodness motivations. There are some occupations in which one can preach about political positions. One would expect people who wish to preach goodness to be more likely to choose those occupations.

A third implication of our theory follows easily from this second proposition. Relative to private discussions, some people will get a higher proportion of their information about the political views of others from loud activists and "do-gooder" occupations. The imitative behavior of those thus informed will, hence, make them choose political positions with a larger goodness component. As developed in this, the previous chapter, and the next chapter, the information from loud activists and "do-gooder" occupations includes the media, education, and books.

Besides testing these propositions, this chapter discusses a large number of empirical regularities that have gone unexplained. Though most economists studying voting behavior have long been aware of their existence, economists seem a remarkably uncurious lot. If something cannot be easily explained by our simplest models, we just assume it is part of "taste." In the case of voting behavior that means we ignore a lot. "Why are the young, college teachers, and residents of large cities more liberal?" These questions and others have been unanswered, that is, attributed to "tastes." Our goodness theory provides more satisfactory answers, answers that allow us to explore subtler features of these regularities.

Before we can test these propositions and answer these questions, however, we must select a data set that allows these tests and controls for the other relevant variables that also have an impact on political positions.

Data and Issues

Our procedure is to run regressions on answers to public policy questions against characteristics of respondents and their families given by data for the United States from the *General Social Survey, 1972–1996* (NORC 1996). Currently, the preferred procedure in the public choice literature for running such regressions is parsimony, but those working with the simple self-interest model usually cannot resist the inclusion of at least a few variables, such as race, region or city size, that they cannot justify on theoretical grounds. We include a large number of variables. That inclusion is justified by the theory we are testing: that concern with what others are thinking is crucial in the determination of voter behavior. There are two main manifestations of that concern: (1) political positions as imitation; (2) political positions chosen to be "good." In this chapter we concentrate primarily on the latter, since the former has been more thoroughly examined in chapter 5.

Our approach is to examine seventeen different issues, opinions about which will be potentially affected by goodness. We use the commonly accepted liberal versus conservative characterization of views about these issues. On all these issues one can display one's goodness by being liberal. On a few, being conservative offers morality-displaying opportunities. What is crucial, though, is that, with a few exceptions, those groups that have an incentive to be "good" liberals on one issue will have the same incentive on the other issues.

In the previous chapter we provided a rationale for goodness being one-sided for many of the issues examined here: expenditures on the poor, the environment, health, education, for blacks, and for the aged. (We treat expenditures for roads as "antienvironmental" and expenditures on mass transit and large cities as "proenvironmental," following most professional environmentalists.)

The case is more complicated for *two-sided goodness* issues: abortion, expenditures on the police, and defense. But, as we shall see, on these issues the same variables that determine liberal goodness tend to operate with opposite sign in determining conservative morality.

The regression results we report are for ordinary least squares, though we use other procedures as well, with no substantial difference in results.[1] Most of the problems with regressions cannot be solved by different techniques. Confidence can be generated only by consistent results over different kinds of data. That is why we have looked at so many issues in this study.[2]

Surveys

We use polling data. As discussed in chapter 5, the same person can have different political positions at the same time: a position for discussions with friends, which could vary with the friend, a position for polls, and a voting position. Variation in those positions is at least somewhat limited by the conscience cost of lying and in some cases the probability that the lie will be discovered. Each of these positions has in its own way an impact on public policy.

Polling data, which are important in their own right, can be biased as an estimator of other political positions. We expect polling data to be affected more by goodness variables and less by group variables than discussions with friends. Relative to the latter, polls are more affected by desires to please strangers, the interviewer. Respondents might believe that there is some chance that the interviewer might leak the respondents answers to his friends, but that chance of discovery by friends is certainly less than when the respondent directly talks to friends. Since goodness is defined as greater general trustworthiness at the expense of trustworthiness to the group, people have a greater incentive to display goodness relative to imitative behavior to strangers than to friends.

The one case of greater goodness displays to friends than to strangers occurs when one is a member of a particularly high-goodness group. But that greater display is attributable to imitative behavior and is counterbalanced by the paucity of goodness displays to friends when one is a member of a particularly low-goodness group.

But one of the big results of these regressions on survey data is that one adopts political positions to please one's friends rather than other people. All of the results emphasized in chapter 5 are of this character, as are many of the results of this chapter. If respondents were just lying to please the interviewer, we would not get these results. These results hold for all the questions asked no matter how vague, so it does appear that real information is being conveyed in the answers.

Our reputational theory does not apply directly to the other form of political expression, voting, because of its secret nature. However, voting is at least somewhat predictable by that theory if a substantial number of people do not lie about how they vote. This condition holds if the returns from voting and then lying about how one voted are not larger than the costs of lying.

This issue is discussed in detail in chapter 5. To the extent that it pays to lie, narrow self-interest is more important in voting than in public political positions. Because of the free-rider problem, our model of political behavior predicts small returns to voting one's narrow self-interest. However, the self-expression model of Kuran (1995) predicts substantial returns. The evidence examined in chapter 5 is not decisive enough to distinguish between these two theories, but it does show no massive difference between aggregate votes and aggregate polls in the usual voting cases in the United States. It would certainly not be surprising if our model that predicts behavior for public political positions also predicts voting behavior, though the latter might well have a greater self-interest component.

There is some evidence that polling data systematically overweight goodness compared to other ways to express political positions. Many of the survey questions asked are of the form, "Should the government spend more, the same amount, or less" on some good, scaled by 3, 2, or 1 respectively. If democracy simply translated these wishes to reality, one would expect the mean of these answers to be roughly equal to 2.

For issues with one-sided goodness implying greater expenditures, there are nine cases of means greater than 2 and only one case of a mean less than 2. There is also one case of a mean greater than 2 when goodness implies less expenditures. (See table 8.1.) The probability of getting nine out of eleven positive outcomes by chance is .032.[3]

There are two obvious explanations for these results. (1) Indirect democracy prevents the full expression of the goodness desires of the electorate. (2) Surveys exaggerate those goodness desires. We present evidence in chapter 9 that is inconsistent with the first hypothesis. Evidence provided in chapter 5 on interviewer bias supports the second hypothesis.

This polling bias means that our actual regression results will not be fully applicable to other forms of political expression. However, the bias itself is some confirmation of the reputation theory that we are trying to test. If the theory works for polls, the theory itself suggests that it ought to work with lower weights for goodness variables for discussions with friends. As we have indicated in chapter 5 the evidence suggests that the theory also works for voting itself.

The scorn that some economists might have for survey questions about political attitudes arises from a misunderstanding of the determinants of voting behavior. "Answers to surveys are designed to impress interviewers, but voting is to influence policy." If both surveys and other forms of political expression are designed to impress others, then they do not stand in such marked contrast. (Voting can be affected by desires to impress others even though it is not so designed. Lying costs can keep it at least somewhat in line with public political expression.)

Besides, the analysis thus far predicts biased means rather than biased regression coefficients. Everybody's incentive to be "good" increases. Biased regression coefficients require some differential effect by variable. Those who lie to convince the interviewer that they are "good" substitute one cost of being perceived good for another. The cost of lying is substituted for the cost of losses in the friendship of close associates. Many of the variables we employ—the community involvement variables—focus on this latter cost. On that account they would be less important in regressions for liars than for others. In spite of this, these variables play an important role in the survey regressions. Something real is captured by our survey results.[4]

Surveys are far from perfect instruments. The alternative to asking people how they voted is to use aggregate data about actual behavior. But cross-sectional analysis using aggregate data has real problems of

TABLE 8.1. OLS Regression of Support for Government, Political Parties, and Candidate

Independent Variables	Dependent Variables						
	PROWELF	PROPOOR	PROHEAL	PROED	PROENV	PROSOC	PROARMS
FY	-1.24E-01 ***	-8.67E-02 ***	-4.33E-02 ***	-4.49E-03	-3.01E-02 ***	-7.34E-02 ***	1.74E-02 **
FY2	3.35E-03	-1.62E-02 ***	-1.42E-02 ***	-9.98E-03 ***	-1.60E-02 ***	-2.43E-02 ***	5.87E-03 *
FYSLOPE	-1.26E-01 ***	-7.57E-02 ***	-3.37E-02 ***	-2.25E-03	-1.93E-02 ***	-5.70E-02 ***	1.34E-02 *
SELF	-3.70E-02 **	-1.04E-01 ***	-5.70E-02 ***	-5.22E-02 ***	-4.75E-02 ***	-7.06E-02 ***	-1.57E-02
PROF	-2.36E-01 ***	-1.29E-01 ***	-1.13E-01 ***	-7.53E-02 ***	-1.73E-01 ***	-5.87E-02 ***	7.85E-02 ***
MGM	-4.69E-02 **	-1.96E-02	-1.13E-04	-3.18E-02 ***	-5.71 E-03	-7.27E-03	1.95E-03
CLERK	-4.36E-02 ***	-5.39E-02 ***	-8.45E-03	1.42E-03	-9.09E-03	-2.36E-03	-1.06E-02
SALES	-5.18E-02 ***	-3.88E-02 *	-1.40E-02	-7.44E-03	-3.68E-03	-2.12E-02	1.76E-02
SERVE	2.23E-02	-3.81E-04	-1.96E-03	-8.82E-03	4.37E-03	1.93E-02	2.31E-02 *
AGR	-2.44E-02	-3.49E-02	-8.97E-03	-3.50E-02	-6.59E-02 ***	-4.61E-02	-8.59E-02 ***
BLACK	4.76E-01 ***	2.89E-01 ***	1.49E-01 ***	1.57E-01 ***	6.54E-02 ***	1.05E-01 ***	-1.85E-01 ***
UNION	-1.35E-03	-6.60E-03	1.32E-02 *	1.59E-02 **	8.07E-03	2.93E-02 ***	-6.17E-03
GOVR	8.15E-02 ***	0.00E+00	3.27E-02 **	-4.34E-03	3.33E-02 **	0.00E+00	-1.22E-02
MAIN	-1.19E-02	2.19E-02	1.55E-02	-5.15E-03	2.22E-02	-1.63E-02	-1.26E-02
JEW	2.16E-01 ***	8.42E-04	6.41E-02	1.81E-01 ***	8.20E-02	5.45E-02	-1.58E-01 **
JSLOPE	1.33E-01 *	6.96E-03	9.60E-02 *	1.47E-01 ***	9.71E-02 *	2.21E-02	-7.90E-02
CATHOLIC	2.02E-02	1.10E-02	2.13E-02	1.84E-03	2.69E-02	2.57E-02	-2.14E-02
CSLOPE	4.72E-02	-2.28E-02	1.57E-02	1.05E-02	5.32E-02 *	2.53E-02	-7.99E-02 **
NOREL	1.52E-02	-1.21E-01 ***	-2.13E-02	-5.36E-04	1.56E-02	-7.80E-02 ***	-1.05E-01 ***
OTHREL	1.19E-02	-5.33E-02	9.29E-03	6.51E-02 *	4.07E-02	-4.19E-02	-1.06E-01 **
ATTEND	-1.12E-02	1.88E-02	-1.27E-02	-8.50E-03	-2.72E-02 ***	-5.37E-03	1.67E-02 *
ATTENDSL	-1.03E-02 ***	-2.11 E-04	-1-13E-02 ***	-5.55E-03 ***	-8.02E-03 ***	-9.66E-03 ***	4.85E-03 **
PATT	5.47E-03	-2.65E-02 **	-4.31E-03	1.08E-04	8.06E-03	-2.50E-03	-1.18E-02
CATT	6.76E-03	-8.49E-03	-1.42E-03	2.18E-03	6.61E-03	-9.70E-05	-1.47E-02 *
JATT	-2.08E-02	1.54E-03	8.01E-03	-8.39E-03	3.80E-03	-8.12E-03	1.99E-02
FUNDAT	-1.99E-03	-1.15E-04	2.25E-03	1.29E-03	6.40E-03 ***	-1.31E-03	-5.88E-04
FYINCOME	9.59E-02	1.15E-02	-3.77E-02	-8.13E-03	-3.95E-02	-8.73E-02 *	-2.02E-01 ***

FMARRIED	-1.54E-01	-4.99E-01 ***	-1.39E-01 *	-1.02E-01	-1.99E-01 **	-1.02E-01	3.70E-01 ***
MARRIED	-3.30E-03	-2.16E-02	1.13E-02	5.43E-03	-3.52E-02 ***	-1.65E-02	3.12E-03
CHILD	-2.07E-02	8.39E-02 ***	6.05E-03	3.23E-02 **	4.54E-03	4.17E-02 **	2.39E-02
NCHILD	3.14E-02 ***	-2.44E-02 **	-5.90E-03	-8.41E-03 *	-1.03E-02 **	-1.52E-02 **	-3.78E-03
STATMIG	-2.10E-03	1.99E-02	3.85E-03	1.86E-02 **	9.91E-03	-9.82E-03	-2.27E-02 **
CONTMIG	1.13E-02	3.32E-02 *	1.31E-02	2.21E-02 **	3.42E-02 ***	-3.26E-02 **	-1.25E-02
MIGSL	5.40E-03	2.73E-02 *	9.03E-03	2.06E-02 ***	2.35E-02 ***	-2.26E-02 **	-1.70E-02 *
CLERGYSL	1.24E-01	-4.37E-02	3.29E-02	1.93E-02	-1.53E-02	-1.37E-02	3.88E-02
AGE	-1.79E-02 ***	-3.55E-03	1.56E-02 ***	5.63E-03 **	-6.71E-03 ***	1.90E-02 ***	6.29E-03 **
AGE2	9.35E-05 ***	-4.76E-05 *	-1.30E-04 ***	-7.68E-05 ***	3.87E-05 ***	-1.71E-04 ***	-9.47E-05 ***
AGESL	-2.41E-03 ***	-3.30E-03 ***	-1.10E-03 ***	-5.32E-03 ***	-8.21E-03 ***	-6.34E-04	4.41E-03 ***
MEMNUM	-3.36E-04	1.19E-04	1.02E-02 ***	1.27E-02 ***	1.02E-02 ***	4.00E-03	-5.30E-04
LCCIT	1.41E-01 ***	3.28E-02	4.49E-02 **	7.24E-02 ***	9.88E-02 ***	5.04E-02 *	-5.25E-02 **
SCCIT	4.98E-02 **	-1.94E-02	-9.57E-03	1.48E-02	2.90E-02 *	1.72E-02	-1.12E-02
SSURB	5.21E-02 **	-1.50E-02	-2.58E-03	2.86E-02 **	4.82E-02 ***	2.54E-02	3.16E-03
LSURB	8.85E-02 ***	-1.26E-02	5.14E-03	3.60E-02 **	4.41E-02 ***	3.05E-02	4.36E-03
OURB	3.00E-02 *	-1.84E-02	-1.09E-02	-5.12E-03	9.58E-03	1.79E-02	7.86E-03
SCITY	2.01E-02	8.01E-03	3.76E-02 ***	3.89E-02 ***	4.53E-02 ***	-4.67E-03	1.19E-02
MCITY	-4.16E-03	5.30E-02 **	4.49E-02 ***	6.52E-02 ***	7.47E-02 ***	1.44E-02	3.17E-06
SUBRB	2.33E-02	4.17E-02	1.97E-02	4.27E-02 ***	7.08E-02 ***	-3.10E-02 *	-4.11E-02 **
LCITY	6.50E-02 ***	2.94E-02	5.78E-02 ***	5.89E-02 ***	8.03E-02 ***	3.70E-02 **	-1.19E-02
LOWTEACH	-4.25E-03	1.67E-02	3.66E-02 **	5.95E-02 ***	6.94E-03	8.85E-03	-2.39E-02
COLTEACH	1.04E-01 ***	8.27E-02 *	9.40E-03 *	-1.14E-02	9.60E-02 ***	-4.57E-02	-1.12E-01 ***
WRITER	1.71E-01 **	1.34E-01	7.48E-02	-6.89E-02	1.01E-01 **	-3.91E-02	-2.13E-01 ***
LAWYER	2.08E-01 **	5.19E-02	2.07E-02	5.02E-02	5.05E-01	-7.35E-02	-1.46E-01 **
CLERGY	1.22E-01	-4.39E-02	3.09E-02	1.46E-02	-3.08E-02	-2.23E-02	4.24E-02
CLERGYFU	1.11E-02	1.44E-03	1.67E-02	3.92E-02	1.29E-01 **	-9.53E-02	-3.03E-02
PRIEST	1.71E-02	5.82E-02	7.49E-02 *	1.06E-02	1.13E-01 **	1.45E-02	-1.21E-01 **
BLACCL	1.27E-01 *	-5.23E-03	4.92E-02	5.10E-02	1.63E-02	4.14E-02	-1.24E-02
ARMY	-3.68E-02	-1.52E-02	-7.68E-03	-8.69E-03	3.21E-02	9.42E-03	2.11E-01 ***
GOV	4.62E-02	6.81E-03	3.38E-02	-1.03E-02	-9.33E-03	-1.82E-02	-1.72E-01 ***
NCOLYR	-5.82E-02 ***	-3.02E-02 *	3.33E-02 ***	2.28E-02 ***	3.86E-02 ***	1.06E-02	-3.75E-02 ***

TABLE 8.1.—Continued

	Dependent Variables						
Independent Variables	PROWELF	PROPOOR	PROHEAL	PROED	PROENV	PROSOC	PROARMS
COLYR	1.04E-02	-2.38E-02 **	-8.94E-03	3.16E-02 ***	4.68E-03	-3.69E-02 ***	-6.61E-02 ***
AGENCOLYR	6.23E-04 ***	3.89E-04	-4.40E-04 ***	-3.07E-04 **	-4.60E-04 ***	-3.95E-04 **	5.10E-04 ***
AGECOLYR	1.97E-04	1.29E-04	-1.78E-04	-5.39E-04 ***	1.18E-04	-4.16E-05	6.52E-04 ***
NCYRSLOPE	-4.52E-02 ***	-1.30E-02 *	1.38E-02 ***	9.11E-03 ***	1.82E-02 ***	-7.00E-03	-2.67E-02 ***
COLYRSLOPE	1.45E-02 ***	-1.81E-02 ***	-1.68E-02 ***	7.68E-03 ***	9.92E-03 ***	-3.87E-02 ***	-5.24E-02 ***
MALE	-1.95E-02 *	-4.59E-02 ***	-5.63E-02 ***	-6.48E-02 ***	-4.00E-02 ***	-9.40E-02 ***	4.20E-02 ***
YEAR	-2.76E-03 ***	-1.57E-02 ***	2.39E-03 ***	1.38E-02 ***	3.53E-03 ***	-5.70E-03 ***	-4.48E-03 ***
NE	8.83E-02 *	1.64E-01 ***	5.45E-02	4.79E-02	1.12E-01 ***	4.30E-02	-8.38E-02 ***
MA	-2.38E-02	3.09E-02	3.66E-02	3.34E-02	1.04E-01 ***	3.05E-02	-3.06E-02
ENC	-9.59E-03	4.57E-02	-1.30E-02	9.63E-03	5.74E-02 ***	3.08E-02	-5.70E-04
WNC	6.53E-02 *	-7.97E-02 *	-1.23E-02	3.95E-02	7.66E-02 ***	-5.31E-02 *	2.72E-03
SA	-5.28E-02 *	-3.61E-02	-1.43E-02	6.11E-02 ***	5.01E-02 **	3.98E-03	7.41E-02 ***
ESC	5.03E-02	-8.92E-03	-1.57E-02	3.71E-02	8.21E-03	5.51E-02	1.29E-01 ***
WSC	2.55E-02	-8.20E-02 *	-4.47E-02 *	1.76E-02	4.43E-02 *	4.11E-03	1.29E-01 ***
MT	2.28E-02	5.48E-02	-5.57E-03	3.39E-02	-1.39E-02	9.35E-03	7.44E-03
16NE	-4.74E-02	-3.32E-02	1.22E-02	-3.67E-02	2.54E-02	-3.67E-02	2.55E-02
16MA	-4.67E-02	5.63E-03	-1.19E-03	-6.89E-02 ***	1.85E-03	-1.26E-02	8.37E-03
16ENC	5.97E-03	-7.63E-02 *	-1.33E-02	-2.71E-02	-1.16E-02	-4.46E-02	-3.53E-02
16WNC	4.16E-04	5.50E-02	-2.71E-02	-3.06E-02	-1.90E-02	-2.33E-02	-8.17E-02 ***
16SA	2.95E-02	4.09E-02	2.30E-02	-8.85E-03	8.55E-03	6.34E-03	4.37E-03
16ESC	1.94E-02	-6.00E-02	1.75E-02	3.26E-02	9.27E-03	-1.96E-02	-1.52E-02
16WSC	-2.89E-02	-4.54E-02	-2.12E-02	-3.32E-03	-2.48E-02	-1.99E-02	-2.32E-03
16MT	-1.85E-02	-7.49E-02	-4.17E-02	-2.04E-02	-6.76E-02 **	-3.39E-02	6.93E-03
SIGETHNIC	3	2	5	4	7	7	4
N	18,232	7,993	26,798	26,235	25,584	15,482	26,327
RSQUARE	0.119	0.087	0.038	0.095	0.095	0.090	0.071
MEAN	1.69	2.53	2.57	2.56	2.51	2.46	1.87
STDEV	0.767	0.680	0.612	0.611	0.639	0.615	0.712

FY	1.60E–02 **	6.81E–03	2.96E–03	–3.38E–02 ***	–1.25E–02	–2.58E–02	–2.86E–02 ***
FY2	–2.26E–03	–2.27E–03	3.65E–03	–9.06E–03 ***	–2.64E–03	–8.92E–03	–6.65E–04
FYSLOPE	1.76E–02 ***	8.34E–03	4.91E–04	–2.77E–02 ***	–1.07E–02	–1.97E–02	–2.82E–02 ***
SELF	–3.29E–02 ***	–5.48E–02 ***	–2.10E–02	–2.77E–02 **	–4.46E–02 ***	–2.80E–02	–3.12E–02
PROF	–3.26E–02	3.14E–03	–1.16E–02	–2.00E–02	–9.57E–03	–1.25E–02	–5.92E–02 ***
MGM	–2.60E–02 **	4.27E–03	–4.45E–03	–2.10E–02	–5.74E–02 ***	–1.34E–02	–4.89E–02 ***
CLERK	1.88E–02 **	4.15E–03	9.51E–03	–9.75E–03	–7.60E–03	–3.97E–03	–1.66E–02
SALES	1.34E–02	3.19E–02 **	2.87E–03	2.99E–03	–1.92E–02	–1.37E–02	–9.86E–03
SERVE	3.36E–03	3.12E–02 **	6.64E–03	4.17E–03	1.95E–02	1.26E–02	3.49E–02 ***
AGR	–5.34E–02 **	8.77E–03	–3.05E–02	–5.92E–02 **	–9.68E–02 ***	–1.26E–01	2.00E–02
BLACK	4.22E–02 ***	–4.71E–02 **	6.41E–02 ***	1.32E–01 ***	2.58E–01	2.06E–01 ***	0.00E+00
UNION	3.08E–02 ***	3.61E–02 ***	1.32E–02	2.15E–02 **	4.26E–03	–2.18E–03	–2.71E–02 ***
GOVR	–3.73E–02 ***	0.00E+00	0.00E+00	0.00E+00	2.96E–02 **	2.35E–02	–3.78E–02 ***
MAIN	7.72E–03	–3.48E–03	3.48E–03	1.97E–02	1.96E–02	2.99E–02	8.42E–03
JEW	4.53E–02	–1.10E–01	6.32E–03	6.76E–02	1.96E–01 **	1.98E–01 *	2.10E–01 ***
JSLOPE	–2.26E–02	–6.73E–02	–4.46E–02	4.89E–02	2.53E–01 ***	2.08E–01 *	1.91E–01 ***
CATHOLIC	2.01 E–02	–5.25E–03	–3.38E–02	–1.65E–02	2.99E–02	3.77E–02	–3.65E–03
CSLOPE	–1.00E–02	–1.13E–03	–2.45E–02	5.23E–03	2.23E–02	1.26E–02	4.06E–02
NOREL	–9.23E–02 ***	–1.76E–03	2.68E–02	5.10E–02 *	1.65E–02	6.14E–02	9.54E–02 ***
OTHREL	–8.21E–02 **	–5.25E–03	3.31E–03	6.53E–02	8.80E–02	6.24E–02	4.34E–02
ATTEND	6.32E–03	–2.27E–03	7.35E–04	–4.06E–03	–1.02E–04	1.10E–02	–1.20E–02
ATTENDSL	–1.59E–03	–3.27E–03	9.33E–05	–5.94E–03 ***	2.46E–03	–2.24E–05	7.37E–03 ***
PATT	–7.37E–03	2.77E–03	–4.86E–03	–2.48E–05	–4.22E–03	–1.00E–02	8.00E–03
CATT	–7.56E–03	1.04E–03	2.32E–03	5.46E–03	–1.90E–03	–6.32E–03	1.11E–02
JATT	–1.71E–02	1.07E–02	–1.28E–02	–4.69E–03	1.42E–02	2.60E–02	–4.71E–03
FUNDAT	–5.39E–04	–1.66E–03	1.09E–03	–1.61E–03	1.56E–03	–1.61E–02	6.00E–03 ***
FYINCOME	–6.06E–02	4.36E–02	1.13E–01 **	–1.54E–02	–9.14E–04	–4.68E–02	4.07E–02
FMARRIED	6.59E–02	1.02E–01	–3.10E–02	–2.00E–02	–9.77E–02	–7.17E–02	8.37E–02
MARRIED	1.65E–02 **	9.80E–03	–1.36E–02	–2.35E–03	–1.79E–02	–1.05E–02	2.25E–03

TABLE 8.1.—Continued

Independent Variables	ANTICRIME	PROROAD	PROMASS	PROPARK	PROCITY(O)	PROCITY(I)	PRORACE(O)
					Dependent Variables		
CHILD	1.16E-02	2.24E-02	-2.29E-02	-4.42E-03	1.48E-02	1.85E-02 ***	-3.07E-02 ***
NCHILD	-6.52E-03	-2.16E-02	9.61E-04	1.78E-02 **	-1.18E-02 *	3.91E-03	1.18E-06
STATMIG	-9.60E-04	-7.69E-03	3.71E-02 ***	-1.76E-03	2.70E-03	-1.03E-02	-6.83E-03
CONTMIG	-1.93E-02 **	-8.87E-03	6.32E-02 ***	1.58E-02	3.65E-02 ***	2.53E-02	1.28E-02
MIGSL	-1.12E-02	-8.35E-03	5.18E-02 ***	8.07E-03	2.16E-02 **	9.65E-03	4.17E-03
CLERGYSL	4.81E-02	-1.36E-03	-1.26E-02	-5.38E-02	-3.24E-02	1.40E-02	7.75E-02
AGE	1.91E-03	2.59E-03	-1.64E-03	-1.30E-02 ***	-1.23E-02 ***	-3.53E-04	-1.42E-02 ***
AGE2	-1.21E-05	-4.96E-05 ***	-2.09E-05	3.27E-05 **	6.48E-05 ***	-1.73E-05	1.09E-04 ***
AGESL	-9.38E-05	2.99E-03 ***	1.05E-03 ***	-4.71E-03 ***	-3.72E-03 ***	-1.55E-03 **	-4.73E-03 ***
MEMNUM	1.54E-03	-6.24E-04	7.64E-03 **	1.24E-02 ***	-1.58E-03	7.82E-03	7.39E-05
LCCIT	5.84E-02 ***	-4.22E-02	1.01E-01 ***	6.67E-02 ***	0.00E+00	1.17E-01 ***	8.32E-02 ***
SCCIT	3.33E-02 **	-8.08E-02 ***	4.38E-02 **	9.11E-03	0.00E+00	0.00E+00	1.68E-03
SSURB	1.98E-02	-7.45E-02 ***	3.87E-02 *	-1.47E-02	7.65E-02 ***	0.00E+00	7.06E-03
LSURB	2.41E-02	-6.48E-02 ***	6.22E-02 ***	2.62E-03	1.20E-01 ***	0.00E+00	-7.13E-03
OURB	-1.73E-04	-5.34E-02 ***	1.60E-02	-5.10E-03	4.98E-02 ***	0.00E+00	2.74E-02 **
SCITY	3.19E-02 ***	-1.02E-02	3.37E-02 **	3.73E-02 ***	3.08E-02 **	-3.03E-02	5.32E-02 ***
MCITY	4.10E-02 ***	-4.41E-02 ***	3.42E-02 **	6.35E-02 ***	4.63E-02 ***	-3.87E-02	3.19E-02 **
SUBR13	9.68E-03	-4.55E-02 **	2.61E-02	3.29E-02 *	8.15E-02 ***	-2.52E-02	4.10E-02 **
LCITY	4.76E-02 ***	-2.77E-02	6.29E-02 ***	7.30E-02 ***	1.00E-01 ***	1.14E-02	4.41E-02 ***
LOWTEACH	5.50E-03	-4.06E-02 *	-3.43E-02	1.73E-02	5.89E-02 **	6.22E-02	7.05E-04
COLTEACH	-7.49E-02 ***	1.36E-02	-6.22E-03	2.51E-02	8.77E-02 ***	4.78E-02	9.88E-02 ***
WRITER	-2.83E-02	2.73E-02	2.97E-02	-3.90E-02	-3.19E-02	1.06E-01	1.09E-01 **
LAWYER	-5.51E-02	3.34E-02	1.15E-01 **	3.41E-03	4.77E-02	9.34E-02	7.06E-02
CLERGY	4.62E-02	3.94E-03	1.82E-03	-6.09E-02	-8.48E-03	-5.25E-03	7.38E-02
CLERGYFU	1.59E-02	-4.42E-02	-1.20E-01 *	5.97E-02	-1.99E-01 **	1.60E-01	3.06E-02
PRIEST	-2.67E-02	6.60E-02	1.30E-01 **	-1.91E-02	5.04E-02	5.40E-02	5.38E-02
BLACCL	3.99E-02	-9.01E-02 **	1.61E-02	4.46E-02	-1.20E-02	-4.66E-03	1.06E-01

ARMY	4.84E-02 *	-3.93E-02	2.93E-03	-3.43E-02	-1.68E-02	-8.85E-02	-1.50E-01 ***
GOV	-4.49E-02	4.48E-02	2.10E-02	6.62E-02 *	-8.94E-03	1.00E-01	1.42E-01 ***
NCOLYR	1.75E-02 **	-1.33E-02	-1.93E-02	-2.41E-02 **	-7.18E-03	2.89E-03	1.80E-03
COLYR	-1.51E-02 **	-1.17E-02	3.36E-02 ***	-1.90E-02 ***	-6.84E-03	4.57E-02 ***	3.34E-02 ***
AGENCOLYR	-8.91E-05	4.01E-04 *	4.29E-04 **	4.40E-04 **	2.21E-04	1.12E-04	-6.35E-06
AGECOLYR	4.33E-05	2.66E-04	-1.58E-04	3.69E-04 **	3.10E-04 *	-6.75E-04 **	-1.16E-04
NCYRSLOPE	1.35E-02 ***	4.53E-03	-2.24E-04	-4.55E-03	2.63E-03	7.88E-03	1.52E-03
COLYRSLOPE	-1.32E-02 ***	1.01E-04	2.66E-02 ***	-2.61E-03	6.95E-03 **	1.57E-02 ***	2.83E-02 ***
MALE	-5.44E-04 ***	9.68E-02 ***	8.63E-03	3.47E-02 ***	-7.16E-02 ***	-3.15E-02	-6.03E-02
YEAR	-1.44E-04	-3.91E-03 ***	4.20E-03 ***	-6.32E-05	-8.04E-03 ***	-9.50E-03 ***	-1.25E-03 *
NE	2.24E-02	4.58E-02	-8.12E-02 **	-3.42E-02	1.99E-01 ***	-3.66E-02	9.14E-02 **
MA	2.10E-02	1.17E-01 ***	-9.07E-02 ***	-1.25E-02	4.37E-02 ***	1.95E-01 ***	-2.73E-02
ENC	3.24E-02	5.74E-02 **	-9.10E-02 ***	-4.31E-02 *	8.45E-02 ***	4.52E-02	-2.87E-02
WNC	1.96E-02	1.54E-02	-1.04E-01 ***	-1.18E-01 ***	8.11E-02 **	1.90E-01 ***	1.16E-03
SA	4.63E-02 **	-3.42E-02	-1.16E-01 ***	-4.09E-02	-2.78E-02	1.72E-03	-1.16E-01 ***
ESC	4.99E-02 *	2.60E-02	-1.47E-01 ***	-4.94E-02	-8.84E-03	-4.90E-02	-1.65E-01 ***
WSC	2.47E-02	-3.04E-02	-1.25E-01 ***	-7.26E-02 **	-1.16E-02	-1.63E-03	-1.37E-01 ***
MT	-5.78E-03	2.26E-02	-2.32E-02	-8.81E-02 ***	-4.81E-02	-1.49E-02	1.51E-02
16NE	-1.42E-02	3.19E-02	3.55E-02	9.23E-02 **	-7.92E-02 *	3.15E-02	-5.37E-03
16MA	-1.83E-02	1.07E-02	-2.39E-03	5.56E-02 *	-1.10E-02	-3.33E-02	-1.87E-02
16ENC	-3.03E-02	-7.87E-03	-2.60E-02	1.11E-02	-6.04E-02 *	4.47E-02	-1.32E-02
16WNC	-3.94E-02	-2.23E-02	1.60E-03	2.57E-02	-4.95E-02	-4.25E-02	-1.42E-03
16SA	-1.46E-02	8.26E-03	-2.63E-02	4.64E-02 *	-2.00E-02	-1.83E-02	-4.25E-02
16ESC	1.92E-03	8.59E-03	-1.69E-02	3.35E-02	-5.14E-02	-3.92E-02	-3.18E-02
16WSC	-1.25E-03	2.83E-02	-3.47E-02	1.78E-02	-7.40E-02 **	-3.45E-02	-4.31E-02
16MT	-5.24E-02 *	-3.62E-03	4.88E-04	-3.67E-02	-1.69E-02	9.49E-03	-3.95E-02
SIGETHNIC	3	5	4	6	5	3	12
N	26,839	16,280	16,175	15,508	6,240	20,669	23,501
RSQUARE	0.018	0.030	0.045	0.053	0.051	0.070	0.058
MEAN	2.55	2.31	2.22	2.25	2.16	2.36	1.99
STDEV	0.596	0.609	0.611	0.535	0.738	0.724	0.684

TABLE 8.1.—Continued

Independent Variables	Dependent Variables				
	PRORACE(I)	ANTIABORT	PROREPUBL	PROCONSERV	PRESR
FY	-3.02E-02 *	-3.85E-01 ***	2.11E-01 ***	1.57E-02 ***	5.62E-02 ***
FY2	-7.72E-03	-3.53E-02	7.73E-02 ***	5.94E-03 ***	1.66E-02 ***
FYSLOPE	-2.50E-02 *	-3.62E-01 ***	1.59E-01 ***	5.95E-02 ***	4.50E-02 ***
SELF	-8.06E-02 **	-1.24E-01	1.92E-01 ***	4.12E-02 *	3.04E-02 ***
PROF	-6.63E-02	-5.13E-01 ***	-1.57E-02	2.99E-02	-8.27E-02 ***
MGM	-3.30E-02	-4.67E-02	2.22E-01 ***	3.50E-02	4.52E-02 ***
CLERK	1.05E-02	-2.33E-01 ***	1.46E-01 ***	4.52E-02 **	4.14E-02 ***
SALES	1.41E-02	-1.77E-01 *	2.38E-01 ***	8.26E-02 ***	3.92E-02 ***
SERVE	-1.55E-02	1.69E-01 *	6.34E-03	-4.68E-02 **	1.24E-02
AGR	3.08E-02	-2.05E-01	2.07E-01 ***	-1.41E-02	6.45E-03
BLACK	0.00E+00	-7.07E-02	-1.29E+00 ***	-3.10E-01 ***	-4.12E-01 ***
UNION	4.97E-02 ***	-1.61E-01 **	-2.33E-01 ***	-7.16E-02 ***	-4.43E-02 ***
GOVR	-1.80E-02	9.02E-03	-1.59E-01 ***	-1.59E-01 ***	-3.96E-02 ***
MAIN	-7.26E-02	-3.17E-01 ***	-8.05E-02 **	-1.13E-03	-2.67E-02 **
JEW	-4.84E-01 *	-3.06E-01	-1.27E+00 ***	-5.38E-01 ***	-2.93E-01 ***
JSLOPE	-1.68E-01	-1.06E+00 **	-1.37E+00 ***	-4.82E-01 ***	-3.17E-01 ***
CATHOLIC	1.23E-02	-2.72E-01	-3.15E-01 ***	-1.21E-02	-6.29E-02 ***
CSLOPE	2.38E-02	3.50E-01	-3.84E-01 ***	-8.15E-02	-1.17E-01 ***
NOREL	-2.71E-02	-5.79E-01 ***	-8.51E-02	-3.14E-01 ***	-1.36E-01 ***
OTHREL	5.08E-02	-2.91E-01	-1.47E-01	-9.46E-02	-1.57E-01 ***
ATTEND	-8.97E-03	3.20E-01 ***	4.51E-04	8.34E-02 ***	1.73E-02 ***
ATTENDSL	-4.13E-03	5.16E-01 ***	4.14E-02 ***	4.67E-02 ***	1.12E-02 ***
PATT	8.37E-03	-1.29E-01 **	5.91E-02 ***	2.60E-03	-3.90E-03
CATT	2.88E-03	1.56E-01 ***	-1.74E-02	-1.74E-02	-1.36E-02 **
JATT	7.93E-02 *	-1.90E-01	-2.54E-02	1.40E-02	-6.01E-03
FUNDAT	-1.41E-03	-1.33E-01 ***	4.36E-03	-1.77E-02 ***	-5.90E-05
FYINCOME	5.79E-02	-1.42E+00 ***	2.98E-01 **	-1.21E-01	3.03E-02

FMARRIED	1.10E-01	3.74E-01	1.23E+00 ***	2.41E-01	8.58E-02
MARRIED	4.02E-02 **	5.29E-01 ***	1.37E-02	9.59E-02	1.09E-03
CHILD	-1.38E-02	-2.36E-01 **	-9.90E-03	-2.27E-02	-4.22E-03
NCHILD	-1.22E-03	3.05E-01 ***	1.56E-02	3.30E-02 ***	2.65E-03
STATMIG	-4.69E-02 *	2.28E-02	7.16E-02 **	2.90E-02	8.32E-03
CONTMIG	-1.76E-02	-7.38E-03	1.02E-01 ***	-1.04E-03 *	8.04E-03
MIGSL	-3.05E-02 *	5.90E-03	8.86E-02 ***	1.21E-02	8.16E-03
CLERGYSL	-1.67E-01	1.92E+00 ***	2.02E-03	2.33E-02 *	4.73E-03
AGE	3.12E-03	-3.63E-02 *	-8.29E-02 ***	5.96E-03 ***	-7.16E-03 ***
AGE2	-2.93E-05	1.07E-04	5.60E-04 ***	-9.67E-05 **	5.93E-05 ***
AGESL	-3.79E-04	8.31E-06	-1.02E-02 ***	7.74E-03 ***	-1.40E-03 ***
MEMNUM	9.42E-03	-8.80E-02 ***	-2.01E-02 **	-7.98E-03	-1.97E-03
LCCIT	2.50E-02	-6.87E-01 ***	-3.00E-01 ***	-1.95E-01 ***	-7.26E-02 ***
SCCIT	7.42E-03	-4.75E-01 ***	-1.68E-01 ***	-8.08E-02 **	-5.74E-02 ***
SSURB	5.27E-02	-3.60E-01 ***	-1.88E-02	-8.55E-03	-9.42E-03
LSURB	7.97E-02 *	-4.28E-01 ***	4.57E-02	-3.51E-02	-1.72E-04
OURB	-2.19E-02	-1.01E-01	-9.45E-02 ***	-3.12E-02	-3.03E-02 ***
SCITY	5.79E-02 **	-1.37E-01	-4.87E-02	-6.35E-03	-1.19E-03
MCITY	5.00E-02 *	-4.54E-01 ***	-3.81E-02	-6.33E-02	2.73E-03
SUBRB	-6.82E-03	-4.95E-01 ***	5.69E-02	-7.51E-02 **	3.65E-03
LCITY	4.38E-02	-5.71E-01 ***	6.39E-03	-1.97E-02	5.27E-03
LOWTEACH	4.20E-02	2.36E-01	-4.02E-02	-5.84E-03	-4.75E-04
COLTEACH	3.59E-02	-1.87E-01	-3.00E-01 ***	-1.17E-01 ***	-6.39E-02 ***
WRITER	-4.00E-01	-6.28E-01	-5.59E-02	-1.52E-01	-2.61E-02
LAWYER	-2.24E-02	-6.56E-01	-2.17E-01	-1.34E-01	-1.06E-01 **
CLERGY	-1.40E-01	1.85E+00 ***	-1.50E-02	3.78E-03	6.08E-03
CLERGYFU	-2.23E-01	5.47E-01	1.42E-01	1.63E-01	-1.13E-02
PRIEST	-1.10E-01	3.68E-01	-1.08E-01	-1.17E-01	-1.16E-03
BLACCL	5.70E-02	-1.21E+00 ***	-4.70E-01 ***	-1.73E-01 **	-3.63E-02
ARMY	-7.22E-02	-3.60E-01	9.76E-02	1.26E-01 **	4.62E-02 **
GOV	5.13E-02	2.37E-02	-2.14E-01 **	-1.65E-01 **	-7.63E-02 ***
NCOLYR	1.37E-02	-3.36E-01 ***	-8.94E-02 ***	-4.72E-02 ***	7.01E-03

TABLE 8.1.— Continued

Independent Variables	Dependent Variables				
	PRORACE(1)	ANTIABORT	PROREPUBL	PROCONSERV	PRESR
COLYR	-1.67E-03	-3.27E-01 ***	-4.26E-02 **	-9.50E-02 ***	-2.79E-02 ***
AGENCOLYR	-9.12E-05	1.98E-03 *	1.83E-03 ***	-5.29E-04 *	-1.58E-05
AGECOLYR	8.89E-05	3.62E-03 ***	1.97E-03 ***	1.28E-03 ***	4.94E-04 ***
NCYRSLOPE	9.62E-03 *	-2.48E-01 ***	-8.14E-03	2.37E-02 ***	6.31E-03 **
COLYRSLOPE	2.28E-03	-1.66E-01 ***	4.48E-02 ***	-3.80E-02 ***	-6.02E-03 ***
MALE	-3.06E-02 *	3.35E-01 ***	1.59E-01 ***	1.39E-01 ***	4.56E-02 ***
YEAR	-3.89E-03 ***	2.52E-02 ***	2.29E-02 ***	1.20E-02 ***	-6.85E-04
NE	2.06E-01 ***	3.64E-01	1.09E-01	-3.46E-02	2.02E-02
MA	1.05E-01 **	5.54E-01 ***	4.96E-02	-3.75E-02	8.40E-03
ENC	6.94E-02	1.08E+00 ***	-3.12E-02	4.89E-02	1.67E-02
WNC	1.12E-01 *	1.23E+00 ***	-8.40E-02	2.62E-02	-1.75E-02
SA	3.85E-02	4.66E-01 **	4.61E-02	3.65E-02	4.16E-02 **
ESC	3.50E-02	7.78E-01 ***	-4.63E-03	1.30E-01 **	3.16E-02
WSC	7.02E-03	6.62E-01 ***	1.91E-02	9.41E-02 *	7.89E-02 ***
MT	-2.91E-01 ***	5.56E-01 ***	-6.61E-02	8.08E-05	2.37E-02
16NE	-3.32E-02	-4.09E-01	2.41E-02	-6.40E-02	-1.19E-02
16MA	4.28E-02	-3.48E-01 *	2.60E-01 ***	-3.10E-02	2.51E-02
16ENC	9.40E-02	-1.43E-01	1.51E-01 **	-7.19E-02	6.88E-03
16WNC	2.65E-02	-2.36E-01	5.65E-02	-1.04E-01 *	-1.85E-02
16SA	3.81E-02	5.58E-02	-1.57E-01 **	-4.08E-02	-2.39E-02
16ESC	9.80E-02	4.41E-01 *	-1.99E-01 **	-6.92E-02	-2.15E-02
16WSC	1.14E-01 *	7.94E-02	-2.49E-01 ***	2.77E-03	-1.98E-02
16MT	2.71E-01 **	5.22E-01 **	2.04E-01 **	6.19E-02	4.60E-02 **
SIGETHNIC	7	3	11	4	11
N	3,393	17,210	27,407	24,290	24,327
RSQUARE	0.084	0.242	0.160	0.087	0.155
MEAN	2.77	12.43	2.6	4.08	0.55
STDEV	0.465	4.640	1.998	1.310	0.496

Key to Table 8.1

I. Dependent Variables

PROWELF: Are we spending too little (1), about the right amount (2), or too much (3) on welfare?

PROPOOR: Are we spending too little (1), about the right amount (2), or too much (3) on assistance to the poor?

PROHEAL: on improving and protecting the nation's health?

PROED: on improving the nation's educational system?

PROENV: on the environment?

PROSOC: on Social Security?

PROARMS: on the military, armaments, and defense?

ANTICRIME: on halting crime?

PROROAD: on highways and bridges?

PROMASS: on mass transportation?

PROPARK: on parks and recreation?

PROCITY(0): on solving the problems of big cities? (for those living in cities)

PROCITY(1): on solving the problem of big cities? (for those not)

PRORACE(0): on improving the conditions of blacks? (for nonblacks)

PRORACE(1): on improving the conditions of blacks? (for blacks)

ANTIABORT: Should it be possible for a pregnant women to obtain a legal abortion under 7 different conditions? Dependent variable runs from 7 (all no) to 14 (all yes).

PROREPUBL: identifications with Republican Party from strong Democrat (1) to strong Republican (7)

PROCONSERV: political views from extremely liberal (1) through extremely conservative (8)

PRESR: vote for or would have voted for Republican presidential candidate

II. Independent Variables

FY = ln of family income relative to mean family income estimated by a Pareto distribution

FY2 = the square of the FY

FYSLOPE = the coefficient of FY evaluated at the mean levels of variables it interacts with

SELF = self-employed

PROF = professional or technical workers

MGM = managers and administrators

CLERK = clerical workers

SALES = sales workers

SERVE = service workers

AGR = farmers and farm laborers, etc.

BLACK = blacks

UNION = union membership by self

GOVR = recipient of government assistance

MAIN = Protestant and not Baptist, Holiness Pentecostal, or other

JEW = Jewish

JSLOPE = the coefficient of JEW evaluated at the mean levels of the variables it interacts with

CATHOLIC = Catholic

CSLOPE = coefficient of CATHOLIC evaluated at mean level of variables it interacts with

NOREL = no religious preference

OTHREL = religious preference other than Jewish, Protestant, or Catholic

ATTEND = from 0 (never) through 8 (several times a week) for attendance at religious services

ATTENDSL = attend slope

PATT = interaction of ATTEND and MAIN

CATT = interaction of ATTEND and CATHOLIC

JATT = interaction of ATTEND and JEWISH

FUNDAT = interaction of ATTEND and (1 – MAIN)

FYINCOME = the average income of the religious denomination to which one belongs

FMARRIED = the percentage of one's religious denomination either married or widowed and never divorced

Key to Table 8.1—*continued*

MARRIED = married
CHILD = parent of a child at some point in life
NCHILD = number of children parented
STATMIG = located elsewhere in the state at age 16
CONTMIG = located in a different state at age 16
MIGSL = the coefficient of migratory status evaluated at mean
CLERGYSL = CLERGY slope.
AGE = age
AGE2 = the square of age
AGESL = age slope
MEMNUM = number of memberships in 16 voluntary organization types
LCCIT = resides in a central city of 1 of 12 largest standard metropolitan statistical areas (SMSA)
SCCIT = resides in a small city of next largest central SMSA
SSURB = resides in a suburb of 1 of 12 largest SMSAs
LSURB = resides in a suburb of one of next 88 largest SMSAs
OURB = residence in counties having towns of 10,000 or more
SCITY = resides in suburbs of smaller central city
MCITY = resides in central city of any but the top 100 SMSAs
SUBRB = resides in suburbs of central city of any but the top 100 SMSAs
LCITY = resides in central city of a smaller central city
LOWTEACH = employed as a teacher other than in college or university
COLTEACH = employed as a college or university teacher
WRITER = editors or reporters
LAWYER = lawyers and judges
CLERGY = clergypersons
CLERGYFU = clergy interacted with (1 – MAIN)
PRIEST = clergy interacted with CATHOLIC
BLACCL = clergy interacted with BLACK
ARMY = membership in the armed forces and police
GOV = employed by government but not in the police, army or education
NCOLYR = number of years of formal schooling at grade 12 or below
COLYR = number of years of college
AGENCOLYR = interaction of age and number of years of non-college education
AGECOLYR = interaction of age and number of years of college education
NCYRSLOPE = the coefficient of noncollege years of education evaluated at the means of the variables it
  is interacted with
COLYRSLOPE = the coefficient of college years of education at the means of the variables it is interacted
  with
MALE = male
YEAR = 1972 = 1
The region abbreviations = resides in one of 8 regions of the United States NE (Northeast), MA (Mid-
  Atlantic), ENC (East North Central), WNC (West North Central), SA (South Atlantic), ESC (East
  South Central), WSC (West South Central), MT (Mountain).
The region abbreviations preceded by 16 = resided in one of 8 regions at age 16.
SIGETHNIC = There are dummy variables for each of 38 ethnic groups specified in Nelson 1994, and this
  refers to the number of such that were significant at the 5% level or better.
N = sample size
RSQUARE = multiple correlation coefficient squared
MEAN = mean voter participation
STDEV = standard deviation
  *Significant at 10% level. **Significant at 5% level. ***Significant at 1% level
  Note: This table is reprinted with permission from Table 1 (pp. 436–42) of Kenneth Greene and Phillip
Nelson, "Morality and the Political Process," in *Method and Morals in the Constitutional Economics,* ed.
Geoffrey Brennan, Hartmut Kliemt, and Robert Tollison (New York: Springer-Verlag, 2000), 413–43. ©
Springer-Verlag 2002.

its own, particularly for voting. Most of these problems are generated by nonlinearities. Population density plays an important role in political decisions, as we shall see, but we do not know how to provide an adequate summary measure of that density by area. Voting regressions by area frequently lead to serious anomalies. For example, high-income areas tend to vote Democratic rather than Republican.

Self-Interest Variables

In studying political behavior most economists focus exclusively on narrow self-interest: how one would vote if solely concerned with the consequences of the policies voted for. As discussed in chapter 6 this approach is unsatisfactory theoretically because of the free-rider problem. Still, narrow self-interest variables do have an impact empirically. The narrow self-interest of the associates whom one is trying to please magnifies the effect of one's own self-interest because there is a positive correlation between the two, as seen in chapter 5.

The most important narrow self-interest variables we use are income and its square. With the exception of abortion, all of the issues have a redistributive component. For most of the programs examined the rich pay more than they receive. But that is probably not true for defense or police or roads. In the latter half of the twentieth century the Communist Soviet Union was the main external enemy of the United States. Presumably, the relative costs to the rich of its success would have been large. An important function of the police is the protection of property, and the rich own more than do the poor, though the poor are crime victims more frequently. The rich are also less likely to be criminals or charged with crimes, so the interests of this latter group will weigh less in their decisions. There is also a positive income elasticity of demand for automobile travel and for the goods transported by trucks. It is not clear whether this more or less counterbalances the share of taxes paid by higher-income groups to finance roads.

In the regression results reported in table 8.1, in eleven out of the nineteen cases the slope of log income at its mean is significant in the conservative direction: only in one case is it in the liberal direction. In this case—the rich are more proabortion—the liberal cause does not involve greater government expenditures.

Another self-interest variable is whether a person is self-employed (SELF = 1) or not. While business and regulatory costs may ultimately shift to either consumers or owners of capital, there will be some short-run costs borne by current owners of businesses. Furthermore, one expects the self-employed to be more knowledgeable about this tax burden and many self-employed to be imperfectly aware of tax shifting. There are eleven cases in which the self-employed are significantly conservative. There are only two cases where they adopt significantly more liberal positions, in each case being opposed to greater government expenditures, first on roads, our iffy issue, and on the police.

Consider broad occupations as given by the 1968 Standard International Codes as specified in table 8.1. One expects higher-income occupations and those associating with high-income families to behave similarly to high-income families, even controlling for family income.

Using "Production and Related Workers" as the control group, we looked at the behavior of dummy variables for professionals, managers, clerical workers, sales workers, service workers, and agricultural workers, including their spouses. The first four occupations are white-collar occupations. The positive and significant coefficient for each indicates that each behaves more conservatively than the control group.

Race is another self-interest variable in the United States. Blacks are likely to be in favor of greater expenditures for blacks. There are often indirect costs associated with government-generated beneficence, and that beneficence is not uniformly distributed to all members of the group. However, these indirect costs are generally less well known to the group involved than the direct benefits themselves. Also party and conservative-liberal identification and votes for president have a direct self-interest component for blacks because of party differences over affirmative action. There are other issues that are not explicitly about race, but because of imitation blacks should vote the same way low-income groups vote, even though family income is one of the control variables. Blacks are significantly more liberal on ten issues and are significantly more conservative on one issue: crime.[5]

Community Involvement: Theory

At the beginning of this chapter we stated one of the hypotheses that we wanted to test, and the way in which we could test it. The lower the cost of "signaling" goodness, the more people will adopt "progoodness" political positions. As discussed in chapter 4, this proposition holds both for public and private political positions, though it will be more important for public positions. The major cost of signaling goodness is signaling friendship less effectively. The more friends one has, the greater the cost of goodness. Similarly, the greater the cost of acquiring new friends, the more one values old friends relative to any return to goodness. We call both of these *community involvement* effects.

This process works in spite of an obvious objection. Suppose the signaling of friendship just involved imitating others' political positions. Then, increasing the incentives for such signaling, just yields a greater tendency for people in the aggregate to adopt the average political position in the previous period. If political positions in general were in stable equilibrium, that average past position would be equal to the average current position. In consequence, greater friendship signaling would apparently have no impact on the role of goodness in determining political positions.

There are two objections to this objection. First, we are not in stable equilibrium. As seen in the next chapter, the role of goodness in determining political positions is increasing. Those who help slow down that change will display relatively less goodness.

Second, as we saw in chapter 5, there is likely to be at least a small narrow self-interest component in a person's signal that he wishes to be the friend of another. That is, the friend will expect the other person to adjust his imitation a bit by including a little narrow self-interest in determining his political position. Given that expectation, that is roughly what he will do. As a result, the greater use of friendship signaling moves political positions somewhat away from average political positions toward average narrow self-interest positions. Hence, those who use more of that signaling will display relatively less goodness.

There is another process that produces a positive relationship between community involvement and asymmetric goodness—the third hypothesis developed at the beginning of this chapter. People can get information about the political position of others through political expression designed for a wide audience, or they can obtain their information through contacts with others. The former source has a much larger goodness component than the latter. The greater one's number of contacts with others, the greater the expected ratio of information from contacts with others to wide-audience information.

These processes hold for both liberal goodness and conservative morality, and, therefore provide only limited predictions for those issues where goodness is two-sided, but do provide simple predictions for asymmetric goodness.

But even in those cases of two-sided goodness we expect community involvement to make a person more conservative because we expect community involvement to have other effects increasing the probability of conservative morality signaling. One expects there to be a positive relationship between community involvement and sexual probity. One pays a bigger price in social ostracism if others disapprove of one's sexual practices. The more one's sexual behavior is in line with group morality, the lower the costs of advocating such morality. We predict a positive effect on antiabortion positions.

The negative association of community involvement with goodness contrasts dramatically with a major implication about standard charity. In chapter 3 we saw that the greater the community involvement, the more a person contributes to the latter. This difference in behavior is produced because community involvement increases the cost of goodness, but it does not increase the cost of standard charity.

In the case of defense spending community involvement works through imitation rather than goodness. Those who are more involved in the community and their friends have a self-interested motivation for increased expenditures for defense. Because they are community leaders, they have more to lose from a change of government by force.

Except in a criminal society, community involvement also reduces the probability that a person and his friends will be criminals. This decreases the cost of favoring greater expenditures to fight crime. But for some community involvement variables, like living in a rural area, the probability of being a victim of crime also decreases. So for those variables the effect is ambiguous.

Community Involvement: Tests

We study several variables that are related to community involvement. Probably the purest such variable is migration, as Glaeser, Laibson, and Sacerdote (2000) show. Migration reduces community membership, and the further one moves the less the network of friends and relatives one is likely to have at one's destination. We use two migration variables: whether one is an intrastate migrant (STATMIG) in the sense that one lives in a different town but the same state that one lived in when sixteen, and CONTMIG, whether one was an interstate migrant in the same sense. There are three cases where intrastate migrants are significantly more liberal than nonmigrants, and there are no cases where intrastate migrants are more conservative than nonmigrants. Interstate migrants are significantly more liberal in five cases and are not significantly more conservative in any cases.

As discussed in chapter 3, we posit that the costs of developing new friends increases with age. We also believe that signaling goodness is particularly cheap to the very young who choose both friends and political positions *de novo*.

We would also expect age over most of the range of adulthood to increase the ratio of information about the political position of others that comes from contact with those others compared to the information that comes from public expression associated with wider audiences. The young build up a stockpile of such information coming through education. After the period of formal education is over, the stream of the two sources of information might very well come in at a constant rate. But such a timing pattern implies that the ratio of contact information relative to wider audience information increases with time.[6]

The slope of the age variable at its mean and the mean of other relevant variables is almost always significant. There are thirteen cases where older people are more conservative; three where they are more liberal: they are more Democratic, vote for Democratic candidates for president, and are in favor of greater expenditures on mass transportation.[7]

Another community-involvement-related variable is city size. The denser a community's population, the harder it is to be an active member. The anonymity of the city has long been recognized. Currently, city residence in the United States also makes a person more liberal because her neighbors will be more liberal and may consist of more blacks, migrants, singles, and the nonreligious.

Suburbs also create unfavorable conditions for community involvement, since a substantial portion of their population commutes long distances to work with a resulting separation of the social life of work and residence. Holding density constant, suburbs should have less community involvement than other city types. Suburbanites are also affected by the attitudes of central city residents, since the latter are often the work associates of the former. This too should make suburbanites more liberal.

City-size categories make a significant difference in the predicted direction for most of the issues investigated. In three of the cases, mass transit, roads, and the environment, there are clear differences in self-interest by city-size categories. But the city-size effect is significant for most of the other issues as well. There are thirteen issues where those in the largest central cities (LRCIT) and seven where those in the next largest (SCCIT) are significantly more liberal than those in rural areas, the control group. There are three issues for which no city-size category is significant—Social Security, aid to the poor, and expenditures for blacks (among blacks). For roads, all city-size categories are significant except large central cities (a surprising exception). For police expenditures, results are reversed, and significantly so. The larger the city the more its residents adopt the conservative position—more expenditures to fight crime. The explanation is obvious.

For six issues the suburbs of the largest cities (LSURB) are significantly more liberal than the comparable density group, other urban: the environment, welfare, abortion, education, city expenditures, roads, and mass transit. This is also true for the suburbs of the next largest cities (SSURB). Three of these positions can be explained by self-interested connections to the city: the environment, city expenditures, and mass transit. One is just the reverse of what one would anticipate in terms of self-interest: opposition to spending on roads. Commuters are heavy users of roads as well as mass transit. For party identification suburbanites are more conservative than residents in the category "other urban."

There is an alternative explanation for the city-size effect. The association between large cities and reduced family ties has a direct impact. Families are less capable of providing a variety of services: child care, education, health care, and insurance. So there is an increased incentive to substitute public services for family services (Holsey and Borcherding 1996).

Along the same lines, one expects less reciprocal relations the greater the population density. People know less about each other as population density increases. In consequence, there is less reputational loss from being a moocher in big cities compared to rural areas. Indeed, Glaeser et al. (1999) find significantly less social capital for big cities. Public services could be substitutes for help from others.

While this alternative hypothesis might explain part of the city-size–liberal relationship, it cannot explain all of it. Not only does the current city size in which the respondent lives make a significant difference in political positions, but so too does city size of the respondent when sixteen. For three of the issues—aid to the poor, health, and parks—there are more significant coefficients for the latter than the former. For four others the lagged city coefficients are roughly equal those for current cities: the environment, crime, education, city expenditures (for those not in central cities). There are, however, five issues on which the current coefficients are bigger: welfare, abortion, party identification, presidential votes, and mass transit.

In chapter 5, we showed that imitation produces lags in voter response to underlying conditions. In the United States married people typically migrate together. When a person is single or moves with his immediate family from a city size, that city size no longer affects the reality he confronts, though it might still affect his extended family. It is hard to believe that the weight he gives to his extended family will be more important than the weight he gives his immediate family. His attitudes move with him, however, and it is possible that early attitude formation could be more important than what happens later.

There is one community involvement variable that is positively related to goodness: the number of organizations to which one belongs (MEMNUM). It has a significant liberal coefficient in seven cases and there are no significant conservative coefficients.

The difference between MEMNUM and the other community involvement variables is that MEMNUM can be a function of a person's activism rather than simply influencing the activism. One may join the ACLU or the Sierra Club in one's desire to be good. One may also join the John Birch Society, but there is a greater return to being a good liberal compared to being a good conservative. The relationship of activism to goodness was discussed in detail in chapter 7.

Religion

Religion has assorted effects on political positions of its practitioners. (1) Preachers can directly preach political activism. This runs the gamut of sermons against abortion to exhortations for government action to fight poverty. Knowledge of the nature of those sermons will help predict systematic differences in the political positions of the listeners. These consumers of sermons can be affected by persuasion. Alternatively, they can be selected on the basis of their willingness to be subjected to such sermonizing. It is known, for example, that mainline Protestants preach more liberal activism than do Fundamentalists. (2) Preachers can preach private morality. Fundamentalists on the whole emphasize sexual probity and family commitments more than do mainline Protestants. We would expect Fundamentalists to be more likely to practice such behavior, and in turn we would expect such practitioners to be more involved in the community, because the more one is involved in the community the greater the return from following the approved mores. As we have seen, community involvement leads to more conservative political positions. (3) Those who attend church are more involved in the community than others, as shown in chapter 3. There is the obvious direct effect—church attendance and its accompanying activities are socializing experiences. The indirect effects are also important, since church-based friendships often open up other friendship opportunities. The details of the regression results we employ using religious variables help show these processes at work.

Probably the most questionable of these listed effects is the second. We try to get at that effect by creating a special measure of the pro-family orientation of the narrowly defined religious denomination of a respondent: the sample percentage of those in the denomination who are either married or widowed and have never been divorced.[8] We call this measure FMARRIED. We also use a dummy variable for mainline Protestants called MAIN, classifying the NORC narrow denominations using the guidelines developed by Kellstedt, Lyman, and Green (1993). Similarly, we would expect those who have no religion, NOREL, to engage in more goodness than others, especially when Fundamentalists are the religion of comparison.

In addition, we include a measure of a person's own profamily behavior: whether the respondent is married or widowed and has never been divorced. That variable is called MARRIED. MARRIED also has a direct community involvement effect in the same direction. As shown in chapter 3, married people jointly have more friends, since they pool their friends by marrying. We also include a variable called ATTEND, the frequency of church attendance.[9]

Table 8.1 shows that FMARRIED has a significant (at the 5 percent level) impact in the predicted direction on policy preferences in six of the nineteen cases examined, and does not have any significant impacts in the opposite direction. Being a mainline Protestant relative to being a Fundamentalist Protestant, MAIN, leads to a significant effect in the predicted direction in only three cases, but there are no significant cases in the opposite direction. Greater values of NOREL lead to significant effects in the predicted direction in six cases and only one in the opposite direction—against greater Social Security expenditures.

Greater values of MARRIED lead a person to be significantly more conservative, significantly antiabortion, and against more expenditures on the environment. There is one opposite case, but, as we shall see later, it is not very important as an indicator of goodness. For blacks, MARRIED leads to greater support for government expenditures on blacks.

There is a significant slope for ATTEND at the means of other relevant variables for twelve issues. In only one of these cases does greater church attendance lead to the more liberal position: for greater expenditures to help blacks among whites.

ATTEND also has a community involvement feature that is required to explain a seeming paradox. Returning to chapter 3, we see that church attendance is the single most important variable explaining standard charity for non-church-based contributions as well as contributions through the church, and yet it produces less goodness. The usual altruism explanation for both charity and goodness makes no sense in terms of this result.

Belonging to a minority religion could also generate less community involvement. Jews, other non-Christians, and Catholics, to a lesser extent, have been victims of past social discrimination, placing some restrictions on their community involvement. Jews are significantly more liberal on nine issues and are significantly more conservative on none. Catholics are significantly more liberal on defense, party identification, and votes for president, and significantly more conservative about abortion. OTHREL—membership in other religions—leads to significantly more liberalism on two issues: defense and crime—and is not significantly more conservative on any issue.

Religion: The Literature

The question of the impact of religious views on political positions has been investigated before, but most of the past studies confine their attention to environmental issues (for example Guth et al. 1995). The main conclusion from past studies is that Fundamentalists are more opposed to environmental expenditures than are members of more mainstream, liberal churches (with a doctrinal rather than political definition of the latter). These results are consistent with our finding that the cross-product of church attendance with a measure of the liberalism of the church is quite significant.

The literature has explained this role of Fundamentalism doctrinally. The argument is that those who take the Creation story seriously are more likely to believe in a man-centered universe, and, hence are less likely to cherish the environment in its own right (Lowry 1998) or those who believe in the Apocalypse give less weight to the future.

Clearly, one does not need such interpretations. Without reference to doctrine, our theory predicts that the sexual probity associated with Fundamentalism would be associated with more community involvement in its believers. In the one case where there is clearly a doctrinal message—opposition to abortion—the β coefficient for the cross-product of church liberalism with attendance is almost three times as great as the β coefficient for this cross-product for the environmental question.[10] In addition, the environmental β coefficient is about the same value as the β coefficients for the other independent variables that are significantly related to this cross-product (expenditures on blacks for whites and conservatism). Furthermore, whether one was a mainline Protestant (with being a Fundamentalist Protestant the control group) was not significant for the environment, while it was significant for the abortion issue, party identification, and how one voted for president. Among the variables significantly related to Fundamentalism, environmentalism does not stand out. Also, there are many other religious variables that play a role in our regressions, including the environmental regression. It is more difficult to explain their role in terms of simple doctrine. For example, opposition to welfare and aid to the poor significantly increases with church attendance, in spite of the "compassion" message of much sermonizing. One suspects, then, that doctrine does not fully explain the role of Fundamentalism in the environmental regression.

Occupational Choice

We hypothesize that one of the determinants of occupational choice is the desire to display goodness. Those occupations that provide a platform for espousing "good" views or an opportunity to fight "injustice" will tend to be chosen by those with such views and those who are convinced about these injustices. For those issues where goodness is asymmetrical we expect these occupations to adopt the goodness side. (However, college teaching could also provide a platform for espousing conservative morality.) For issues in which goodness is two-sided, the occupational position will be governed by the demographic characteristics of the occupational group. College teachers should be more proabortion, for example, because they are less religious. They should be antidefense because they are less involved in the community than others as well as having a higher proportion of Jews.[11]

We concentrate our attention on college and other teachers, journalists, clergymen, and lawyers. Our technique is to look at the regression coefficients of the dummy variables associated with whether one or one's spouse is a member or not of the respective occupations, controlling for all the other determinants of political preferences.[12] We define college teachers by industry rather than occupation because there is a serious problem with the occupational definition in this case. Many college teachers would not so classify themselves. They would call themselves economists, physicists and so forth. However, use of the occupational definition does not change the essence of our results.

It comes as no surprise that college teachers are liberal. In no other occupation are there so few outside constraints placed on advocacy. (Any internal constraints placed by other college teachers, such as political correctness, would just exaggerate the effect of any variables influencing their political position. In other words, the effect of goodness in occupational choice is strengthened by imitating others who also so choose the occupation for goodness sake. The professors with opposite views have those views dampened by the academic norms antithetical to those views.) Academic freedom virtually removes employer monitoring of college teaching. College teachers are significantly liberal on nine issues, and there are no issues on which college teachers are significantly more conservative. Others have found college teachers even more liberal (Trow 1975).

Our regressions show what is at least in part an important consequence of the liberal proclivities of academics. The political position of those who have been to college is affected by what was taught long after they leave college. There are eleven issues on which people adopt significantly more liberal positions the greater the number of years they attended college.[13]

However, there are four cases in which those who have been to college are significantly more conservative, and that is enough to make it unlikely that these latter results are just attributable to chance. This is hardly surprising. The greater one's education, the more likely one associates with others of higher income. Through imitation this should make those who have been to college more conservative even controlling for their own income. We have seen that prediction work by broad occupations. In chapter 5 we showed it works by ethnic groups. We are not able to predict whether the income associates or the college experience effect will dominate. However, two of the liberal positions produced by college do not meet resistance from high-income groups, who are also proabortion and neutral as far as increased expenditures on education are concerned.

Though our theory does not predict the sign of the year of college slope, it does yield more subtle predictions. Holding constant the general age effect, one expects years of college to have a greater liberal effect the younger the person. A college student starts out being indoctrinated by his teachers and his peers. He then starts associating with people with higher incomes, and he gradually moves toward the political position of that group. To test this hypothesis we create a cross-product variable: age times years of college: AGECOLYR. There are six cases where AGECOLYR is significant in the predicted direction and only one case where it is significant in the wrong direction: parks, hardly a burning campus issue.[14]

There is one more testable implication about the effect of college indoctrination on the political position of those with college experience. If indoctrination works, one would expect those with college to be most liberal on those issues on which college teachers are most liberal and least liberal about those issues on which those with higher income are least liberal. Indeed, this is the case. Since one expects the slope by issues to be sensitive to the variance by issue, we compare standardized regression coefficients—betas—by issue. We then regress the beta for years of college (COLβ) against the log income beta (INβ) and the college teaching beta (COTEβ). The results:[15]

$$COL\beta = .0087 + .367 \, IN\beta + .241 \, COTE\beta \qquad (1)$$
$$(3.58) \qquad (3.18)$$

With nineteen observations, these t values (in parenthesis) are significant at the 5 percent level.[16]

Possibly, all of the results on college teaching and college education could be explained by an alternative hypothesis: knowledge makes one liberal. Where does knowledge end and indoctrination begin? Are classes devoted to information about the benefits of government activity without a concern for costs indoctrinating or transmitting knowledge? Economists—the one group that focuses on cost-benefit analysis—are the most conservative group of social scientists (Lipset and Ladd 1971). While self-selection could explain some of this difference, the self-selection requires a preexisting difference in political views between economists and other social scientists. This strongly suggests that at least some of the college effect is attributable to indoctrination. In addition, the aged are more conservative. To the extent that this is attributable to the greater knowledge of the aged, this result is inconsistent with the knowledge explanation for the liberalism of college teachers. This evidence will hardly convince those who believe the contrary. Let the unconvinced present evidence in support of their position.

While teaching at lower than the college level also offers a platform for the espousal of political positions, it is much lower because of the constraints placed on these other teachers by lesson plans and more careful monitoring. They are significantly more liberal on three issues, but are significantly more conservative on two. So this provides little indication that noncollege teachers are more liberal.

Nevertheless, increases in years of below-college education make people significantly more liberal on five issues, and it makes them significantly more conservative on five issues. In the absence of an indoctrination effect, increases in years of below-college education would be positively associated with conservative positions because increases in education lead to greater associations with people with higher incomes.

Educational indoctrination together with income imitation should make older, less than college educated people more conservative, even controlling for the general effect of aging on political positions. This prediction is significantly confirmed in five cases, while there are two cases in which the sign of the age-years of noncollege education coefficient is significantly in the opposite direction. This evidence seems to us somewhat supportive of the below-college indoctrination hypothesis.

It is possible to get a liberal indoctrinating effect even when there is no net selection of liberals among noncollege teachers. There can be some tendency for those who teach social studies to be more liberal than other teachers, a tendency noted for college teachers. Furthermore, as implied by the material in chapter 7, there will be some tendency for liberal social studies teachers to do more preaching than conservative social studies teachers.

Stigler (1982) proposed a far different explanation for the liberal proclivities of educators—self-interest. Most of education is publicly financed. Hence, educators have a self-interest in a larger public sector.[17] Indeed, this argument has some merit when it comes to expenditures on education, and it is no surprise that educators advocate greater educational expenditures. However, educators do not have a self-interest in most of greater government expenditures elsewhere, and yet college teachers are in the forefront of liberal advocacy on these issues as well. The only way to rationalize this latter result in terms of self-interest is to argue that an expansion of government activity in other areas helps generate an expansion of government in education as well. But college teachers are opposed to greater expenditures on defense, as are nonteaching, nonarmy, nonpolice government employees. Furthermore, those educators with the greatest self-interest in more government expenditures, those below the college level, are not the most liberal educators. The percentage of public financing of education is far greater for noncollege education than for college education. Along the same lines, college teachers are far more liberal than nonteaching, nonarmy, nonpolice government employees, who are significantly liberal on only five issues, in contrast to the nine for college teachers. Furthermore, government employees who are in the army or the police are significantly conservative on four issues and liberal on none. Among college teachers, those in the sciences get far more government grants than nonscientists, and yet they are the least liberal college teachers (Lipset and Ladd 1971). The obvious explanation for this latter phenomenon is a goodness explanation. Science provides less of a platform for preaching goodness.[18]

Writing—and journalism in particular—is another occupation that could provide a platform for "do-gooders." Because of the relatively small sample size of journalists in the NORC study, our study can yield only limited information on this subject. Writers, including journalists, are significantly more liberal than others on four issues. They are not significantly more conservative on any issues.

Some lawyers might choose that occupation to help right the world's injustices. There are four cases where lawyers are significantly more liberal and no cases where they are more conservative.

These results could explain in part the consistently liberal stance of the American Bar Association in the 1990s. Consider the evidence given by Lexis under the rubric "American Bar Association: partisan," and by looking at the newsletter *ABAnetwork.* While the issues so documented are not a random sample of issues on which the American Bar Association has taken a stand, evidence so gathered should be unbiased with respect to the question of whether the ABA takes liberal or conservative positions. In the sample the relevant issues are identified by people with liberal, conservative, and moderate views. In our sample we find that the ABA advocates sixteen liberal positions and one conservative position that are not in the obvious self-interest of lawyers.[19] Eight of those positions are about criminal rights. But even excluding those positions, eight liberal positions out of nine is significant at the 5 percent level.

The liberal bias of the ABA on issues is so strong that it has been recognized by liberals and conservatives alike. (This unanimity of views is in marked contrast to views about ABA bias in rating judicial nominees.) Said the former president of the ABA, John Curtin, "If you say that support for a greater voice for women and minorities, support for legal services to the poor or support for the Civil Rights Act is liberal, then I guess we have to plead guilty" (Podgers 1992).

It would appear, in fact, that this bias is so large that it is hard to explain simply by the mild liberalism of lawyers revealed by our regression results. We believe that views expressed to the public in general as in ABA conventions will have a larger goodness component than will the usual voting behavior of participants. The latter will correspond more closely with the views of close associates whose friendship one values. As we have seen, a signal of goodness is a signal that one is more trustworthy to most people at the expense of being less trustworthy to one's close associates. In consequence, signaling that is directed more to people in general will tend to have a bigger goodness component. This is an example of what Kuran (1995) calls preference falsification.

Clergy is another occupation where sermonizing goodness is a determinant of occupational choice. But in this case the possible range of sermons is large. A clergyman can focus on piety and family values as well as social issues. In consequence, it is not clear, a priori, whether clergymen, in general, will be liberal or conservative. Our study yields only one significant coefficient out of nineteen.

Gender

A variable that is consistently significant issue after issue is gender. There are thirteen issues where males are significantly more conservative than females; two where they are significantly more liberal: crime and parks. It is easy to understand one of the latter results. Women are more likely to be victims rather than perpetrators of crime.

Why are women generally more liberal than men?[20] Conceivably, the underlying cause is women's lower wages. But, one would expect the imitation effect to be much less with a sex variable than with most others employed. In general, imitation magnifies any underlying regression if one associates dominantly with people like oneself. Compared to low- and high-income groups, women and men do a lot of associating with one another. Yet, the sex variable has more significant liberal coefficients than does income itself (thirteen compared to eleven).

The only explanation for this sex difference that we can see is not really part of our theory. Wilson (1993) claims that women are more compassionate than men. The compassion that is a useful tool of child rearing is transferred to other settings. *Compassion* is a word often used in defense of liberal positions, and it would seem to have particular relevance to the liberal position on crime and defense, as well as all the propoor positions.

Two Experiments

For two of the issues investigated we separate our observations into two categories: beneficiaries of government largesse and net losers from these government programs. For the question, "Should there be an increase in expenditures to improve large cities?" we divide the sample into residents of central cities in metropolitan areas versus everybody else. For the question, "Should there be an increase in expenditures to improve the condition of blacks?" We divide the sample into blacks versus everybody else. We expect advocates of increased expenditures to display more goodness if they are not the beneficiaries of those expenditures. Therefore, the goodness variables should play a bigger role for the sample of losers than for the sample of beneficiaries.

For both the residential and racial divisions we look at the variables that have been established empirically to have a goodness component—those discussed in the previous sections of this chapter under the categories of community involvement, religion, gender, and specific occupational choice. In both cases we confine our attention just to the subset of those variables that are significant at least at the 10 percent level in either subsample for the specific issue being investigated.[21] We then compare the coefficients of these variables by subsample to see whether the loser subsample has larger coefficients in the predicted direction than the winner subsample.

Table 8.2 records the results. For expenditures on cities there are six cases of greater goodness coefficients for losers compared to winners and two in the opposite direction. For expenditures on blacks there are twelve cases of greater coefficients for losers and three cases of greater coefficients for winners. Combining these experiments, the probability of getting these results by chance is .005. Goodness variables do, indeed, behave as we would predict.

Results by Issue

A healthy distrust of our data requires us to answer the question, "Do our results make sense?" One simple requirement is that we get more significant results with respect to the issues that people regarded as more important over the time period 1972–96. Table 8.3 shows that that requirement is, indeed, fulfilled. The fewest significant coefficients occur for the aid to large cities for large city residents and for blacks among blacks respectively. We saw in the last section why goodness plays only a minimal role in these cases. The next fewest significant coefficients occurred for the minor issue equations—expenditures for roads, parks, and mass transit. The smaller number of significant coefficients for these groups can be attributed in part to the smaller sample sizes associated with those issues. But even when we compare major and minor issues with comparable sample sizes, the minor issues yield fewer significant coefficients.

TABLE 8.2.   Relevant Coefficients for Donor versus Beneficiary Groups for Pro-city and Pro-black Issues[a]

Variable	Pro-city Donor	Pro-city Beneficiary	Pro-black Donor	Pro-black Beneficiary
Community				
AGESL	–3.72(E–3)	–1.55(E–3)	–1.42(E–2)	–3.79(E–4)
STATMIG			–6.83(E–3)[b]	–4.69(E–2)[b]
CONTMIG	3.65(E–2)	2.53(E–2)		
MIGSL	2.16(E–2)	9.65(E–3)		
MARRIED			–2.25(E–3)	4.02(E–2)
City Size				
LCCIT			8.32(E–2)	2.50(E–2)
RB			2.74(E–2)[b]	2.19(E–2)[c]
LSURB			–7.13(E–3)	7.97(E–2)
SCITY16			5.32(E–2)	5.79(E–2)
LCITY16			4.41(E–2)	4.38(E–2)
MCITY16			3.19(E–2)	5.00(E–2)[c]
SUBRB16			4.10(E–2)	–6.82(E–2)[b]
Faith				
JSLOPE	2.53(E–1)	2.08(E–1)	1.91(E–1)	–1.68(E–1)
CLERGYFU	–1.99(E–1)	1.66(E–1)[b]		
NOREL			9.54(E–2)	–2.71(E–2)[b]
ATTENDSL			7.37(E–3)[b]	–4.13(E–3)[c]
FUNDAT			6.00(E–3)	–1.41(E–3)[b]
"Goodness"				
LOWTEACH	5.98(E–2)	6.22(E–2)[c]		
COLTEACH	8.77(E–2)	4.78(E–2)	9.88(E–2)	3.59(E–2)
COLYRSLOPE	6.59(E–3)	1.57(E–2)[c]	2.83(E–2)	–1.67(E–3)[b]
WRITER			1.09(E–1)	–4.00(E–1)[b]
MALE	–7.16(E–2)	–3.15(E–2)	–6.03(E–2)	–3.06(E–3)

Note: The 16 with city abbreviations signifies residence at age 16. For definitions of other variables, see key to table 8.1.

[a]Regression coefficients for "goodness" related variables that are significant at the 10% level for at least one of the pairs that are being compared.

[b]The particular coefficient has the wrong sign from that predicted by the "goodness" effect itself. Sometimes that wrong sign is generated by the "self-interest" effect.

[c]Test fails because beneficiary coefficient is the larger.

Table 8.3. Number of Significant Coefficients with the Predicted Signs, by Issue and Category[a]

Issue	Self	Faith	Community	City	City Lag	Good	Ethnic	Reg	Reg Lag
PROENV	6	5(1)	3	4	4	7	9	6	1
PROWELF	10	1	1	5	1	7	5	3	0
PROPOOR	7	0	3	0	1	0	4	2	1
ANTIABORT	9	9	1	4	3	5(1)	2	7	3
ANTICRIME	7	1	0	2	3	3(1)	6	2	1
PROARMS	4	5	3	2	3	9	9	4	1
PROREPUBL	9	7	4	3	1	5	16	0	6
PROCONSERV	11	4	3	2	3	5	5	1	0
PRESR	8	8	1	3	0	5	7	1	0
PROHEAL	5	1	1	1	3	5	7	1	0
PROED	4	2	3	3	4	8	7	1	1
PROCITY(0)	4	3	2	3	4	4(1)	8	3	3
PROCITY(1)	1	0	1	1	0	2	4	2	0
PRORACE(0)	5	3(1)	1	2	4	4(1)	16	4	0
PRORACE(1)	1	0	0(1)	1	2	0	6	4	2
PROROAD	3(2)	1	1	4	2	2	7	2	0
PROPARK	4	1	1	1	4	2(3)	6	4	2
PROMASS	1	1	2(1)	5	3	2	6	6	0
PROSOC	7	2	2	1	1	2(1)	9	1	0

Note: For definitions of variables see key to table 8.1. Self-interest variables: BLACK, GOVR, ARMY, SELF, PROF, MGM, CLERK, SALES, SERVE, AGR, UNION, GOV, FYSLOPE, NCYRSLOPE, COLYRSLOPE. Faith variables: MAIN, PATT, CATT, JATT, FUNDAT, CLERGYFU, PRIEST, BLACCL, FYNCOME, ATTENDSL, JSLOPE, CSLOPE.

[a]Significant at the 5% level. Number of wrong signed significant coefficients in parentheses. We did not distinguish the self-interest variables by right or wrong sign when one could not clearly predict the sign either *a priori* or by the sign of the income variable.

CHAPTER 9

The Growth of Government

In the course of the past century government expenditures, including transfer payments, in developed democracies grew from at most a sixth to generally over two-fifths of national income. We believe the standard economic explanations for this growth are inadequate. That belief is shared by others such as Holsey and Borcherding (1997).

The standard explanation views public activity as income redistribution to the politically powerful. In this context the poor are regarded as politically powerful, in the sense that the rich do not have the votes to protect their dollars. Anything, then, that would increase the political power of the poor would increase the size of government's redistributive activity. Kristov, Lindert, and McClelland (1992) reason that some economic development frees lower-income classes to devote political effort for redistribution to themselves.

While this increased power of the poor could well be part of the story, we do not believe it is the whole story. We offer an alternative theory of the growth of government, one that leads to different testable implications than does the standard theory. Our theory passes those tests.

Our own explanation for the growth of government is simple. "Goodness" increases the role of government, and virtually all the variables that reduce goodness have declined over time, and those that increase goodness have increased over time. Community involvement has been on the decline, and on the decline in a way particularly conducive to the growth of political goodness. Increasing mobility reduces the cost of goodness, which is the cost of friendship lost by offending others who do not share this desire to be "good." Starting over, one can specialize in friends who also want to be good.

This process is important for college students, particularly those who live away from home, and there has been a huge increase in college education in the world. College students would tend to be "good" whether or not they were indoctrinated by their teachers. Chapter 8 showed college education making people more liberal on eleven issues and more conservative on six. However, these conservative positions have a quite different intertemporal effect than the liberal positions. The conservative positions occur because those with college education associate with high-income groups. This association is a function of one's education relative to others rather than one's level of education per se. In contrast, the liberalizing tendencies of a college education are a function of that level of education. Therefore, an increase in the level of education will increase votes for greater government activity.

The growth in urbanization and the increase in commuting time for the general population increase the growth of government. It is harder to be an active member of the community as it becomes denser in population. Community involvement is also reduced by a significant difference between one's work and residential location. Both reduce the costs of being politically "good."

Indirect Democracy

In the United States the growth in goodness has generated a sea change in the effect of assorted institutions on government expenditures. Historically, indirect democracy was considered a bulwark against mobocracy. Hamilton reasoned that if we "[g]ive all the power to the many they will oppress the few" (in Madison 1989) and the few should be protected by an upper house chosen by special electors to serve for life. The U.S. Constitution was constructed in part to reduce the redistributional role of government by appointing, rather than electing, the Senate and the Supreme Court. It was the populists—those in favor of the poor—that were the driving force in the movement to convert appointed offices to elected offices.

Part of the rationale behind this belief in the conservatism of appointed offices is still correct. Appointed officials are less constrained by voter preferences than elected officials (Tabarrok and Helland 1999), especially where their terms of office are longer (Elder 1987). But it was also assumed that the preferences of appointed officials would be more conservative than voter preferences. Officials tend to come from higher-income classes than voters in general. Class loyalty would, then, generate more conservative preferences for officials compared to voters. But, this careful statecraft on the part of conservatives and liberals alike did not reckon with the growth of goodness. Many of those working as appointed government officials will be "do-gooders." In the last chapter we found evidence that, in part, lawyers choose their occupation to be "good." We found similar evidence for of a subset of government officials: those not involved in teaching or the protective activities of defense, fire protection, and policing.[1]

The reduction in the cost of goodness over time increases the proportion of people choosing goodness occupations in order to signal goodness. In consequence, lawyers and public servants become more liberal relative to the general population.

The Founding Fathers and the later populists were right in believing that there were processes that made more direct democracy more liberal. One cannot predict a priori whether their processes or goodness will be more important at a moment in time. One can predict, however, that the goodness effect will become more important over time as its price goes down. That we observe goodness in the occupational choice of lawyers and the relevant government employees is evidence that the goodness effect may be sufficiently strong to dominate over the Founding Fathers' effects.[2]

The behavior of the Supreme Court over time is subject to changes generated by fluctuations in the party of the president when Supreme Court appointments are made and the political makeup of Congress.[3] The present, more conservative court compared to the more liberal court in the recent past can be so attributed. Over a longer time span that encompasses party-to-party fluctuations, however, there has been a decided increase in the liberalism of the Supreme Court. For example, one cannot envision the present court finding the income tax unconstitutional had there been no constitutional amendment to undo a previous Supreme Court decision. Currently, a judge is deemed a conservative if he advocates noninterference with legislative decisions. Before World War II a judge was called a liberal for the same position. The reason for the difference is not hard to find. In the period between the Civil War and World War II judges were declaring liberal legislation unconstitutional. Now, if legislation is declared unconstitutional, it is generally conservative legislation.

Some confirmation of these results comes from examining the behavior of lawyers over time relative to the population as a whole. There seems to be unanimous agreement that the current American Bar Association is a much more liberal institution than it used to be, though some would cavil at the exact language. For example, past president of the ABA D'Alemberte said, "We've clearly moved from a narrow definition of what is involved in justice issues, and to the extent that they are seen as liberal issues, then I suppose we're liberal, but not in a partisan sense" (Podgers 1992). The last clause probably refers to the ABA's neither endorsing candidates nor making campaign contributions. Liberal former judge and congressman Abner Mikva (1996) said, "Where earlier criticisms had come from the liberals, who complained that the ABA was always looking backward to the status quo ante as its position of the day, now the criticisms came from conservatives, who complained that the ABA kept pushing all these new ideas."

As a result of the increasing relative goodness of both the judiciary and other appointed government officials, one of the important bulwarks against the tendency of democratic governments to redistribute and augment its size has been severely weakened. This helps explain the growth of government. This prediction of the goodness hypothesis is of particular interest because it is not a prediction of the standard explanation for the growth of government. There is no reason that we know why the increasing political power of the poor should produce more liberal appointed government officials relative to elected government officials.

The Media

There have been other dramatic changes in the character of institutions that have resulted in an increased role of government. Consider the media. Before we can analyze what has happened to media bias over time, we first must examine the forces generating media bias at any point in time. Much has been written about political bias in the media. There have been three main approaches: (1) determining the political position of journalists; (2) examining the political bias in stories; and (3) discussing the properties of ownership.

Our own study of the positions of journalists is of the first type, and finds them to be significantly liberal on four issues and significantly conservative on none. But though our study has a large sample size, the number of journalists in our sample is small. The studies specializing in a comparison of the position of journalists and others are likely to produce more reliable results. On the whole they tend to show that relative to the population as a whole, journalists are strongly Democratic, proenvironment, proabortion, pro–affirmative action, pro–homosexual rights, and mildly liberal on nearly all other issues. None of these studies provide any rationale for their results.

The studies about ownership conclude that the size of the firms owning newspapers has grown over time. They also conclude that advertisers try, and sometimes succeed, in influencing stories that affect their sales. These studies, as exemplified by Lee and Solomon (1990), assert that these facts impart a probusiness bias to newspapers. Their evidence is that newspaper stories are less radical than their own interpretation of the truth.

The dominant motive for business firms is profit. Profit maximization encourages firms to give readers the kind of reporting they want. Given readers with diverse political views, that boils down to entertaining reporting that at least appears unbiased. But Demsetz and Lehn (1985) found that the corporate structure of newspapers suggests that there is a psychic income from owning and managing newspapers. One source of psychic income is just being important. But another source is the possible joys from influencing public opinion. For this latter joy goodness motives will conflict with class solidarity. This is similar to the lawyer case, but the average newspaper publisher is probably richer than the average lawyer, so that class solidarity has a bigger chance of winning out in the case of newspaper owners.

The bias in news coverage generated by advertising is unlikely to be significant on the big issues. Advertisers are interested dominantly in profits. To threaten to cut advertising from its optimal level is to threaten the advertiser's profits. She will do so only if a newspaper story also has a significant effect on the firm's profits. Those stories will be stories about the advertiser or the advertiser's industry. Such stories may only rarely have a significant effect on the big issues such as welfare expenditures or expenditures on health or the environment or defense. All of the examples we have seen of advertiser muscle have been about industry- or firm-specific stories. Occasionally, that might have some effect on a big issue, for example, if an advertiser tried to suppress a story on his particular polluting activities or to encourage favorable reporting on a particular defense system. But we would not expect an advertiser to suppress a story on pollution or against a defense initiative in general.

The literature has also addressed the content of news reporting. The conclusion is that there seems little blatant bias. Newspapers have an incentive to provide at least an unbiased appearance because now they usually have a politically diverse audience. For the same reason journalistic ethics now emphasize fairness in reporting. There can, however, be unconscious bias. For example, a journalist can give more attention to candidates the journalist likes. Havick (1997) found that for both newspapers and television considered separately there is a lot more attention given per candidate for Democratic female candidates than for Republican female candidates even controlling for such variables as incumbency. Or journalists can seek sources that correspond to their own point of view. Lichter, Rothman, and Lichter (1986) reported that journalists found more reliable sources that are liberal than conservative ones.[4] Linsky (1986) documents that self-designated liberals among federal legislative and executive officials were far more likely to initiate stories about themselves and their activities, feel comfortable with the media, and spend more than five hours a week with them than self-designated moderates and conservatives.

Journalistic values, themselves, can create biases. One can sell papers more easily by writing about a potential environmental disaster than by writing about the low probability of its occurring. Lichter, Rothman, and Lichter (1986) found that journalists were far more convinced of a nuclear power disaster than were scientists. Dunlap, Gallup, and Gallup (1993) show an interesting consequence of disaster reporting of the media and education. In twenty-three out of twenty-four developed and underdeveloped countries, surveys of individuals throughout the country evaluated the environmental quality of their locality as better than the environmental quality of their nation. (Turkey was the exception by a narrow amount.) Important components of a person's assessment of the environmental quality of the locality are direct observations and word-of-mouth generated by the direct observation of others. These components also put constraints on what the media and educators can say about local environmental quality. In contrast, a person depends almost exclusively upon educators and media for their ultimate source of information about nonlocal environmental quality. Pollution makes for more interesting stories than nonpollution. More importantly, newspaper stories are more likely to focus on the direct consequences of a policy rather than the indirect consequences. These indirect consequences include the deadweight loss of redistribution and the shifting of assorted costs and taxes to consumers. The latter information is more difficult to obtain and convey, and, hence more expensive.

The one place in a newspaper where owner interference is consistent with journalistic ethics is on the editorial page. Currently in the United States, the dominant editorial motif is determined by lack of political specialization in readers. Bosses make an effort to provide something for everybody, syndicated columnists with a diversity of political views. Few take offense from columnists, since we suspect that readers tend to read only those columnists with which they agree. The cost to owners of choosing a less-than-profit-maximizing mix of columnists will be less than the costs to them of interfering with the news department. Because news is in the hand of journalists and the editorial page is more in the hand of owners, we would expect the first to be more liberal than the latter in the sense that there should be a higher proportion of liberals among journalists than among editorial writers.[5] But any editorial bias is much less important in influencing readers than any news bias. Readers are aware of the former and adjust to the bias mainly by reading only the editorials with which they agree. Currently, it is not clear whether editorial writers are more liberal than the average reader. Our theory suggests that reporters are, and our evidence supports the contention that the sum of reporters and editorial writers are also more liberal.

It is generally believed that radio is more conservative than other media. The explanation may be the large number of radio stations in most markets. Radio stations can specialize in the political views of its audience. That such mirroring of the political views of its audience produces the most conservative media says a lot. It implies that the rest of the media must be more liberal than radio's audience. Unless radio audiences are markedly different politically from the audience for other media, that in turn implies that other media are more liberal than their audience.

The Media over Time

There has been a considerable change in the character of media bias over time. Virtually all of the changes have made the media more liberal now than in the past. These changes, then, have contributed to the growth of government.

First of all, the costs of a journalist's being "good" have fallen in part because the costs of anybody's being "good" have decreased.[6] But there is a special reason for an increase in journalistic goodness: the vast increase in the proportion of journalists with college degrees. The importance of the college experience in generating goodness is strongly supported by data and by theory.

Fundamental changes in the character of the media business have also contributed to an increase in the liberalism of newspapers (and the media in general, though at the moment we will focus simply on newspapers). Some of these changes are exactly the changes that leftists have complained about. There are fewer newspapers per city and newspaper firms have grown larger.

The first change has mixed effects. An increase in monopoly power allows owners to pursue more nonprofit objectives. This by itself would lead newspapers to become more conservative, supposing that class solidarity is more important to newspaper owners than goodness.

But this effect seems swamped by another consequence of fewer newspapers in a city: less specialization. In the past, with several newspapers in a city, newspapers could specialize in readership. One newspaper could cater to Democrats, another to Republicans. Significantly, party identification was often part of newspaper titles. Prior to the latter half of the twentieth century reporting could be blatantly biased because that is what their specialized readers wanted. The important feature of that world is that the bias was dominantly owner determined. He could dictate and easily monitor the newspaper's content. Monitoring problems could arise, since the owners could not read what was *not* in the newspaper. But the newspaper's political bias would dominantly express that of the owner. To the extent that the owner wished to sacrifice profits, that bias was dominantly conservative.

Now we have moved to a world where, with rare exceptions, there are too few major newspapers per city for newspapers to specialize in the politics of their readers. Readers probably react more unfavorably to reporting the greater the distance between their views and the views represented in a story. In consequence, newspapers can maximize readership by reporting that is somewhere in the middle of the views of their potential audience. On issues where that potential audience has quite mixed positions, the newspaper tries to appear unbiased. This helps explain the current code of journalistic ethics that tries to do exactly that.

The peculiar aspect of this code is that it is more binding on owners than it is on journalists. A violation of this code by owners is more easily discovered than a violation by reporters. Owner's bias usually requires a censoring of a story for political reasons or explicit personnel policies. Either would become generally known if it occurred often. The reputation of the newspaper would suffer considerably as a result. In contrast, journalistic ethics cannot control for unconscious bias. As discussed earlier, we expect this unconscious bias to be a liberal bias. Hence, there is even a stronger reason to believe any bias would become more liberal through time.

The facts of the changes in the newspaper industry come largely from Lichter, Rothman, and Lichter (1986). They report that in their interviews no reporters complained of current interference from their bosses on political grounds, but old-timers reported frequent past interference.

The current hands-off policy of bosses is fortified by an increase in the size of the firms owning newspapers. This increase in size has led to a reduction in the importance of firms controlled by owner-managers, with a consequent increase in emphasis on profit maximization. A single-owner firm was freer to choose to lose profits by political preaching. But stockholders who are not management are almost exclusively interested in profits. They would object to money-losing preaching by their newspaper.

This analysis would not be affected by television prior to the recent growth in the number of cable channels. Now, there are enough television channels that one—Fox News—can specialize in a more conservative audience. One would expect that prior to this growth in the number of channels, television was somewhat more liberal than newspapers because the average income of its audience is lower. Its advent and partial displacement of newspapers strengthens the trend toward a more liberal bias.

The increase in radio stations and television channels and the development of the Internet are the only changes in the media that could produce a decrease in its liberal bias on average and through time. That would hardly counterbalance until quite recently the many forces increasing the media's liberal bias and the growth of government.

College

College has been one of the primary sources of political goodness training. Its importance stems from two institutional arrangements. Academic freedom provides a platform for goodness preaching with few constraints. Many college students live away from home. They do not have to pay a big price for goodness in terms of alienating past friends and family by a "good" political position. Changes in such an important source of goodness are likely to play a crucial role in the growth of government.

We have noted before the general reduction in the cost of goodness. This should increase the proportion of college teachers choosing that profession in order to signal goodness. There has also been an increase in the number of people going to college. This has reduced the relative average income of the parents of college students. Just as in the lawyer case college teachers are faced with a conflict of class versus goodness, though in the past, the class was more the class of the teachers' parents. The lowering of the income barrier to college has reduced the class bias of college teachers. The cost of signaling goodness by college teachers has gone down. Moreover, there have been changes in the demographic composition of college teachers. There are now higher proportions of women, who are compassionate, and ethnic minorities, who identify with liberal positions. The census reports that the proportion of female teachers in colleges and universities rose from less than 22 percent in 1960 to over 42 percent in 1999. Similarly, the percentage that were black or Hispanic rose from 4.4 percent to 10.7 percent during the same period. Such changes should have increased the liberalism of the profession (U.S. Census 1960, 2000) .

In addition to these general trends, there have been changes within fields of study, not all of which have contributed to the growth of government. For instance, a major change producing more conservative political positions has occurred within economics. The field has become much more technical with the full flowering of mathematical economics and econometrics. One of the consequences of these changes is that there is less opportunity for preaching. The higher ratio of technical material to policy analysis requires teachers to devote most of their teaching to the former. Even the policy analysis has become more technical, with less and less time spent on issues of "social justice." As a result, economics has grown more conservative relative to other college disciplines. It does not appear, however, that economists have grown more conservative absolutely. Using the data of Alston, Kearl, and Vaughan (1992), we find that U.S. economists gave more liberal answers to six questions in 1990 compared to 1979, and more conservative answers to three questions. The more liberal answers were for questions regarding microeconomics, while two of the three more conservative answers had to do with macroeconomics. The consensus belief is that macroeconomic theorizing experienced much greater changes than microeconomic theorizing during this period. So one would expect the internal changes in the field to have a bigger effect on policy views about macroeconomics, and this may explain why on net they did not become more liberal.[7]

This trend in economics has been mirrored to a lesser degree in the other social sciences. Political science has been invaded by economists with a consequent reduction in preaching. Statistical analysis plays a bigger role in sociology than it used to do. Whatever the results of this development is in its own right, it would tend to reduce the emphasis on goodness for want of time.

But we believe that whatever has been happening in the social sciences has more than been made up by developments in the humanities. The increasing number of students and teachers seeking goodness had to go somewhere. The humanities have been transformed. The focus has shifted from aesthetics to studying the class, race, or gender basis for literature and the arts. The theme has been that this is an unjust world that requires an enormous dose of goodness to set aright. Contrary to what is happening in the social sciences, we see no intellectual basis for this transformation in the humanities. It appears to be completely goodness driven. Moreover, new fields have been established whose raison d'être is goodness preaching: black and women's studies for example.

One would predict from the above that the political position of college teachers in the humanities has become more liberal over time relative to college teachers in the social sciences. Unfortunately, we do not know of any data available that would test this proposition.

No doubt, there have been historical events that influence the liberalism of colleges. Many ascribe a unique importance to the Vietnam War. College students' goodness combined with college students' self-interest to radicalize the campus in the late sixties and early seventies. But our data suggest that college students' liberalism dissipates significantly over their lives. So it would be hard to explain current goodness by even a substantial proportion of the faculty being students during the 1960s. Besides, the Vietnam War cannot explain the shift in the focus of goodness to the humanities.

There were two other events that had an impact on college liberalism: the Great Depression and the demise of Communism. The Great Depression was ascribed at the time to a failure of capitalism. The first of these events certainly encouraged the development of antimarket sentiment among economists. The second had the opposite effect. But any reduction in the number of Marxists in economics has been more than compensated for by the increase in Marxists in the humanities, where there has never been a concern with a relationship of evidence to notions of goodness.

Some evidence for the overall shift of goodness in college campuses can be seen by the nature of curriculum requirements. D'Souza (1991) documents the changes that took place at Stanford, Temple, Mankato State, and San Diego State. Sykes (1990) does the same for Dartmouth. Kors and Silvergate (1998) document the assorted costs paid by faculty who took positions contrary to goodness at the Universities of New Orleans, New Hampshire, Alaska, Delaware, and elsewhere. Experiences were similar at Binghamton University, our campus. Prior to 1993 there were no course requirements with a political cast. In that year students in Arts and Sciences were henceforth required to take two diversity courses dealing with "ideas of race, ethnicity, culture, religion, gender, life styles, language and caste." This year all undergraduates are required to take a course in "pluralism" and "global interdependencies." While this is hardly a random sample of universities, we know of no university whose required courses have become less politically correct over time. On the whole, changes in colleges have contributed to the growth of government.

CHAPTER 10

Environmental Policy

What determines a person's political position on environmental issues? In chapter 6 we developed a theory of asymmetric "goodness" applicable to environmental issues as well as redistributive policy. A person is considered "good" if he supports environmental causes, but is not considered "good" if he opposes those causes. Group survival is the ultimate cause of that asymmetry. The long-term nature of the payoffs to environmental expenditures causes underinvestment in environmental amenities (from a group survival point of view) by a thoughtful democracy. In addition, the externalities of environmental amenities could produce goodness advocacy of more expenditures in an era without big government. With lags in determining good causes, environmental expenditures as a good cause could continue even with the externality corrections produced by big government.

In chapter 8 we found that those who had the greatest return from goodness were, indeed, those who supported environmental causes in addition to other causes with asymmetric goodness. In chapter 7 we saw that environmentalists engaged in more demonstrations than those opposed to environmental expenditures because the good demonstrate more than others. In this chapter we look for more evidence of asymmetric goodness for environmental issues. We also examine the policy consequences of that asymmetry in terms of positive economics.

The Phenomenon of Nonuse Value

There is strong evidence that some kinds of verbal behavior cannot be explained by the standard narrow self-interest model. Consider the literature on nonuse evaluation by environmental economics: where people are asked how much they are willing to pay (WTP) as their share of the costs to preserve some feature of the environment that they and their heirs will never use or see.[1] That literature is filled with controversy about whether such nonuse values are valid parts of the social

179

benefits of preserving environmental resources. But most agree that the answers cannot be explained by narrow self-interest. Those that believe in the importance of nonuse values often make their arguments in terms of altruism, or the inclusion of other entities' welfare in an individual's utility function.

The observed positive nonuse values to environmental amenities have an important property: asymmetry. There are both potential external benefits and costs when an individual successfully advocates for an amenity financed at public cost. The external benefits are others' use value of the amenity. The external costs are the costs or taxes that others incur because those who support a tax in favor of an amenity are supporting that tax for others as well as for themselves. If respondents to a questionnaire were simply using a cost-benefit assessment of the amenity and being altruistic, those external costs would be considered as well as the external benefits (Milgrom 1993). There is no evidence that users reduce their advocacy for the amenity in response to altruistic considerations toward nonusers. There is no reason a priori to expect this asymmetry in altruism.

Moreover, often the nonuse value assessed by nonusers is higher than the individual use value claimed by current and potential users. The required kind of altruism to fit such a picture gets extremely odd. To make nonuse value consistent with reasonable utility functions requires "planet love" or the inclusion of nonhuman welfare in the utility function. That goes beyond any altruism as normally defined to mean love for one's fellow humans rather than love for assorted environmental characteristics over and above the use of those amenities.[2] Those who believe that such an attitude exists would seem required to explain how it is consistent with evolutionary processes, since it would seemingly have nothing to do with either individual or group survival.

At first glance, it would appear at least conceivable that these estimated nonuse values could be produced by this expansive altruism that includes "planet love." However, the free-rider problem prevents either altruism or narrow self-interest from directly affect voting decisions. But the way nonuse values are estimated, a person is asked in effect, "If you were king, how much would you be WTP for an amenity if others also paid." His decision determines the hypothetical outcome. The free-rider problem appears to be avoided. Or has it?

The person knows that he is not king, that what he says in a survey will have even less impact on policy than his vote. Altruism cannot explain his survey answers as long as there is any private return from those answers.

There is, of course, a private return for claiming nonuse values: the desire to signal "goodness." By asserting a WTP more for the amenity than its use value to them or even its value to potential users, people show that they are in favor of "good" causes, with the returns from that assertion previously discussed. There would be no similar payoff to concern about the taxpayers who bear the burden of environmental expenditures. The asymmetry of goodness explains the asymmetry of behavior between users and nonusers. That goodness is not free, however. It is constrained by the return to imitating the political positions of friends and one's narrow self-interest.

What makes nonuse value so interesting is that there are so many ways in which it is inconsistent with utilitarianism—either narrow self-interest or altruism. Most of these ways have been summarized or developed by Diamond and Hausman (1993) and Diamond et al. (1993). We shall focus on some of their results. We add to their work in only two respects. The Diamond articles focused on nonuse value. But the behavior Diamond et al. found for nonuse value has far wider ramifications. They saw the connection to charity, but they did not explore the even more obvious connection to political behavior. What generates nonuse value generates a significant part of the demand for environmental legislation and for other "good" causes.

Second, Diamond et al. provided a convincing rejection of utilitarian explanations for nonuse values. But they did not provide a satisfactory alternative theory. Their alternative theory was "warm glow." But, again, all warm glow means without further specification is nonaltruism. Warm glow by itself does not predict that nonusers would get a warm glow by supporting environmental legislation, but that users would not get a warm glow opposing more expenditures for amenities. Warm glow must be more specific to yield such implications and other features of nonuse value. Our theory of asymmetric goodness does provide a sufficiently specified alternative to altruism to explain the behavior of nonuse value.

A consistent feature of nonuse values is that they increase little or not at all with increases in the size of the amenity in question. For example, as Diamond et al. showed, the amount people are WTP to save three specified wilderness areas is little more than the amount people are WTP to save any one of them. Different people are WTP roughly the same amount to protect two hundred thousand birds as two thousand birds. They also are WTP the same amount to prevent a decline in fishing in all Ontario lakes as to have the same effect on fishing in a subset of those lakes. These results are quite similar to the findings of Palfrey and Prisbrey (1997) discussed in chapter 2. In their experiments net contributions to a public good do not increase with the productivity of the public good.

The embedding problem is a related finding from WTP studies. The amount people are WTP for an amenity is greater if they are asked separately how much they are WTP for that amenity than if that amenity is part of a list of amenities about which they are asked.[3]

Neither of these results makes sense as long as utilitarianism governs WTP. Our theory of charity, however, explains both results. The total amount of charitable contributions—where charity is broadly defined to include all prosocial acts—is determined by an individual's signaling needs and his conscience, an internalized form of signaling. He is roughly indifferent between charities that are equally satisfactory for signaling. Under those circumstances he makes little effort to discriminate between charities. In particular, he generally adopts the low-cost strategy of giving only to charities that seek him out. If, for example, he confined his total charity to protecting wilderness areas, he would give the same amount to protecting three wilderness areas as to one. In any case, a solicitation for a wilderness area must reduce the amount he is willing to give to any other wilderness area.[4] From the point of view of charitable contributions, these two cases—greater size of the amenity to be protected and more causes from the same solicitor—are really the same case.

Desvousges et al. (1993) found another behavior inconsistent with WTP as a product of altruism. They found that when they asked about WTP in two different ways there was a consistent difference in the answers. They first asked people directly how much they were WTP to protect a given amount of waterfowl from oil spills (the open-ended form). They then asked others if they were WTP at least some amount for this protection, and then varied the amount (the dichotomous form). They found that these two procedures yielded very similar values of WTP at small and medium values of WTP. But there was a significantly greater percentage of people with high WTP values for the dichotomous form than for the open-ended form. This result is inconsistent with a utility-based WTP, which should produce the same WTP in both cases.

However, it is what we would expect if WTP is a signal. In chapter 3 we argued that a person's charitable contribution depends on that of associates. When others are choosing a reciprocity partner, they want the most trustworthy partner they can find. Hence, relative charitable contributions matter. In choosing their charitable contributions people often want to know what is a reasonable amount of charity to give, that is, what others are likely to contribute. By asking whether one's WTP is greater than some large amount, the interviewer indicates to the respondent that that large amount is not a totally unreasonable amount. "Why, otherwise, would the interviewer bother to ask the question?" one queries. In contrast, the open-ended procedure provides the respondent no guide to a reasonable price. In consequence, we should observe, as we do, higher percentages of the WTP for the larger amounts given the dichotomous procedure.

"Above All Do No Harm"

Diamond and Hausman (1993) discuss a well-known paradox facing those who believe in a utilitarian explanation of contingent valuation.

> Consider the issue of visibility at the Grand Canyon, recognizing how visibility varies throughout the year. Consider a costly project that can decrease pollution from power plants and thus improve visibility on some of those days. Next, consider a CV [contingency valuation] survey that asks respondents how much they are willing to pay (WTP) to fund this project to improve visibility. Instead of this survey, consider an alternative survey in which the respondents are told that the costly project has actually been approved (rather than just being proposed). Then tell the respondents that the government is considering saving money by canceling the project. In this alternative survey, the respondents are asked a *willingness-to-accept* (WTA) question: How much money would the respondents have to receive to be in favor of canceling the project (thereby accepting worse visibility)?
> The two question involve the same change in visibility. Thus one might reason that the two questions should receive the same answer, but, in fact, CV studies frequently find that WTA greatly exceeds WTP. (21)

Diamond and Hausman further show that this difference cannot reasonably be attributable to the most obvious explanation utilitarianism has to offer: the income effect. Goodness signaling, however, with a reasonable specification does provide an explanation.

Consider the design of mores to constrain individual self-interest in such a way as to maximize group survival. In some social interactions a person benefits others. In other interactions a person harms them. Many of the beneficial social interactions can be accomplished with the minimum intervention of social rules. Trade or the reciprocal exchange of favors does the job. Harmful interactions are another story. Reciprocity will not work very well. In the absence of enforced social rules there are several strategies that a person can use to avoid harm. He can bribe somebody not to harm him. Unfortunately, this encourages threats of harm. Alternatively, a person can protect himself by counterthreats. But there will be many circumstances where it pays to make the threat a reality. Miscalculations can also occur, generating violence and counterviolence.

There is also a big difference in the side effects of social rules encouraging beneficence compared to social rules discouraging malevolence. Enforced beneficence produces the well-known disincentive effects of income redistribution. That mores are enforced by ostracizing rather than by the powers of the state should not change the direction of that effect. Proscriptions against harmful behavior reduce the resources required for either defensive or offensive behavior and, hence, tend to increase group survival. Therefore, we expect a far greater emphasis in mores against harmful behavior than in favor of beneficent behavior.

In consequence, it is a much more serious offense to violate the mores against harmful acts than to violate those in favor of beneficence. A person needs a greater compensating return to malevolence than she requires for not being beneficent.

WTP measures the worth of *increasing* an environmental amenity. WTA measures the worth of avoiding a *decrease* in the amenity. In the first case one is beneficent, in the latter case one is malevolent. Or is one? This characterization of the WTP and the WTA require asymmetric goodness about the environment. It is "good" to spend more for the environment; it is not "good" to save others the taxes required to finance the amenity. The difference between WTA and WTP is further evidence for asymmetric goodness on environmental issues.

Opaluch and Grigalunas (1991) and Boyce et al. (1992) argue that ethics generates the difference between WTA and WTP. However, they do not try to rationalize this moral value; they just state its existence. Kuran (1998) and Sunstein (1997) maintain that the WTP context forces the individual to focus on preferences and practical trade-offs, but WTA leads him to focus on the values he uses to evaluate preferences and choices. Socialized to consider it a moral obligation to preserve the environment in this latter case, the individual places less weight on his own preferences.

Though the details of their argument differ from ours, its logic has the same essential feature—asymmetric goodness in the social rules. The value system must place more emphasis on preserving the environment and less on supporting tax savings to others as well as oneself.

This discrepancy between WTA and WTP has wider ramifications. It would be much harder to rescind any proenvironment legislation than to prevent its enactment. It is harder to reduce a benefit to the poor than to prevent that benefit in the first place. Any effort to reduce tax rates to the rich are regarded as "redistribution to the rich" in spite of the progressiveness of the tax-benefit structure that would still exist even after such a reduction.

Of course, there is inertia associated with much legislation that increases the cost of change. This inertia generated by the goodness effect would, however, be an added source. One would expect more of it to be in evidence for issues involving asymmetric goodness than for other issues.

There is an alternative hypothesis that possibly could explain the difference between WTP and WTA—what Thaler (1980) called the endowment effect and Kahneman and Tversky (1984) called loss aversion. In a wide variety of experimental settings people's utility for a state is increased when that state is ascribed to be the actual state. WTA is supposedly about how much one requires to give up an actual state, while WTP is about how much one is willing to pay to get the state, so this alternative hypothesis seems applicable to explaining the difference between the two.

Some of these results can be explained by nontrivial costs to switching consumption patterns. But some of the experiments focus on ownership rather than consumption. For example, people are reluctant to sell stock that they have inherited even though they are reluctant to buy the same stock with cash they have inherited and they are told that brokerage costs are trivial (Samuelson and Zeckhauser 1988).

To determine whether the endowment effect is really applicable to the difference in the WTA and WTP case it would be helpful to understand the reason for the endowment effect. Psychological decision costs might be the explanation. There can be a cost to our ego in making a wrong decision that is not fully compensated by ego returns from making a right decision. Look at the example cited in the last paragraph. In one case one decides whether to buy stock; in the other case one decides whether to sell the same stock. One can seemingly reduce the psychological decision costs in both cases by doing nothing. But this requires that the ego costs of the wrong decision to do nothing be less than those costs of the wrong decision to do something. That condition would be satisfied if sins of omission are regarded less seriously than sins of commission even when there are no external consequences of those sins.

If that were the explanation for the endowment effect, it does not appear applicable to the difference in WTA and WTP cited by Diamond. There the government is either considering approving the environmental project or canceling the project. Neither of these decision processes is initiated by the respondents. They are confronted by decision costs in any case.

Environmental Federalism: Theory

Oates and Schwab (1988) looked at the regulation of environmental externalities confined to a locality. Given several reasonable simplifying assumptions, local governments will adopt efficient environmental standards. There will be no "race to the bottom" of environmental standards. The fiscal benefits from attracting capital by lowering standards below the efficient level will be more than offset by higher wages and reduced amenity levels.

There are important reasons why under these circumstances regulation should be localized, and they are related to Oates's decentralization theorem (1972). They concern the greater ability of local regulation to respond to variation in local conditions as compared to federal regulation. The benefits from regulation and the preferences for these benefits are likely to vary by locality. The costs are also likely to vary. It would appear, then, that local regulation of "local externalities" is preferable to national regulation.

Nevertheless, there are many cases where regulation occurs for a wider area than the nature of the externalities justifies. This regulation also often imposes more stringent standards rather than less stringent standards than the local residents prefer. To our knowledge, nobody has asked why, much less provided an answer to the question. We review some pertinent evidence.

Such an answer is easy to generate given asymmetric goodness signaling for environmental issues. Suppose there are two geographic areas and all the benefits and costs of the "localized externality" are confined to one of these areas. If there were only localized regulation with voting by citizens of each separately, the residents of that area would choose a level of regulation consistent with those costs and benefits in addition to the goodness returns they get from voting for proenvironmental causes. If there were regulation of both areas voted upon by the citizens jointly, the nature of the voting in the affected area would not change. But those in the unaffected area would not be indifferent. They get a return to signaling goodness with none of the costs associated with putting the regulation into effect. They will opt for a higher level of regulation than would be chosen by those in the affected area, even though they receive none of the benefits from the regulation. In the unaffected area the demand for environmental regulation is unlimited, since there are no cost constraints. In consequence, the two areas together will vote for more regulation than the affected area would prefer.

Furthermore, there is an incentive for the unaffected area to advocate regulation on the basis of the joint areas in order to get more opportunity to signal goodness. This might be sufficient to overcome the opposition of the affected area to nonlocalized regulation, especially if the population of the unaffected area is large relative to the population of the affected area. It is by no means certain, however, that two-area regulation will occur. However, if it does, it will impose stricter standards than localized regulation for "localized externalities."

There is another process that can lead to the same set of conclusions. It also depends upon goodness asymmetries. The analysis of Oates and Schwab assumed that local voters were motivated either by narrow self-interest or altruism confined to local borders. Goodness signaling changes their conclusions. The locality would vote for more environmental regulation than the utilitarian interests of its voters would dictate. This excessive amount of regulation will not generate a fully compensating reduction in wages because the value of the increased amenity is less than its costs. There will be some combination of capital and labor flight in response to a loss in real income produced by the excessive regulation. It is possible that those in the locality would show by their votes that they prefer national regulation of all localities to reduce this capital and labor flight. If in this case national regulation occurs, it will involve a higher level of regulation than would have been imposed locally. The prospective flight of resources would constrain local regulation in a way that it would not constrain national regulation.

There is one important difference between this second process and the one previously discussed. The second depends upon areas being similar; the first depends upon areas being dissimilar. Suppose that one locality is the only one that would be affected by a regulation. Then, making the regulation national would not stem the flight of capital or labor. It would simply make that flight greater by increasing the level of regulation. There can be no local majority for nationalizing the regulation.

In contrast, if all areas were affected equally by the regulation, the first process would not work. There would be no areas where voters could costlessly signal their goodness because all areas would have to bear the costs of the regulation.

But whether the two areas were the same or different, we would get the same result—stricter regulation at the centralized level. Furthermore, that same result requires goodness asymmetry in both cases. When the areas are equally affected, more joint regulation is generated by the reduced flight of capital compared to localized regulation. This flight occurs only because the overregulation at even the one-area level implies that the reduction in wages does not fully compensate for the cost of regulation. When only one area is affected, the greater centralized regulation is produced by goodness advocates in the unaffected area.

The entire analysis of this section has made an assumption that is roughly appropriate for most environmental regulation. There is not an important redistributive component of the regulation. One does not need asymmetric goodness to explain the centralization of laws that are primarily redistributive in character.[5] Centralization can be produced to avoid the movement of harmed people and capital out of a locality and the movement of the beneficiaries into the locality. This has been the usual explanation for national as opposed to local taxes. But even in this case "asymmetric" goodness contributes to this centralization.

Some cases where redistribution is involved are better understood in terms of asymmetric goodness than in the flight of resources—cases where resource flight is probably not very important. Take the demands of developed countries for restrictions on child or prison labor in less-developed countries. The products of this kind of labor in less-developed countries are usually not close substitutes for the products of developed countries. Therefore, the developed countries probably have more to gain in terms of lower prices from child labor than they lose from a flight of capital. Part of developed countries' opposition to such labor can be attributed to the power of unions. But there are many nonunion opponents in developed countries to such labor in less-developed countries. Asymmetric goodness seems a required part of the explanation.

Similarly, the European Union requires of its member countries that they have no death penalty. Surely, there are no direct benefits or costs to people outside the country involved. Goodness must be operating, though in this case there could be an opposite morality signal.

Environmental Federalism: Evidence

Those in localities that are the primary beneficiaries of the benefits and bearers of the cost of regulation oppose the stricter environmental standards that others would impose. Kalt and Zupan (1984) analyze senatorial support on roll call votes for stricter standards associated with the Surface Mining Control and Reclamation Act (SMRCA) in 1977. One of their results: the higher the state's surface coal mining resources as a fraction of state income, the greater the opposition to stricter standards.

Durden, Shogren, and Silberman (1991) study votes in the House of Representatives in 1974 on support for controls of strip mining. They too find a significant negative effect of mining employment. Even without asymmetric goodness in their theoretical arsenal, neither set of authors was surprised by their results. Obviously, the cost of these stricter standards fall primarily on the localities in which surface mining is important. However, they fail to see that the benefits of these stricter standards also fall on these localities.

Nonlocals are benefited only to the extent that they visit the areas adjacent to the surface mines. For the purposes of either tourism or hiking, these surface-mining areas tend to have close substitutes. In consequence, nonlocals are unlikely to benefit much from the grooming of former coal mines. And nonlocals bear some of the cost of more expensive surface mining in the form of more expensive coal. We suspect these direct nonlocal costs are greater than the direct nonlocal benefits. Asymmetric goodness is required to explain these results.

Even without goodness it is conceivable that locals would favor national regulation. While a coal mine cannot move from area to area, the amount produced can shift. The reduced mobility of production with national regulation could make it desirable to the area affected. But that is not the case, as witness the local area's opposition to this regulation. Asymmetric goodness does operate.

Kahn and Matsusaka (1997) explain support for environmental initiatives in California during the period 1970–94. For a number of issues it is likely that all externalities were local. These included a 1982 vote on mandated bottle deposits, a 1990 vote on forest preservation and its counterinitiative, and a 1990 initiative to ban hunting of mountain lions. In nearly every case the coefficients of the variables meant to control for local residence were significantly negative in explaining support.

Mandated bottle deposits express a concern with unsightly trashing of the countryside. Those visions are almost exclusively for local eyes. In the case of the forest preservation initiative the apparently nonlocal effects are not very important. Nonlocal hikers like to hike in forests, but nearly all that hiking from the outside occurs on public land, and the forest preservation proposals are only relevant to private land. There is a worldwide concern with the preservation of forests to reduce CO_2 levels in the air, but California forests would only have a trivial impact on that goal. The only people that are likely to see a mountain lion are locals. They, too, are the ones who pay the price for any mountain lion attacks on livestock, and are most likely to enjoy hunting the lions. Of course, some nonlocals would also like to hunt mountain lions. But in this case this nonlocal interest is at variance with the nonlocal goodness interest, and clearly cannot explain nonlocal opposition to hunting mountain lions.

Asymmetric goodness is the obvious explanation for these attempts to centralize decisions about these "localized externalities." The evidence also indicates that the opposition to these initiatives was concentrated in the localities that would be affected by them—another prediction of asymmetric "goodness." When the authors controlled for the percentage of employment in construction, the percentage of employment in farming or forestry had a significant negative effect on support for environmental preservation ten of twelve times and never had a significant positive effect. Again, people from outside the localities were attempting to impose stricter standards than the locals desired.

Dineen and Twail (1997) document another case of the federal government's imposing minimum standards for a "localized externality." Contamination of water systems by "adjusted gross alpha emitters" that are carcinogens likely to have entirely local costs because only long-term prolonged exposure puts people at risk and because the cleansing capacity of streams is sufficient to assure no downstream contamination if even minimal locally approved standards are enforced. Yet the federal government set minimum standards. Two hundred and eighty water systems failed to meet this minimum standard. For those localities, obviously, the locality preferred to do less than what the federal government required.

Dineen and Twail show that in the case of the water systems that failed to meet the standards, enforcement imposed substantial net costs on the localities, even if the benefits of a cancer prevented is assumed to be a very high $10 million. Of course, this net cost is not sufficient to insure that the localities would fail to meet the standard. Goodness operates on the local level as well as on the national level. It is just that its effects will not be as great locally. Their results, however, show that there is asymmetrical goodness for this environmental issue. Somebody must be getting some benefit from requiring higher standards than can be justified on utilitarian grounds.

In another case Morris (1997) examines federal regulations on pesticide use in agriculture. He documents that the Environmental Protection Agency restricts eradication programs against fire ants and predators that would have little external costs beyond state borders.

There is another case of "localized externalities": animal trapping. The consequences of trapping animals such as beaver are focused almost exclusively in the localities in which they are being trapped. Where animals are not a tourist attraction, it is the locals who experience both the costs and benefits of having the animals around. A National Public Radio broadcast in 1999 indicated that the impetus for more stringent regulations on trapping comes from urban areas; the opposition comes from rural areas. These results make sense only in terms of asymmetric "goodness."

Here is yet another case. The federal government sets aside more wilderness area in Alaska than Alaskans' want, as evidenced by the behavior of their congressman and senators. For example, the Arctic National Wildlife Act was approved in 1979 by the House of Representatives by a vote of 360–65 and approved by the Senate in 1980 by 78–14 (*Congressional Quarterly* 1979, 1980). The entire Alaskan congressional delegation opposed this bill that set aside large wilderness areas in Alaska. Though there were only three Alaskan votes on this bill, that number is sufficient to reject the hypothesis that Alaskan votes were a random sample of all votes.[6] Alaska's isolation from the rest of the United States makes virtually all environmental regulation the regulation of "localized externalities." The number of tourists going to Alaska from the rest of the United States is trivial compared to the U.S. population, and most of them are confined to a narrow maritime strip that is not affected by most wilderness area regulation. One expects the rest of the United States to be affected more by the effect of this regulation on Alaskan exports than on tourist opportunities. And the export price effect would discourage others from supporting more wilderness areas in Alaska. Asymmetric goodness seems required to explain the imposition of wilderness areas on unwilling Alaskans.

Cost-Benefit Analysis

As the name suggests, cost-benefit analysis simply sums up the costs and benefits of any policy to determine whether the policy is a good idea or not. In the "pure" form these costs and benefits are determined by private assessments as manifested through market behavior. The "pure" form also uses market interest rates to discount costs and benefits, where the market interest rate is defined as the interest rate facing investment alternatives (but, as we saw earlier, care must be taken to appropriately estimate the time stream of the benefits and costs).

An impure form of this analysis also includes nonuse value or uses interest rates lower than market rates (never higher). Only the "pure" form is consistent with utilitarianism. As we previously saw, nonuse values have no utilitarian meaning. Furthermore, the use of lower than market rates imposes time preferences other than what people want.

Cost-benefit analysis is utilitarianism at work. Most, but not all, of the criticism of cost-benefit analysis from environmentalists is a criticism of utilitarianism.[7] They argue that environmental values are morally superior to consumer values and, hence, should not be evaluated simply by what consumers want. There is, of course, a difference between environmental values and consumer values in the sense that there are important externalities in the former. But the whole purpose of cost-benefit analysis in this context is to evaluate the externalities, not to ignore them. There has to be something else that gives environmental values their superiority.

Many of the critics go no further than this declaration of the virtues of environmental values, as if they were so obvious as to require no defense. Others provide assorted arguments, all of which are ultimately based on group survival or its natural misinterpretations that have been previously discussed. One of the arguments makes private consumption inferior to public consumption because of the selfish basis of the former (Sagoff 1988). This is a familiar refrain of "do-gooders" who ignore the virtues of selfishness when properly channeled.

Another argument focuses on the long-term benefits of environmental policy. Many environmental regulations have benefits over the generations with costs concentrated in the present. This argument would question the use of market interest rates as an appropriate discount factor for cost-benefit analysis. Indeed, as we have seen, maximizing group survival requires lower discount rates than man would freely choose.

Both of these arguments have one thing in common. They are nonu-tilitarian. They advocate people as a collective buying something that they do not want as individuals. The critics of cost-benefit analysis recognize what they are doing. They also argue that it should be these collective decisions rather than the private decisions of cost-benefit analysis that should count.

The critics are right in believing that these collective decisions will differ from cost-benefit decisions. They are also right in believing that the collective decisions will consistently favor greater environmental regulation than would be produced by cost-benefit analysis. The obvious explanation: it is "good" to be in favor of environmental expenditures by the government; it is "bad" to oppose them.

The beauty of the cost-benefit debate for our purposes is that it is another clear demonstration of a nonutilitarian component of environmentalism. It is also a demonstration of goodness asymmetry. Opponents of environmentalism are more than willing to use cost-benefit analysis in determining environmental policy. The 1994 Republican "Contract with America" proposed replacing public health mandates in with cost-benefit analysis and redoing all past regulation in light of cost-benefit analysis.

Such conclusions will hardly shock anybody except the economists who use a narrow self-interest model of political behavior, but that is, of course, the dominant view of economics. What is more interesting is our explanation for this phenomenon: asymmetric "goodness." It is hard to understand how else moral values would arise that have nothing to do with the costs or benefits to the individuals producing those values.

In discussing the critics of cost-benefit analysis we are not just dealing with radical extremists. This criticism, or the preferences that generated it, is in the mainstream, so much so that it has had a profound impact on public policy. Cost-benefit analysis, so obvious from a utilitarian perspective, has not won the day in determining environmental policy. "Congress has treated environmental risks as impermissible except when required by considerations of feasibility. Rather than cost-benefit analysis, Congress has adopted a proenvironmental baseline for the control of air and water pollution, carcinogens in the workplace, and hazardous waste sites, and has much less often called for cost-benefit analysis" (Farber 1999). For example, the Clean Air Act explicitly rejects considerations of cost in determining the appropriate level of air quality. And even where cost-benefit analysis is used, it has been distorted by President Clinton's executive order to allow "contingent valuation" (nonuse value) in its calculation. As we saw earlier, nonuse values have no utilitarian base. The underlying problem is that goodness has so permeated popular opinion that cost-benefit analysis is not a winning cause. That is why the critics of cost-benefit analysis would prefer political to economic judgments about environmental policy.

The Value of Life

The utilitarian rationale of most environmental regulation is to protect health when the market fails to do so either because of externalities or lack of information of market participants. What regulations are desirable? The cost-benefit answer to this question is to compare the cost of the health benefits from government regulation to the cost of the same health benefits implicit in market behavior. Practitioners tend to focus on one component of those health benefits—the value of life. Obviously, such a focus has its problems. Health affects the quality of life as well as life expectancy. However, that is true for market-determined health as well as government decisions. We do not know of any reason for a systematic difference between the ratio of death to ill-health generated by the two classes of decisions. Hence, we suspect that the order of magnitude of that ratio is the same for the two decisions, and that is all that is required for our purposes.

However, there is one systematic difference between the impact of the government regulations we examine and market behavior. The Clean Air Act, for example, primarily prevented deaths from respiratory cancers, which tend to occur late in life. Many of the market-determined behaviors examined are related to deaths from injuries that occurred throughout life, but mostly in adolescence and young adulthood. We do not propose that one substitute a standard of years-of-life saved for the number of lives saved. The emotional and financial investments in very young children are substantially less than in older ones. But those investments have mostly already been made for young adults. Saving their lives must, certainly, be more valuable than saving lives of the average lung cancer patient. So the benefits of saving a life by market behavior probably exceed the value of saving a life under the Clean Air Act, possibly by a substantial amount.

Keeping these reservations in mind, we will follow the standard practice of cost-benefit analysis. It says that a regulation is better than no regulation if it saves a life at lower costs than does the market. If, then, the cost-benefit approach were the single principle governing health-related environmental regulation, one would predict that absent mistakes, the value of life for all regulations would be lower than or equal to the market-generated value of life. Given mistakes in regulations, this proposition is not easy to test directly. However, it does imply that for any class of economic regulation, the expected value of life will be less than the expected market value of life.

For regulations under the Clean Air Act just the opposite occurred. Miller (1989) summarizes twenty-nine high-quality studies of the value of a life determined by market behavior. He finds in 1989 dollars that that the mean value is $2.25 million. Van Houtven and Cropper (1996) find that the mean value of a cancer prevented for fourteen banned uses under the Clean Air Act was $348 million, also in 1989 dollars.

The concepts used in the two studies are not quite the same. A cancer prevented is not a life saved. Not all cancers are fatal, and the air pollution that produces cancers reduces life expectancy in other ways, such as increasing emphysema. These differences work in opposite directions. We estimate that at most the number of cancers saved should be increased by 40 percent to be equivalent to the number of lives saved under the Clean Air Act.[8] That would mean that the average value of a life saved under the Clean Air Act would fall at the most to $249 million, still substantially greater than the market-determined mean value of life. This large difference is statistically significant at the 1 percent level.[9]

This result is hardly surprising. The Clean Air Act prohibits the EPA from using cost-benefit analysis. However, the EPA seems to have somewhat violated that prohibition. Van Houtven and Cropper show that in twenty uses considered under the Clean Air Act but not banned and where banning could save lives, the mean value of a life saved was $11,571 million, substantially more than the value of a life for banned uses. That result is also not surprising. Congressmen could signal their goodness by voting to prohibit cost-benefit analysis, but the enormous waste of resources involved in totally ignoring costs was too much even for the EPA.

There is an alternative explanation for the discrepancy between market-determined values of life and Clean Air Act values of life: lack of information by market participants. The relatively low standard deviation in market-determined values of life calculated in considerably different ways ($.58 million in Miller's twenty-nine studies) suggests that this is not a terribly serious problem. The values of life under the Clean Air Act are significantly greater than the largest market-determined value of life. Furthermore, even if there were a serious information problem, values of life saved by government regulations should be less than market-determined values of life if government regulations were determined simply by cost-benefit calculations. The regulations would focus on those areas where the information problem produced the greatest downward bias in market-determined values of life.

Goodness signaling has another implication. Since it is not about consequences, there is no reason for regulations in various areas to generate the same utilitarian consequences. In particular, the values of life should be quite different regulation to regulation. Of course, one would expect some of this just by the all-or-nothing character of government regulation. A use is either banned or not banned. It is sensible to ban higher value of life uses as well as lower values as long as both are less than the market value of life. But given the goodness motivation for banning, one would expect to see some uses that are not banned having lower values of life than uses that are banned. And such cases cannot be explained on utilitarian grounds. Some of this could be explained by mistakes. However, if one were to find a class of nonbanned uses that have a significantly smaller value of life than a class of banned uses, the mistake hypothesis can be ruled out.

Van Houtven and Cropper (1996) find that the 149 unbanned uses considered by the EPA under the Federal Insecticide, Fungicide, and Rodenticide Act had a mean value of life of $15.697 million, considerably less than the banned uses for the Clean Air Act—$348 million. The published data do not permit a statistical test given the nonnormality of the distributions. But the large difference in means is suggestive. The most obvious explanation for the difference in results under the two different acts is that the Insecticide Act did not prohibit the use of cost-benefit analysis.

Animal Rights

In previous chapters we developed one big consequence of this nonintellectual approach to "goodness." Often the goals of goodness will be understandably derived in an emotional sense from group survival, but they will not in fact contribute to that survival. From the point of view of group survival the culprit is misplaced compassion. In chapter 6 we saw this in the case for criminals, war victims, and women, among others. A similar compassion operates in the case of environmental policy: compassion toward animals. Such compassion is required to rationalize the Endangered Species Act, which cannot be defended either in terms of cost-benefit analysis or maximizing the survival of humans as a group. Indeed, the Endangered Species Act specifically rejects consideration of costs except under very special circumstances.

The best man-oriented defense is Wilson's (1992). Diversity in DNA is potentially useful to man for medicines and other products, and there is user value in biological diversity. Having said this, however, he reveals his nonutilitarianism: "We should judge every scrap of biodiversity as priceless."

The DNA that has been found useful thus far comes to our knowledge exclusively from plants, not even remotely related to the animals that have been protected under the aegis of this act. The animals that man has found useful as models to test medicines are also not protected. There is evidence that the DNA argument is not the driving force behind this act. Given recent developments in biology, DNA can be preserved and multiplied without keeping the plant or animal alive. There has been no great movement to eliminate the Endangered Species Act on that account. And even without DNA preservation there are such things as zoos and botanical gardens that permit DNA preservation but that do not require large tracts of land to be set aside for that purpose.

It is quite likely that there exist species worth preserving in terms of costs and benefits appropriately calculated. But it is also likely that there are species that are not worth preserving by the same standard. A blanket protection for all species seems singularly inappropriate from a utilitarian perspective.

Environmentalists do not rest their case for the Endangered Species Act on specious utilitarian grounds alone. For example, Farber (1999), a moderate on environmental issues, assesses the general attitude of the population as a whole, including environmentalists.

> Most people today recognize that nature has value, quite apart from any immediate utility. Even beyond aesthetic appeal, we can recognize that nature is the result of a process beyond human scale, whether in the form of divine intervention or the sheer extent of a billion years of evolution. Together with the more utilitarian reasons for preserving biodiversity to provide direct human benefits, these values deserve a place in our societal pantheon. (109–9)

There is at least a modicum of a utilitarian defense for the Endangered Species Act. It would be hard to explain other features of goodness behavior toward animals on pragmatic grounds. What utilitarian goal—when utilitarianism is confined to humans—would be achieved by the animal rights activists? Where is the gain that can compensate for the human losses that would be produced by restricting the use of animals for medical experiments?

Paraphrasing a frequent argument made by environmentalists and animal rights activists alike, "This universe consists of more than just humans. Other animals also have the right to live and thrive on this planet." Indeed, there is no reason to suspect that this is a man-centered universe. But that is not a good argument for why man should not be man centered. We are talking about decision making by and for man, not by and for seals. From a survival or a utilitarian perspective there is no more reason for man to be concerned with seals than seals for man except for man's joy in watching seals or wearing sealskin coats.

This widespread compassion toward animals is a recent phenomenon. It is associated with television's making us aware of details in their lives, anthropomorphizing them, and claiming man's "cruelty" in endangering their habitat. A substantial percentage of the nature programming on PBS and the Nature Channel has this as its theme. As discussed in the last chapter, when preferences were being developed, individual survival was enhanced by being compassionate toward friends because that compassion was reciprocated. Friends were people whose lives we know a lot about. That compassion has mistakenly been transferred to animals that we know something about. This process started with pets, who originally served utilitarian purposes, and has now extended to the animal kingdom in general.

The contents of this chapter have a special importance. We have developed a theory of asymmetric goodness based on group survival and its misinterpretations. There is a competitive theory, which supposes that big business dominates the political process (for example, Chomsky 1989) but does not dominate the development of mores. Then, we would also expect asymmetric "goodness." (If big business dominated both, then political outcomes and goodness would be the same.) It would be "good" to be opposed to big business. But this kind of goodness would have one big difference from the goodness we have discussed up to now. The new goodness would be based on what people *want* that big business is preventing them from getting. In consequence, it would be utilitarian in nature. But in this chapter we have seen that the goodness ethic is the antithesis of the utilitarian ethic. This provides additional support for our theory of the origins of asymmetric "goodness."

Summation

Much of this book focuses on the concept of asymmetric "goodness": for issues such as child care, health, the environment, and redistribution to the poor a person advocates greater government expenditures in part to signal that he is "good," that is, generally trustworthy. Asymmetric goodness has a wide range of implications.

1. There are activities that "loudly" proclaim a person's political views in such a way that strangers can be aware of such views. Such activities have a bigger payoff to goodness advocates because they are signaling generalized trustworthiness at the expense of trustworthiness toward immediate associates (chap. 7). We find more antimarket than promarket demonstrations, activists, and philanthropic expenditures.

2. Who will support greater government expenditures for these issues (chap. 8)? Our answer: those who have lower costs in doing so and those who choose occupations in part to display their "goodness." The main cost of signaling goodness is offending current friends. Those who have more friends and value them more, therefore, will buy less "goodness." In addition, those who get more of their information about political positions of others from friends than from media addressed to a wider audience will be less goodness prone. The reason is an outgrowth of number 1 above. Those who address a wider audience have more of an incentive to signal their generalized trustworthiness. Consistently, over a fairly large set of variables and issues, those with greater community involvement prefer less goodness-related government expenditures. The goodness occupations are those that provide opportunities to espouse goodness or to put it into practice. We find that members of such occupations support more goodness expenditures than do others.

3. Goodness government expenditures have grown over time because community involvement has declined (chap. 9). Our model has implications different from other "growth of government" theories. In particular, over a time period sufficiently long to avoid short-run party effects, judges and bureaucrats increasingly interpret legislative decisions on the side of goodness.

4. A person's advocacy of environmental expenditures is only loosely related to the consequences of those policies (chap. 10). We find that people's assignment of nonuse values to amenities cannot be explained simply by the value to users of those policies. Indeed, most environmentalists and much legislation reject the utilitarian procedure, cost-benefit analysis, for valuing these amenities. Nearly all the actions taken by the Environmental Protection Agency under the Clean Air Act result in far greater expenditures per life saved than the market's assessment of the value of life.

5. People who bear neither the cost nor the benefit of a government action are generally in favor of goodness-driven government expenditures (chap. 10). They can display their goodness at no cost. In consequence, we find numerous cases of a larger governmental unit enacting environmental regulations that have dominantly localized consequences. In all such cases, the larger unit demands stricter environmental standards than the local unit.

This breadth of consequences not only shows that asymmetric goodness is relevant to a significant number of issues, but permits a wide range of tests of the concept, tests that on the whole it passes.

Most of the rest of the book focuses on another proposition: that people give to charity and vote to enhance their reputation for trustworthiness and to assuage their conscience (chaps. 2 through 4). We believe these two reasons have many similar implications because we expect conscience to increase with increases in reputation variables. Both charity and voter participation increase with an increase in community involvement and with a decrease in the rate of time preferences.

There is a relationship between these latter hypotheses and asymmetric goodness. The same people who give to charity and vote adopt political positions. That a reputation for trustworthiness and conscience is important in determining charity and voting increases the probability that the same will be relevant for voting positions, and vice versa. That the dominant alternative hypothesis—altruism—doesn't work in the charity case strongly suggests that it will not work in determining political positions as well.[1]

Return to the charge in the book's beginning: to explain the more general behavior of which "political correctness" is a current manifestation. Political correctness is just another set of political positions used to signal "goodness." Such positions are an outgrowth of evolutionary pressure to maximize group survival consistent with individuals maximizing individual survival. But since this pressure operates so slowly, social rules can vary considerably from maximizing rules.

We find, however, that in spite of that variation there is a pattern to those rules, a pattern consistent with political correctness. Group survival demands social rules that redistribute income to the poor and give greater weight to the future than do market decisions. Compassion to other groups that is part of the political correctness creed is often inconsistent with group survival objectives, but appears to be explicable as an extension of compassion for the poor. The other groups so chosen do have certain common characteristics, but our theory does not predict the exact groups. Nor do we explain why these groups have been chosen now in the United States, but not earlier and not at all in certain other countries. Indeed, signaling theory predicts multiple equilibria until the slow process of group selection determines a winner. We do predict, however, that the social rules that help group survival are more likely to be observed than the social rules that do not. Political correctness is peculiar to the latter half of the twentieth century in some Western countries, but goodness signaling is a far more general phenomenon, a phenomenon that has a profound effect on public policy.

Government policy is in part determined by the political positions of its citizens. That those positions are in part determined by goodness signaling means that government policy will be similarly influenced. Hence, government does far more than correct for market failures as revealed by utilitarian analysis, since goodness signaling is essentially nonutilitarian in nature. That the importance of goodness signaling is growing over time means that even more of government policy will be so based in the future.

Appendix 1: Reciprocity

In reciprocity, one player i does the other player j a favor and, at best, receives a favor only later. To keep the analysis simple, a number of assumptions are required. We assume that there exists a large set of alternative players who are identical to i and j as far as the other can determine a priori. While most people do not know exactly when they will need a favor, we simplify by assuming that the period between granting a favor and receiving a favor in exchange is a fixed period t. We further assume that there are two groups in the population: one whose favor needs occur in even time periods and whose willingness to do a favor if it exists occurs in odd time periods. The other group has the reverse time characteristics. Furthermore, who belongs to each group is known by all the participants. We will also assume that there is a strict one-to-one correspondence between favors. Two favors are never granted for one favor. In consequence, the period between favors given to the same person in a given reciprocity relationship will be $2t$. For the ith individual the discount rate over period t is r_i, the cost of a favor is f_i, and the returns of receiving the favor in any one period are g_i. This gain includes any emotional returns from the relationship. We also assume that a person wants only one reciprocity relationship at a time. The game is started by j asking i to do him a favor; and there is risk neutrality.

There must be some costs imposed on the person asking the favor, or nobody would be the first to do a favor. Asking people to do favors takes time, so one is limited in the number of people one can ask before it is too late to have the favor done. As shown later, this time constraint implies that those who ask for a favor first have a lower probability of getting their favor done when they need it than those who do the favor first. To simplify, we will assume that one can only ask one person for a given favor before it is too late to have the favor done.

When j asks i to do him a favor, an unmatched i can refuse for two reasons: (1) reciprocation does not pay, (2) he does not want to be the first favor giver. In deciding about (1), i has two alternatives to reciprocity: *(a)* he can not play the favor game or *(b)* he can be a moocher—always asking for favors but never reciprocating.

We assume that conditions are constant over time. As a result, if one adopts a given strategy for the initial period, one will continue using that strategy thereafter. But for conditions to remain fixed, the probabilities of getting partners in various ways must be time invariant. (We will show shortly how these probabilities enter the decision process.) These probabilities will only be constant in a steady state. But a steady state requires people entering and leaving the market, and doing so at the same rate. Let k be defined as the probability of staying in the market in a single period. Though $k < 1$ is required for a steady state, such a k considerably complicates the analysis without adding much to the issues on which we focus. We present equations assuming $k = 1$. The corresponding equations for $k < 1$ are available from the authors by request.

The expected present value of the returns for mooching (M) is

$$M = Pgs, \tag{A.1}$$

where P = the probability of i getting his favor if he asks somebody that he has neither previously helped nor refused to help, which is the proportion of partnerless favor initiators in the whole population; and s is the expected stream of returns generated by mooching every other period. Remember, the unsuccessful moocher must wait two periods to ask again because he only can ask once per period and he needs a favor every other period.

$$s = 1 + 1/(1 + r)^2 + 1/(1 + r)^4 \ldots = (1 + r)^2 / [(1 + r)^2 - 1].$$

The expected present value of the return from i reciprocating a favor when i asks somebody else to do the favor first (R) is more complicated to construct. There are two components: (1) The expected present value of a partnership determined by interest rates and the probability of getting a partner, and (2) what happens if the partnership does not start times the probability of not getting a partner initially: i begins the process afresh at his next opportunity—a two-period delay. This gives him what he expected to get initially but with a lower present value given the two-period delay.

$$R = Pas + R(1 - P) / (1 + r)^2,$$
$$a = g - [f / (1 + r)]. \tag{A.2}$$

The expected present value of the returns from i doing the favor first (F) is even more involved.

$$F = P^*[-f(1 + r) + P_2 as] + (1 - P^*)Pas + ZF,$$
$$Z = [(1 - P^*)(1 - P) + P^*(1 - P_2)] / (1 + r)^2, \qquad (A.3)$$

where P^* = the probability of being asked to do a favor, which is the proportion of all players who are moochers, partnerless favor initiators, and partnerless reciprocators. P_2 is the probability of a person reciprocating i's favor, which is the proportion of people asking for favors who are reciprocators or favor initiators. P^* is the probability that at least one request from these groups will be received by a given favor initiator.

To keep the time periods comparable to the other decisions, the time the favor initiator would in turn receive a favor is period 0, and the time he initiates the favor is period -1. If in period -1 the would-be favor initiator is not asked to do a favor, he will in turn ask somebody else for a favor in period 0. The first two terms determining F are the present values at period 0 of these two ways of getting into a partnership. When he is not in such a relationship, he starts all over with the usual cost of the time delay. There are two reasons for starting all over: he doesn't succeed in starting a partnership the first time or his would-be partner is a moocher.

Individuals can vary by any of the determinants of F, R, and M. To simplify our analysis we will assume that a person deals only with a group all of whom have the same r, f, and, perhaps, some common characteristics that help determine g, but g varies within the group.

As long as i gains from receiving favors ($g_i > 0$), i will be a player. Given that i is a player, he will be a moocher if $M_i > R_i$ and $M_i > F_i$. He will be a favor initiator if $F_i > R_i$ and $F_i > M_i$. The text provides the rationale for $\partial(R - M) / \partial g$, $\partial(F - R) / \partial g > 0$ and note 1 the mathematics.[1] One can determine by the gs where $M = R(g_1)$ and $R = F(g_2)$ how to classify anybody for a given r and f.

The variables g_1 and g_2 are determined in part by the probabilities that have entered into equations (A.1)–(A.3), but g_1 and g_2 help determine those probabilities. To fully model the reciprocity process this latter effect must be analyzed. However, as we show later, probabilities are not so determined in the simple charity case, so we can examine charity now.

Appendix 2: Charity

We assume that people who are asked to give a favor know with certainty the amount of charity that others have contributed. Suppose others believe that if a person contributes charity of amount C, she will be a reciprocator forever, and if she contributes $C^* > C$, she will be a favor initiator forever, and if she gives less than C, she will be either a moocher or a nonplayer. Are there a C and a C^* that will make that belief self-fulfilling? Calculate the maximum C that any moocher will be willing to pay in charitable contributions to be confused with a reciprocator. The expected present value of the moocher's return if she gives less than C is 0, since nobody will do her a favor. If she gives C, her expected gross return (not including her charitable contribution) is given by equation (A.1), assuming initially that everybody remembers forever how much everybody has contributed to charity. So set C equal to that gross return at a gain level that just separates moochers from others. Now set C^* so that it is the smallest distinguishable value greater than C. Reciprocators do not gain from being confused with favor initiators, since they would refuse an initial request for a favor if it were made. However, favor initiators do gain from being identified as favor initiators because it pays for them to initiate such favors. Hence, the slightest contribution above C will serve to separate reciprocators from favor initiators.

To determine C from equation (A.1) it is necessary to determine the maximum g_i such that i will be a moocher. In the simple charity case—where only g_i varies—the g_i such that people are indifferent between mooching and reciprocating is the same as the g_i such that they are indifferent between mooching and favor initiating. Hence, $g_1 = g_2 = g_3$, where g_1 is the g_i such that $M_i = R_i$; g_2 is the g_i such that $R_i = F_i$; and g_3 is the g_i such that $M_i = F_i$.

$$g_1 = g_2 = g_3 = f(1 + r) / (1 - P). \tag{A.4}$$

The key to equation (A.4) is that P_2, the probability that a favor will be reciprocated, is now equal to 1 for both favor initiators and reciprocators, since favor initiators will confine their largesse to those who have contributed to charity, who are either favor initiators or reciprocators. Bygones are bygones. Reciprocators act as if they were favor initiators when it is their turn to reciprocate. With certainty that their favor will be reciprocated, favor initiators get the same return for a given g_i as do reciprocators at the time that reciprocators reciprocate. In consequence, the g_i that is required to induce either to assume their respective roles will be the same.

Then C is simply the expected returns to mooching at g_1: equation (A.1) calculated at g_1, or

$$C = Psg_1. \tag{A.5}$$

Now consider the relationship between the gains of players and charity. Some determinants of gains vary within a distribution of gains if these are characteristics that are unknown to the players. On the other hand, known characteristics are parameters determining a particular distribution. (We assume that people sample at random within a distribution or within a subset determined solely by signaling. This assumption is appropriate only if they sample within a distribution for which the only information about trustworthiness known to others is the signal.)

Within any given distribution of gains, those with greater gains are more likely to give to charity, since they are more likely to be favor initiators. But what happens to charity as the whole distribution of gains changes? The variables affecting C in equation (A.5) are not related to the distribution of gains, not even P, the probability of a favor request's being granted, even though without charity, P is a function of that distribution. In the charity case both the requests for favors and the responses come from the same group: favor initiators. There will be no pure reciprocators, and moochers are screened out. P, then, depends solely on the ratio of unmatched to total favor initiators. In the steady state that ratio will be determined solely by the probability that people stay in the market another period.

But though C is unrelated to the distribution of gains, the expected amount of charitable contributions per capita will be closely related. C is the amount given by those who give to charity. The expected per capita amount of charity is C times the proportion of the group that gives to charity—the proportion of the group who are favor initiators, that is, people with gains greater than g_1. This proportion should increase as the distribution of gains is shifted upward, since g_1 is invariant with respect to the distribution of gains.[1]

Suppose that instead of g varying by an amount unknown to the participants, r varies and g is a parameter. Then, at levels of g and f where R, M, and F are positive, $\partial F/\partial r < \partial R/\partial r < \partial M/\partial r < 0$. The favor initiator is distinguished from the reciprocator by a greater likelihood of both his giving the favor first and his getting a partner. The former is a present cost; the latter is a future return. The lower the interest rate, the more important the latter relative to the former. A reciprocator is distinguished from a moocher starting with the second period. He pays the present cost of returning a favor in anticipation of future returns from a partnership. The lower the interest rate, the more important the latter relative to the former.

Equation (A.4), determining the required g_1 and g_3, can be converted into an equation determining the required r_1 and r_3 by converting g_1 and g_3 into the parameter g. Since $g_1 = g_3$ if r is a parameter, $r_1 = r_3$ when g is a parameter. The analysis that predicted that expected charitable contributions will increase for high g distributions can be repeated to imply that expected charitable contributions will increase for low r distributions. Similarly, expected charitable contributions will increase for low f distributions.

While there are no problems using different variables as the unknown variable for which charity serves as a signal, the *simple* charity model does not work when the participants are unaware of more than one of the variables determining reciprocal behavior. Suppose that both f and g vary, are unknown to the participants, and are not perfectly correlated with each other. Then there is no C that would fully separate moochers from reciprocators. The required C to separate the two by their gs would be different for different levels of f. (From equations (A.5) and (A.4) C is directly proportional to g_1, which in turn is directly proportional to f.) If the value of f were unknown to the participants, then either of those Cs would only imperfectly screen. The lower C would not screen out some of the moochers who have a higher f. The higher C would screen out some of the reciprocators who have the a lower f. C would still screen in the sense that a higher proportion of reciprocators would give to charity than would moochers.

Appendix 3: Political Positions with "Goodness"

We extend the imitation model of chapter 5 by adding an additional term: the "goodness" return to political positions. To make the model more concrete, suppose the issue is some environmental problem like clean air and suppose some scale to measure the cleanliness of the air. An individual has to decide on how much clean air he advocates. We assume that the ith person adopts his preferred position on this scale (P_i) to maximize

$$U_i = c_i \sum w_{ij}[-(P_i - P_j)^2] - h_i(P_i - S_i)^2 + d_i(P_i - A), \qquad (A.6)$$

where $\sum w_{ij} = 1$. S_i is the degree of air quality that maximizes i's self-interest considering i's share of the costs. A is the average position of everybody other than i, which roughly is the position on air quality adopted by government. The idea is that one displays one's "goodness" by advocating higher air quality standards than proposed by others. Notice that the last term of equation (A.6) is not squared, as are the other terms. The reason for that difference is that for the first two terms one's utility is reduced by a position on air quality either more or less than the position that maximizes utility as far as that term is concerned. In contrast, for the goodness return, the higher air quality one advocates the better over the entire range of air quality.

Maximizing the U_i in equation (A.6),

$$(c_i + h_i)P_i = c_i \sum w_{ij} P_j + h_i S_i + .5d_i. \qquad (A.7)$$

Relative to h_i, c_i should be large because the association returns from voting are private returns, whereas the outcomes of elections, which are only remotely affected by i's vote, are public returns. However, the positions of others are not exogenous variables; they are determined by an equation similar to equation (A.7). All of the S_i and the d_i are exogenous, so in the reduced form only they will determine P.

Simplify by assuming just two homogeneous groups: group 1 of size n_1 and group 2 of size n_2. Then the reduced form solution for P_1, and an analogous solution for P_2, will be

$$P_1 = (H_1 H_2 S_1 + .5 H_2 D_1 + n_1 w_{21} S_1 + .5 n_1 w_{21} D_1 + H_2 S_2 n_2 w_{12}$$
$$+ .5 n_2 w_{12} D_2)/x$$
$$x = H_1 H_2 + H_1 n_1 w_{21} + H_2 n_2 w_{12} \tag{A.8}$$

Not surprisingly, the resulting political position is more proenvironment than the position determined in the absence of goodness.

Notes

Chapter 1

1. Some may object to calling the voting problem a free-rider problem. After all, one would be better off if nobody else voted. Where is the public good? But the presence of divergent interests does not prevent a free-rider problem. After all, the term itself originated in a conflict between strikers and strikebreakers. As long as there is a large subset of a group all of whom have the same interests, a free-rider problem exists. There is, indeed, a large subset of voters who would vote the same way. Within that subset any one voter would prefer that others do the voting if voting were motivated simply by the direct consequences of one's vote.

2. Only hunter-gatherers were ever in a state that could even be remotely characterized as long-run equilibrium. So the "invisible hand" should apply at least to the incipient markets developed then. Ofek (2001) provides evidence of widespread trade even in that stage of man's development.

Chapter 2

1. This term must have the standard mathematical properties: marginal utilities that are positive and diminishing.

2. This proposition holds only for those contributors to charity that give more than or the same amount of charity than the government does in their stead. The others have their charity reduced to zero. In the aggregate this does not necessarily yield perfect crowding out.

3. Suppose for simplicity n individuals with identical incomes (Y) and identical altruistic preferences with an income elasticity of demand for charity of 1, and each gives the same share of his income to some charity. (The assumption of an income elasticity for charity of 1 exaggerates the altruistic effect on charity. Clotfelter [1985] estimates that income elasticities are less than 1. As becomes clear below, the greater the income elasticity, the greater the altruistic effect. Furthermore, as can easily be shown, the assumption of identical potential donors exaggerates the expected amount of charity when that expectation is taken in terms of the amount of charity that would be given by the potential donor who would give most to charity if there were no other potential donors.) Let $x = aY$ be the amount of charity that each would give in the

absence of anybody else. Suppose one person gives that amount, x. The real income of all the other would-be donors goes up by that amount, just as their own utility needs to give to charity go down by that same amount. On the basis of that real income increase, if there were only one other contributor, he would give ax. Suppose one person decides that he will bite the bullet and take it upon himself to give that amount. That, then, has the same effect as above on other charitable givers. If one of these others, then, decides to give to charity, he will give at most a^2x. This process can stop any time. But it can only go on as long as there are potential donors. The greatest amount of charitable contributions that could be produced would be the sum of the resulting geometric series: $x(1 - a^{(n+1)}) / (1 - a)$. If $a = .03$, then total charity would only be less than 1.03 times the amount of charity that one person were willing to give if he were the only possible donor. With $a = .95$, total charity is at most twenty times this number.

Notice that this argument does not explicitly consider whether an altruist is concerned for the well-being of the other potential donors or not. If he is, one effect is to reduce the income effect on other donors from a person's contributions. The well-being of other potential donors is reduced somewhat by the reduction in the well-being of the donor who transferred his income to beneficiaries. On the other hand, a donor who takes the well-being of other potential donors into account is less likely to choose the zero charity option than donors with other preferences. This latter result, however, does not affect the range of possible solutions, just the probability of various solutions within that range.

4. By an analysis similar to that in the last note total charitable contributions to a specific charity would be $x / (1 - b)$ where $b = a(n - 1) / n$.

5. "Warm glow" reduces our estimates of the amount of altruistically derived charity in another way. As we saw above, the greater the hypothetical altruistically motivated charity-to-income ratio, the greater total charitable contributions will be relative to that ratio for an individual. We have used the actual charity-to-income ratio as our estimate of this hypothetical ratio. If, however, much of this actual ratio is motivated by warm glow, then the altruistically motivated charity-to-income ratio must be substantially less than the actual ratio.

6. In general, it is in the interest of firms to disclose even unfavorable characteristics of their products to consumers if the cost of such disclosure is negligible. If knowledge of total charitable contributions were important to potential donors and a charity did not include that information, potential donors would think the actual amount was the expected amount among charities that did not include their total contributions. Hence, any charity with less than this expected amount has an incentive to disclose. But this increases the expected value of total contributions among the charities that do not disclose. Now charities with donations less than that higher expected value disclose. This process goes on until all charities disclose except the one with the greatest contributions.

7. The foregoing suggests that one reason more charities do not disclose their total contributions is that their contributors form a group sufficiently diverse that they are not status competitors.

8. Economists have also tried to show how altruism can survive. But Eshel, Samuelson, and Shakel (1998) focus on a different definition of altruism than do we, and even that kind of altruism is only survivable within small groups. Bester and Guth (1998) show that altruism can triumph over short-sighted self-interest, but in terms of their model sensible self-interest triumphs over altruism.

9. What people believe has some relevance because it is their behavior that we are trying to predict. Often, people can use some rough rule of thumb, whose existence depends upon some fundamental principle of which they are unaware. But even, then, the rough rule will generally generate some unique implications.

10. There are two seemingly contradictory statements that are both correct in the right context: "Only the past matters." "Only the future matters." The first statement is right for intergenerational comparisons. It is the preferences of past generations that have survived that determine present preferences. The second statement is right for a given generation, the present context. The future consequences of the preferences of past generations determine whether the preference survives to present generations.

11. In this game the controller is assured of twelve dollars without the cooperation of the other player. With cooperation the total payoff is fourteen dollars with the decision of how it is to be shared to be mutually determined. Equal sharing (seven dollars a piece) requires the controller to give up at the margin a dollar for every dollar going to the other player.

12. Yezer, Goldfarb, and Poppen (1996) present evidence that contradicts this last finding of Frank, Gilovich, and Regan (1993) that the study of economics leads to more beliefs that both self and others will play the envelope games and the mistaken invoice game dishonestly. They also show that when the envelope game is actually played, the data are consistent with students in economics classes being more honest.

13. These proponents of altruism have a very difficult job testing for it on the individual level because on that level there are very few distinctive properties of warm glow. It is easy to show that much prosocial behavior cannot be explained by altruism, but almost impossible to show warm glow's not working. Batson (1991) shows a relationship between the closeness with which a person identifies with another and being helpful, and claims that this demonstrates the existence of altruism. But there may very well be a social rule that says help your own kind more. Following such a rule could create warm glow.

Chapter 3

1. This evidence is not tainted by their serious error in overestimating lying rates among nonvoters. All of the estimates of this paragraph are based

exclusively on National Election Studies data, so their previous mistake in comparing National Election Studies results with population voting rates is not relevant. However, one can object to their not including other relevant variables in their regression, in particular age, income, and the election year.

2. Even if income and occupation variables were included, one would expect these ethnic variables to have reputational consequences because group income is so low for both blacks and Hispanics. As detailed in chapter 5, because of imitation, group variables play a significant role in determining behavior.

3. All of the signaling cases we examine in this book involve many players. Under those circumstances knowing what determines others' reactions to what you do is irrelevant. Those reactions are determined by the behavior of a large set of fellow players. In consequence, a single player can influence those reactions only by a miniscule amount.

4. First, firms face lower discount rates than employees. They can both be better off if the compensation comes first, but is reduced to take into account the expected present value to the firm of such an arrangement. Second, there is the Becker and Stigler (1974) process: delayed compensation increases the incentive to good behavior.

5. The General Social Survey has two different possible measures: number of respondent's friends and number of organizations to which the respondent belongs. Both have problems as relevant measures of friendships. The main problems with the former is that respondents' definitions of friendships vary and many of those definitions will be quite different than the number of people likely to know about one's charitable contributions. To control somewhat for the latter problem we use a dummy variable: whether one has greater than or equal the median number of friends or not. Since a lot of charity is through organizations, the number of organizations probably comes closer to an appropriate measure. Glaeser et al. (Glaeser et al. 1999; Glaeser, Laibson, and Sacerdote 2000) find that number of organizations to which a person belongs is positively related to being married, home ownership, church attendance, and income. (They did not examine whether a person migrated or not, though they find a positive effect of "potential migration.") Restricting ourselves to many fewer variables because of its relatively small sample size, we find that our friendship variable increases with church attendance and income, but is not significantly related to marriage status. However, number of friends of the respondent excludes relatives and the friends of one's spouse that are not common to both husband and wife. This implies that including spouses and spouses' friends, number of friends would increase significantly with marriage. These latter are as likely to know about family charitable contributions as the respondent's own friends.

6. Glaeser et al. (1999) find an inverse-U relationship between age and number of organizations with a maximum at about age fifty, and there is no significant age effect on our friendship dummy.

7. We also experimented with using constants other than $10 ($1, $25, $100). The results of these experiments do not change any of our conclusions.

8. A number of studies have used the *National Study of Philanthropy* to estimate price elasticities using alternative approaches to measure price. The price variable used is $1 - t$, where t is the marginal tax rate. Dye (1978) observed that virtually all the price effect apart from the influence of income on marginal tax rates was produced by whether a person itemized his deductions or not. We use as our price variable this itemization dummy variable.

The true price of charity is 1 minus the marginal tax rate if one itemizes and 1 if one does not. First, consider just the itemization effect. The regression with an itemization dummy exaggerates the effect of itemization on charitable contributions because there is also a reciprocal effect with the same sign.

As a result of this simultaneity, the observed effect of itemization on charity is larger than the true effect. This has an impact on the estimates of the variables correlated with itemization. If itemization is included in the regression, the variables that are positively correlated with itemization have smaller regression coefficients than the true regression coefficients because itemization steals some of their thunder, and the reverse for variables that are negatively correlated with itemization. If itemization were not included, the regression coefficient of variables that are positively correlated with itemization would be overestimated because those regression coefficients capture some of the itemization effect. Reverse results hold for variables that are negatively correlated with itemization. As a result, the regression coefficients taking into account the true itemization effect would be somewhere between the regression coefficients observed with and without itemization included as an additional variable.

9. We classify occupations as having high slopes by observing the 1969 earnings of white males with twelve years or more of schooling and working fifty to fifty-two weeks. We calculate the difference in earnings between those of ages fifty-five to sixty-four and those of ages eighteen to twenty-four. We divide this difference by 38.5. We identify those with below-average slopes as low-slope occupations: operators, laborers, and farmers (U.S. Census 1973).

10. And this comparison understates the appropriate differences by approximately 1.5. Because our dependent variables are in the form $\log(y + \$10)$ and the means of our two dependent variables are different, the differences in $\partial \log y / \partial D$ (where D = an occupational dummy variable) are 1.5 larger than the differences in the coefficients at their respective means of $\log(y + \$10)$.

$$\partial \log y / \partial D = [(y + \$10) / y] \, \partial \log(y + \$10) / \partial D.$$

The values of $(y + \$10) / y$ at the geometric means of $y + \$10$ of charity and volunteer labor are 1.038 and 1.599, respectively.

11. The value of time explains the other "occupational" result peculiar to the volunteer labor regression. "Not in the Labor Force" has a significant positive coefficient for the volunteer labor regression.

12. Number of children has a positive effect on volunteer labor. This may be the manifestation of a small group effect. One is more likely to be a Boy Scout leader if that increases the probability that one's son will have a troop to join.

13. This process will not operate if charity is a perfect screen. In that model one is either trustworthy or not, and the contributions of others would be irrelevant. Our regression results show no group effect as far as race is concerned.

14. The Catholic and Jewish regression coefficients warrant closer examination. The Jewish coefficient is significant for nonchurch contributions but not for church contributions. The latter result, however, may be misleading. Instead of passing the plate at services, Jews pay dues, which may not be counted as charity. In consequence, their church contributions may be understated compared to the contributions of others. In contrast, the Catholic coefficients are significantly negative for church contributions and for volunteer labor but not for nonchurch contributions. One possible explanation for the Catholic charity shortfall is that there is only one Catholic Church while there are numerous Protestant denominations with fewer members per congregation. These denominations tend to have less within-group variation of most congregant characteristics than the one Catholic Church. In consequence, a Catholic is less concerned with his reputation among a random fellow congregant than is a Protestant. Size of congregation would have similar effects. Jewish minority status might make them a tighter-knit group than others. This might make them more concerned with what other fellow congregants think.

15. The relevant benefits for charity to the poor are the external benefits to the nonpoor—insurance against their own potential poverty, reduction in crime, etc. This follows because the poor are, at best, only peripherally members of the group from which most charity comes.

16. With this data set, price and other elasticity estimates at the means as well as the respective regression coefficients are quite sensitive to the choice of x in the dependent variable: log(Charity + x). If x is chosen as $100 rather than the $10 of Boskin and Feldstein (1978) and Clotfelter (1985), the resulting elasticity is .47 that of the latter. (This statement is based on our proxy for the tax price: the itemization dummy.) On the other hand, if $x = 1$, then the resulting elasticity estimate is raised by a factor of 1.41 from $x = 10$. Fortunately, for these data t values are not that sensitive to variation in x, so that tests of the null hypothesis do not depend so heavily on functional form.

Chapter 4

1. The payoff to the Advertising Council is the gain it receives in social approval from funding such advertisement. This gain can only be obtained if people in general believe voting to have positive externalities. The probusiness political positions of advertisers will in general be harmed by a greater voter turnout.

2. Since, as we saw earlier, there is more lying in the data set used by Bernstein, Chadha, and Montjoy (2001) than in our data set, there should be a closer relationship between the results using actual votes and the results using self-reported votes for our data set than his.

3. We use all variables found significant later in chapter 8 when we explain voter positions. Our technique is ordinary least squares. We also ran the same regression just including the statistically significant variables for this regression, and we also used PROBIT. There were no differences in our results worth noting.

4. The relationship between church attendance and number of friends is examined more closely in chapter 8.

5. Since the cross-product of Protestantism and attendance is also an included variable, the interpretation of the coefficient of the Fundamentalist cross-product is that there is no discernable difference in the attendance effect of mainline and Fundamentalist Protestants. This strongly suggests that among Christians the ATTEND effect is dominantly attributable to the greater community involvement of those who attend church rather than the messages received through attendance.

There is further evidence that whether one votes or not is not attributable to the assorted doctrines of the various churches. For those who do not attend church at all, religious affiliation among the major religions makes very little difference in the likelihood of voting. In fact, the only remotely significant coefficient for this group is for those without religion at all. That coefficient is positive at the 10 percent level ($t = 1.82$). Some of these current nonattendees must have attended church in the past. Whatever doctrine they acquired did not significantly affect their current voting behavior. This suggests that it is attendance, not doctrine, that makes the difference in whether one votes. Of course, those who attend a church the most are more likely to accept its doctrine than those who do not attend at all. However, that proposition does not invalidate the previous sentence as long as those who do not attend a church and claim identification with that church have absorbed some of the church doctrine.

6. Of course, reputational returns are an investment. There will be fewer years to reap a return on the investment of voting the older one is, and that should work in the opposite direction. However, there is little evidence that older people are less future oriented than younger people except in training decisions. Much besides time preferences operates to focus training on the young. They are more trainable, and the opportunity costs of their training are less. Furthermore, the decision of whether the young should be trained is heavily influenced by parents. Voting decisions are made by the individual involved. As life expectancy declines with age, people's knowledge that there is a future increases. Drugs and crime are typical disinvestments in the future that are associated with the young. As a result the life cycle hypothesis has problems. Bernheim (1987) finds that "neither single individuals or couples dissave significant fractions of their total resources after retirement."

7. Suppose that x decreases voting. Given our model, there are two reasons for a yearly decline in voting participation. (1) The same set of eligible voters has been exposed to a greater mean value of x. (2) Eligible voters die and are replaced by others with a far higher value of the mean of x. The first of these effects is also what produces the change in voting by cohorts a year apart, by exactly the same amount. Since the second effect is larger than the first effect, the yearly change in voting participation is an upward biased estimate of the cohort effect. That yearly decline in voting participation (–.00016) is far too small to explain the age effect, which at the means of the relevant variables is .00084.

8. In the case of migration there is an even more obvious than usual alternative hypothesis: the time cost of reregistering to vote. Migration is defined in the NORC data set to be living in a different town than where one lived when one was sixteen. In terms of that definition the number of registrations for the same number of votes would on average be greater for migrants than nonmigrants. (It should be noted that any delay in being able to register to vote is irrelevant because only eligible voters are included in the observations we use.) In consequence, migrants should vote less than nonmigrants. One way to control for this effect is to compare the voting behavior of interstate and intrastate migrants. They both have to reregister to continue to vote. However, we would expect intrastate migrants to have more associates and family that they continue to see than their interstate counterparts. Nelson (1959) showed that there were more relatives and friends at closer distances than at longer distances. Indeed, as we have seen, the interstate migrant slope is substantially more negative than the intrastate slope, but the difference is not statistically significant. The results, while hardly decisive, suggest that the migration effect is not entirely due to the higher time costs of registering.

9. The homework idea is not borne out, however, in the insignificant impact on voting of the number of children, a dummy variable for whether one has a child or not, or the cross-product of either of these variables with gender of the respondent. The only household composition variable that makes a difference other than marriage is the number of adults in the household. This significantly reduces the voting participation of the respondent: $b = -.018$ ($t = -3.81$). Conceivably, this is because the earned incomes of each adult is less, holding constant family income, and, hence, the reputational gains from voting are less for each. The cross-product of marriage and number of adults is insignificant.

10. The city-size variables were not included in the reported charity results because they were not significant.

11. Using the NES data, Greene and Nikolaev (1999) show that contrary to the aggregated results of Filer, Kenny and Morton (1993), higher income is monotonically positively related to voter participation.

12. The food at dinner parties is more expensive and the wines better as incomes increase. The jobs acquired through friendship networks are better too.

13. Given the substantial errors in that last estimate, the substantial value of t suggests that this is a reasonably important effect. In spite of the relatively large sample size of NORC, the number of people sampled in some congregations is quite small. See chapter 8.

14. This tends to contradict the findings in the literature. Using crude controls, Bennett and Orzechowski (1983), Jaarsma, van Winden, and Schram (1986), and Greene and Nikolaev (1999) find more voting by all public sector workers.

15. For a more thorough discussion of our tests of their version of the expressive voting hypothesis see Greene and Nelson 2002a.

16. We tested our hypothesis two different ways. First, we regressed the coefficient of the ethnic dummy in the voting regression against various ethnic characteristics, such as the average income of the ethnic group. The coefficient of the ethnic dummy tells us the influence of that ethnic group characteristics on voting, holding constant the individual characteristics that are included in the voting regression. Our procedure would show us, therefore, if ethnic income had an impact on voting, holding constant individual income and other characteristics.

Our second procedure was to add these various measures of ethnic characteristics to the voting regression. At the same time we eliminated the ethnic dummies from the regression, with the exception of the black dummy variable. This would also show us if, for example, the income of the ethnic group influenced voting, holding constant the income and other characteristics of the individual. The reason for eliminating the ethnic dummies from the regression was that we wanted to see how much of their effect was attributable to the ethnic characteristics that we used. We did not, however, eliminate race as a variable, since it was perfectly apparent that the race effect could not be simply explained by the ethnic characteristics we used.

Both procedures yield unbiased estimates of the ethnic effects. The tests of significance, however, make different assumptions about the residuals. The first test is the stronger of the two tests. For the first test we tried various combinations of independent variables out of the set: EBORN, the proportion of the ethnic group that was born in the United States; ERFYN, the average relative family income of the ethnic group; EEDUC, the average years of school of the ethnic group; EDPID, the average strength of party identification of the ethnic group; and AFF, whether the ethnic group received special affirmative action treatment or not.

While EBORN was the only significant variable, it was quite significant, with t values ranging from 5.6 to 3.1. So the effect of increased voting on the part of others in one's ethnic group translates to increased voting on one's own part as well.

Using the second procedure, EBORN is still significant ($t = 2.18$), EDPID is significant at the 10 percent level ($t = 1.83$), and DRAN (black [DRAN = 1]) is also significant ($t = 3.99$). Without the inclusion of DRAN the other variables would be even more significant.

17. In fact, DRAN has a positive coefficient in our voter participation regression (b = .1019 with a t value equal to 8.21). However, our regressions include a cross-product of black with Republicanism with a coefficient of −.0433 and a t value equal to 8.67. The net value of the black effect at the mean of Republicanism would be −.0106. But even that coefficient probably grossly understates the black coefficient when just blacks and whites are compared. In our regression blacks are compared to the control group: "Ethnicity Unspecified" because we explicitly introduce dummy variables for all the other ethnic groups. In addition, some blacks with the lowest expected voting participation are included in other ethnic groups, in particular "West Indian," and to a lesser degree, "Puerto Rican." Black Haitians, for example, may very well identify their ethnicity as "West Indian" when the alternative is "African." Both being a West Indian and being a Puerto Rican have a very significant negative impact on voter participation. Greene and Nikolaev (1999) provide a better idea of the black coefficient in the standard white comparison. They get a b = −.036 (t = −3.82) using the same data set and many of the variables we employ. All of the other variables in common in the two studies have similar coefficients except for those with cross-product terms in our regressions. When those coefficients are evaluated at the mean of the other term, they too are roughly similar. This is consistent with our explanation for the differences in the black coefficient between the two studies.

Chapter 5

1. The model and empirical work in this chapter are from Nelson 1994. The theoretical foundations are new.

2. Many of the propositions of economics depend upon trial-and-error behavior for their widespread applicability. Squirrels do not maximize in a conscious sense, but their nut gathering is consistent with the law of demand through trial and error over many generations. Signaling behavior in animals must be similarly rationalized. In all these trial-and-error cases, there, is always the danger, however, that the local maximum will be somewhat different from the global maximum.

3. How much lying is required if reputation affects verbal statements but not actual voting? Assume x percent of the population lies about their vote. Their stated votes are determined by reputational concerns, but they vote differently in response to their narrow self-interest. The rest tell the truth either because reputation and narrow self-interest coincide or because they choose not to lie in spite of a difference between the two. Since, by hypothesis, voting is not determined by reputation, this last group both speaks and votes in terms of narrow self-interest. Our later results show that reputation dominates narrow self-interest as far as verbal behavior is concerned. In consequence, we would expect fewer people whose speech is determined by narrow self-interest than by reputation when reputation and narrow self-interest conflict. That means that the last group should represent less than x percent of the popula-

tion. Therefore, the percentage of the population for which narrow self-interest and reputation coincide must be greater than $100 - 2x$. Later, we get estimates of x varying between 19 percent and 2 percent. If 19 percent lied about their votes, then for there to be no reputational impact on votes at least 62 percent of voters must have narrow self-interests that coincide with their reputational interests. In the 2 percent lying case, at least 96 percent of voters must be so characterized. Because we have no direct knowledge of this percentage, we do not know how to specify the "considerable lying" criterion of the text more precisely.

4. However, respondents know a great deal about the political preferences of interviewers when they can detect that the interviewers are black. The political preferences of blacks are much more homogeneous than the preferences of whites, at least in the choice between a Democratic and Republican candidate.

5. Additional evidence and a discussion of the reason for such a bias is contained in the next three chapters.

6. The only condition in which this result would not hold is if the marginal utility of friendship quality diminished so rapidly as one approached the ideal set of friends that a person was willing to sacrifice a little of this quality to adopt a political position closer to his narrow self-interest in spite of the free-rider problem associated with the latter. (The quadratic utility function used for simplicity in equation (1) is an example of a utility function with that property.) In that case people will have a miniscule incentive to choose a b_i greater by a small amount than the b_i that others believe he is using. All b_i other than infinity are inconsistent with a signaling equilibrium because no matter how large is b_i, signalers will always use a b_i larger by a small amount than the b_i receivers of the signal expect. However, all b_i are consistent with "almost" equilibrium, that is, a position where people have exceedingly small incentives to change behavior from what others expect. It is not clear that anybody adjusts his behavior to obtain such a small return. If the person does respond, one would expect the response to be quite slow. Under those circumstances, the starting belief about behavior may be a better predictor of behavior than the equilibrium belief. The most straightforward way to signal desired friendship is simple imitation. It is also the signaling solution that requires least information about the signaler's narrow self-interest. On those grounds imitation is likely to play a more important role in signaling friendship than narrow self-interest. For all practical purposes the conclusions of the text would not change even in this case.

7. The utility function of the previous note generates some weight to narrow self-interest even if "mistakes" did not occur.

8. The same can be said for altruism if it exists. The utility function of a person would incorporate an altruistic component, and people could very well believe that others are using such a utility function in part in determining how they vote. The evidence of chapter 2, however, makes us believe that altruism is both not very important and confined to friends and relatives. That latter feature of altruism yields predictions similar to those we examine in the

"Implications: Group Effects" section in this chapter but does not imply the effects we discuss in the subsequent "Implications: Lags" section.

9. For details see Nelson 1994.

10. This result follows from equation (4) if one simplifies the problem by assuming that a person confines his association just to members of his group and that the group has just two subgroups, with $S_1 = O$, $S_2 = x$ and with n_1 and n_2 members respectively. (These simplifications reduce the analysis to the two-group case for which equation (4) is appropriate.) Then both dP_1/dn_2 and dP_2/dn_2 are positive even though the determination of the sign of each from equation (4) is complicated by the constraint that the sum of the weights must equal 1. However, we expect the following reasonable responses of the components of this sum to n_2:

$$dn_1w_{12}/dn_2 = z > 0,$$
$$dn_1w_{12}/dn_2 = m < 0.$$

Then

$$dP_1/dn_2 = x(bz + n_1w_{12}z - n_1w_{12}m) / (b + n_2w_{12} + n_1w_{21})^2 > 0,$$
$$dP_2/dn_2 = x(n_1w_{21}z - n_2w_{12}m - mb) / (b + n_2w_{12} + n_1w_{21})^2 > 0.$$

11. Kuran (1998) also emphasized the importance of reputation in ethnic identification.

12. In constructing that measure one wants to hold constant those variable included in the Republicanism equation that have big association effects of their own. The average income of those groups would effect Republicanism through these variables rather than through ethnicity. If ethnic associations are within religious and locational groups, one would want to control for variation in locational and religious composition in calculating group average income. We assume the other variables in the Republicanism equation have a relatively small impact on associations, and, hence, with one exception we do not control for them in determining the ethnic income dummies. Since it is group permanent income that is relevant, we also control for age. The assumptions underlying this calculation of group dummies may not be fully satisfied. Fortunately, it makes little difference. When we calculate the regression coefficients for the group dummies not controlling for either location or age, the results reported in the text are not substantially changed.

13. We do not investigate whether these groups were on net actual beneficiaries of affirmative action.

14. This procedure assumes that the ethnic groups harmed by affirmative action are equally harmed. But one expects the losing low-income groups to be harmed by affirmative action more than the losing high-income groups because they are closer competitors for jobs, schools, and residences with low-income affirmative action beneficiaries. So on this account a low income for a losing low-income group would add to support for Republicans. This bias

clearly cannot explain the observed relationship between group income and Republicanism for the ethnic groups that are losers from affirmative action, but our imitation model can do so. Because of imitation, one's political position is determined by the average income in one's ethnic group as well as by one's own income.

The other alternative hypothesis is the permanent income hypothesis: that ethnic group income provides a measure of permanent individual income, even given current individual income. It must be remembered, however, that in our study many individual characteristics—education, age, employment, and so forth, are included in our Republicanism equation in addition to group income and individual income. In Friedman 1957, group income was shown to be an important predictor of permanent income when the only other characteristic considered was individual current income. The other characteristics in our equation are either themselves measures of permanent income or make present income a better measure of permanent income. This would produce a smaller role for ethnic group income as a measure of permanent income. In addition, for ethnic groups Friedman used only black/white distinctions for which one anticipates the largest permanent income differences. So the case for this alternative hypothesis, especially for the regression in which blacks are not included, is probably not strong. It is, of course, still possible that there are some permanent income effects of ethnic group income.

15. Given equation (8) and the assumed values in the text, then

$$P_{1t} = -.010753(.998999)^t + .04301(.969033)^t + .645161,$$
$$P_{2t} = -.010753(.998999)^t - .021505(.969033)^t + .677419.$$

With these equations one can determine the time required to get halfway to equilibrium.

16. In the latter case there is a substantial self-interest gain from technological efficiency. That is one reason we expect technological changes to be the source of other cultural changes rather than changes in the mores inducing technological changes. The imitation that goes on in the production process is dominantly imitation for information. When new information comes to light, there will be less cultural resistance to its implementation than in the case of mores.

17. Higgs (1971) provides estimates of wage rates for the foreign-born by country in 1909 for twenty-four countries of origin for our ethnic groups. In addition we estimate three others—Austria, Spain, and Switzerland—by taking the unweighted average of the wage rates for the countries bordering the country with the missing observation. We use this measure of past income, though wages for the foreign born in 1909 are not the same as wages for a whole ethnic group in 1909. We made extremely rough estimates of the latter. Our statistical results were virtually identical using the wages of the foreign born and our estimates of the wages of a whole ethnic group. Since the measurement errors for the latter are so large, we use the former as displayed in table 5.1.

18. Results of adding 1909 wages (*PI*) as an additional explanatory variable for *B* for the twenty-seven groups for which it is available are

$$B = -.094 + .087 \, I + .0076 \, PI.$$
$$(-1.92) \, (1.23) \qquad (1.83)$$

The regression results are moderately encouraging. R^2 is higher than the R^2 without *PI* when both are taken over the set of observations for which *PI* could be estimated (.2233 rather than .1094) and the former is significant at the 5 percent level for 27 groups. The *t* value of 1.83 is also significant at the 5 percent level. There is some evidence, then, that past income in the distant past of an individual's ethnic group has an impact on his political affiliations.

Chapter 6

1. Imitation plays no independent role. Without "goodness" it would just make people vote in terms of the narrow self-interest of others as well as themselves.

2. "Narrow self-interest" by definition excludes some self-interested returns. But in our definition what is excluded are the signaling returns from political positions, not the external benefits of the policies one advocates.

3. We are looking at the formulation of social rules rather than the decision to obey social rules. We saw in the last chapter that individual survival is irrelevant in determining the survival consequences of the formulation of social rules.

4. As discussed later, we expect a dollar redistributed from rich to poor to increase the population of the group practicing such redistribution if one does not also consider the deadweight loss associated with that redistribution.

5. For example, we expect the same kind of proenvironment emotionalism as we predicted for redistribution to the poor.

6. In the short run there is a trade-off between quality of descendants and numbers, but the quality is only relevant insofar as it increases the ultimate number of descendants.

7. It is important to note that we are considering social rules in long-run equilibrium. Some actual present social rules may have the opposite effect, for example, social rules that encourage conspicuous consumption. In hunter-gatherer societies conspicuous consumption would not be a serious problems because that consumption would add little to other's knowledge of individual income because that knowledge was already fairly complete.

8. There would still be a role for charitable expenditures aimed at any externality correction, since the deadweight loss of a voluntary contribution is less than the deadweight loss of the involuntary contribution produced by taxes.

9. The conclusion of Fischer and his modern followers does not follow, that within wide limits virtually any sexual selection criterion is self-

confirming. They are right as far as individual selection is concerned. But group selection is also operative. Groups in which females use mating criteria that lower group survival value will have lower survival probabilities than groups in which sexual selection enhances group survival. In this case female preference for big-game hunters increases group survival.

10. This is a version of Becker's (1976) rotten kid theorem. This version should be called the "somewhat rotten parent theorem." Given the social rules, the nonaltruistic child is forced to help the parents later, and the parents know that the child will be forced to help in order to induce the imperfectly altruistic parents to give better child care earlier.

11. Group survival is more about the survival of the rules of the society than about its genes if the issue is what rules will continue in the future.

12. To the extent that child care is confined to the immediate family, the homosexual makes no contributions to child care.

13. This behavior is counter to what would be expected with insurance motivations for compassion. More people have a chance to be one of the unknowns that is helped than the knowns.

Chapter 7

1. Voting does increase the probability that a person has strong political views (as shown in our empirical results developed in chapter 8), so, indirectly, one learns something about political positions from the fact that a person voted. Furthermore, conversations with voters are more likely to reveal the content of their vote than conversations with nonvoters. But of all political activities voting least reveals a person's political position. It is the signal that has least to do with that position.

2. There is one qualification. As shown in the chapter 8, voters have stronger political views than nonvoters. It is conceivable that a voter for party A feel so antagonistic toward members of party B that he would be a less rather than a more reliable reciprocity partner for the latter than a nonvoter of party A. Where party differences are relatively small, such as in the United States, this qualification does not seem to be very important.

3. An analogous question in the Survey is whether marijuana should be legalized. If marijuana were regarded favorably, the question would have involved whether marijuana consumption should be encouraged.

4. Lichter, Rothman, and Lichter (1986) found the ratio of the media elite that were Democrats compared to those who were Republican to be approximately the same as Levite's ratio of liberal to conservative "activists," viz., two to one. But, with the exception of personal liberty issues, party identification is the issue over which the press reveals itself to be most liberal. On all other issues surveys tend to show the media as only moderately liberal (for example, Lichter, Rothman, and Lichter 1986). Besides, most students of the press agree that in the contemporary United States, the press for the most part tries to be unbiased, that the liberal bias is unconscious. They tend to select facts that a

liberal would regard as important, but their professional integrity requires them to be as unbiased as they can.

The Levite results could be attributable solely to media bias, if all Democratic reporters call only liberals "activists" while all Republican reporters reserve that term just for conservatives. This result must hold even though many reporters are quite moderate about other issues and desire to be unbiased. That is an unlikely scenario, though media bias may well explain part of Levite's results. The only scenario that would give some credence to the Levite argument is if the *New York Times* were sufficiently liberal relative to all other newspapers to produce the strong media bias required in this case.

5. This counting is approximate. We count the inches devoted to these organizations and, then, determine the inch, number relationship.

6. The information for these changes in the activist tendencies of these foundations comes from *The Left Guide* (Wilcox 1996); *The Right Guide* (Wilcox 1997); Nielson 1972, 1996; and Lagemann 1989.

Chapter 8

An earlier version of this chapter appeared in Greene and Nelson 2002b.

1. The advantages of ordinary least squares is that it allows comparisons of coefficients across issues and permits one to determine the slope of variables at the means of other variables used in cross-products. There are, however, some statistical advantages of multinomial logistic regressions. We also ran multinomial logistic regressions with no substantial differences in results. Experience has shown that usually there are no big differences in results using these alternative techniques, especially where sample sizes are very large like ours.

Because we will be looking at many regressions, nineteen in all, there is a problem with tests of significance. It would be quite likely that a variable will be significant at the 5 percent level in at least one case just by chance. However, the likelihood that a variable will be significant at the 5 percent level in at least three cases is .067, and the likelihood of this occurrence in at least four cases is .014. In consequence, we will regard an independent variable as significant if it is significant in at least three or four regressions.

One problem faced in these regressions is what to do about the variables in a regression that are not significant but for which there is a prior case for inclusion. We proceeded with two alternative approaches. (1) Including all variables in any given regression that are significant in at least one of the regressions. (2) Including in any regression only significant variables (at the 10 percent level) in that regression. While the detailed results differ somewhat, the overall pattern of the results remains the same. Because of space limitations only the results for (1) are reported in the text.

2. Another objection can be raised to our regression procedures. In formal regression theory the dependent variable is a quantified variable. Yet some of our dependent variables appear to be qualitative variables such as seven degrees of Republicanism from strong Republican to strong Democrat or a

similarly defined conservative measure. Indeed, in doing the regressions for chapter 5 we responded to that objection by providing a quantification for the Republicanism variable—variation in the probability of voting for Republican presidential candidates as the various states of Republicanism varied.

Since performing those regressions, however, we have decided that such a procedure was unnecessary. That decision was governed partly by the results observed by our earlier efforts. Variation in the scale of the Republicanism variable just didn't make much difference in the overall character of our results. But there is a theoretical justification for our present procedures as well.

Though the Republicanism variable appears qualitative, it is unlikely to be a qualitative variable in the minds of a respondent to the survey. An individual must have some rough idea of what he means by strong Republican as opposed to moderate Republican, and that idea has a quantitative component, for example, the percentage of time he votes for Republican candidates. It is possible that he uses something other than a linear scale in translating that percentage to the various degrees of Republicanism. Say his various degrees of Republicanism are even splits in terms of the square of that percentage, but it is really the percentage itself that is determined by our assorted variables. Then we have used the squared relationship to approximate the true linear relationship. But we have no more reason to expect a linear relationship than any other. All we predict is a monotonic relationship in a given direction between Republicanism and our variables. A priori using any monotonic relationship as our approximation for the true relationship is as good as any other.

There is, however, a real drawback in using many of these variables. We expect a lot of noise in the data. Different respondents will be using different underlying variables as the basis for their different scaling of these variables, and their guesses will be exceedingly rough in any case. But we have no reason to suspect that the noise will be systematically related to our independent variables. In that case our estimates are all biased toward zero. That we are able to discover significant relationships in spite of the noise suggests that if we could accurately measure these variables, we would get even more significant results.

3. The one case of a mean less than 1 is an important case: "Should there be greater welfare expenditures?" But, treated as a separate case, answers about greater expenditures to aid the poor have a mean greater than 2. The one case of a mean greater than 2 when "goodness" dictates lower valued answers is our "iffiest" case for "goodness" identification—expenditures on roads.

4. This argument is not airtight, since we know very little about the determinants of the other relevant cost, the cost of lying.

5. It is not surprising that blacks want more expenditures to fight crime, though one could not predict this a priori. While they have a higher probability of being a victim of crime, they have a higher probability of being charged with crime.

6. Conceivably, however, age could also increase information about the consequences of policies as well as information about the political views of others.

7. There is a puzzle in the way the age variable behaves. How could older people support all of the important positions associated with Republicans (mass transportation is not that big a political issue) and still end up supporting Democrats? The answer, we believe, lies in a likely interpretation of the Social Security question in the NORC survey. NORC asks whether expenditures on Social Security should be increased, decreased, or remain the same. We scale the respective answers to this questions as 3, 1, and 2 respectively with "don't knows" being assigned a 2. Not only are older people more opposed to Social Security on this scale, but the aged are particularly opposed. (Age squared is significantly negative.) Nor do these results depend upon the inclusion of all the other variables we employ. The age variable has a significant negative simple correlation with support for Social Security. On its face these results are inconsistent with political wisdom about the aged and Social Security. But, it is not unreasonable for many people to interpret the Social Security question to mean whether *individual* benefits to Social Security should be increased more than they would increase automatically. Given that interpretation, there is a way to explain our results. Most of the Social Security debate has focused on the fiscal difficulties of maintaining Social Security benefits including the COLA, given an aging population. Even Social Security's staunchest advocates in this debate do not advocate an expansion of benefits. Those who are in favor of maintaining the benefits including the COLA would be counted in our survey as 2's. They would be counted as relative opponents of Social Security, since the mean value of the answers is 2.45. We expect the Social Security regression to be dominated by determinants of whether people are aware of this debate or not, rather than narrow self-interest or "goodness" variables. That expectation is confirmed by a closer look at that regression, which we postpone until we discuss all the variables entering into our regressions. Certainly, the aged would be likely to be among the most informed about this debate. If the aged support Social Security, the rest of the puzzle is easily explicable. Support for the Democrats among older Americans flows from the perception that Democrats are the party that supports Social Security.

8. For denominations with just a few members in the sample such a measure is subject to considerable sampling error. To reduce this sampling error we restricted our measure to denominations with thirty or more members in the sample.

9. There are several cross-product terms in our regressions in which one of the terms is ATTEND.

10. The standard way to compare coefficients for independent variables with different standard errors (σ_b's) is to compare their β's ($\beta = b\sigma_x/\sigma_y$, where b = the regression coefficient of the x independent variable on the y dependent variable).

11. Again, even in regressions in which these characteristics are included, the group effects of the characteristics still persist in impacting the coefficients of other variables.

12. For ease of exposition we do not always make the existence of these control variables explicit.

13. Evaluated at the mean of age, the other component of the one cross-product term involving years of college.

14. There is also one issue for which both income and college teaching have the same sign: abortion. On that basis there is no clear prediction about the sign of AGECOLYR. In the abortion case older former college students are significantly more conservative.

15. There is, however, a possible problem of simultaneity in using a least-squares regression procedure. Fortunately, the respective simple correlation coefficients are all significant at the 5 percent level, so whatever the causal process, there does seem to be a relationship by issue between the effect of years of college and the effect of college teaching and the effect of income.

16. One may question the approach of this section to indoctrination. We have focused on the regression coefficients by issues of college and noncollege teachers, holding constant a considerable number of variables. This procedure is appropriate in determining whether do-gooderism explains any part of the political position of these occupations. One would assuredly want to control for the other determinants of political position. However, the issue is somewhat different if one is concerned with the effect of teachers on their students. What difference does it make if a college teacher is made more liberal by his "goodness," if, on net, he is conservative because he is in a higher income group? Whether he makes students more liberal or more conservative would seem to depend solely on whether he is liberal or conservative on net relative to the population as a whole. The appropriate measures of that characteristic would be the simple correlation by issue of measures of his political position and job status.

There is, however, a serious problem with this argument. It does make a difference why a college teacher is a liberal. Those who seek to be college teachers in part because it offers a platform for their political views are more likely to use their teaching as a platform. For one thing they are more likely to teach subjects where political views are relevant. Still and all, nonactivist conservative professors may have some impact in influencing the political position of their students. Both the simple correlations and the regression coefficients would appear relevant in predicting the influence of teachers. Fortunately, the simple correlations yield results similar to the regression coefficients. In terms of the former, college teachers are significantly more liberal on nine issues. There were also nine significantly liberal regression coefficients for college teachers.

17. Not even Stigler is able to maintain a consistent self-interest explanation for the assorted relationships we explore in this section. He explains the greater conservatism of economics compared to other social sciences by the intellectual content of economics (Stigler 1965). Of course, this was a somewhat earlier Stigler.

18. There are some exceptions. Ecologists are often big on environmental-

ism. But on the whole scientists are not involved in public policy questions as scientists.

19. Senator Hatch (Hengstler 1996) lists ten non-self-interest issues on which the ABA has taken a liberal stand: abortion, affirmative action, welfare reform, flag desecration amendment, religious liberty amendment, federal rules of evidence, exclusionary rule reform, habeas corpus reform, prison conditions litigation, mandatory minimum sentences, and expedited deportation of criminal aliens. In addition, from the ABAnetwork (2000), there are three other liberal issues on which the ABA concentrated its lobbying: treatment of immigrants, gun control, Legal Service Corporation funding, and there is one narrowly defined conservative issue: liability reform for the Superfund. The ABA has also taken a position against the death penalty and in favor of universal health insurance.

20. Recently, Lott and Kenny (1999) document the role of women's suffrage in expanding the size of the public sector.

21. We also just used coefficients that were independent of one another. There are two kinds of dependence among our coefficients: (1) the dependence between coefficients and some weighted sum of those coefficients; (2) the dependence between dummy variables that are constructed with the same excluded variable. In the first case, we use the simple sum rather than the individual coefficients. The second case occurs when we deal in the race issue with city-size categories and lagged city-size groupings with rural residence and rural residence at age sixteen, the respective excluded variables. The observed effect of any city-size category is the difference between its effect and the effect of rural residence. Hence, the coefficients of any two city-size categories are not independent of each other, since they both include the rural residence effect. In the case of city-size categories, three yielded greater coefficients for losers and one yielded a greater coefficient for winners. We count this as one case for each side. For lagged city size there was one case of a greater coefficient in the right direction for losers, and two cases of greater coefficients for winners. We count this as one case for each side.

Chapter 9

1. Of course, these latter results can be explained by the alternative hypothesis that such employees are simply operating in terms of group self-interest and that promotions are easier to get the more rapidly government expands. There is evidence that this alternative hypothesis is not sufficient to explain the behavior of this category of government employees. These employees are significantly more liberal on two specific issues. They are for greater expenditures to help blacks, and they are against greater defense expenditures. They are also more Democratic and vote more for Democratic presidential candidates. There is no obvious bureaucratic reason for these government employees to oppose greater defense expenditures. The bureaucratic hypothe-

sis has the same implications for the liberalizing tendencies of indirect democracy as the "goodness" hypothesis, but it has different implications for the growth of government. The growth of goodness would not increase the bureaucratic motivations for government expenditures. One way of distinguishing between these two hypotheses is to examine the behavior of private charity workers, who, if anything, have a self-interested motivation in less government expenditures. We lack the data but would hypothesize that their goodness would dominate.

2. The goodness effect that we observed for lawyers in the last chapter was not very big. But it could have big effects. A lawyer that chooses lawyering because he is a social activist will be expected to have a greater effect on legal philosophy than a lawyer who makes his occupational choice to make a bundle. The former will more likely be involved in those activities influencing legal philosophy than others. He will certainly be more likely to be a professor of law, and probably will be more likely to be a judge. Both require a financial sacrifice that "do-gooders" are more willing to make.

3. Toma (1991) provides evidence that the ideology of Congress has influenced both economic and noneconomic findings of the justices and that Congress used its budget powers to accomplish this.

4. In chapter 7, "Activism," we provide an alternative explanation for this result, though we believe that Lichter, Rothman, and Lichter's (1986) explanation is also part of the story. That alternative explanation is that it is perfectly natural to believe that a source with which one agrees is more reliable than a source with which one disagrees.

5. One would expect the intensity of views represented by editorial columnists to be stronger than the intensity of views of journalists. If both were on the average liberal, by some measure editorial writers could be more liberal even though by numbers they were less liberal.

6. That observation holds for owners of media sources as well.

7. There is, however, somewhat contradictory evidence, also from Alston, Kearl, and Vaughan 1992. On the whole, the later an economist received his Ph.D., the more conservative he is, though the relationship is not monotonic. Those economists who received their Ph.D. before 1961 are clearly the most liberal, but the recipients of Ph.D.'s between 1971 and 1980 are the most conservative, followed by recipients between 1961 and 1970, and, then, recipients between 1981 and 1990.

Chapter 10

1. The equivalent voting format is at what per family costs would they be indifferent between voting for preserving an amenity plus its costs or against it.

2. Conceivably, the large nonuse values are attributable to an inordinate weight placed on the well-being of future generations. But our empirical work

in chapter 8 found that those who might be expected to give greater weight to future generations—married people and those with many children—are more opposed to environmental expenditures than are others.

3. Not surprisingly, the large nonuse value industry has not taken these criticisms lying down. Hanemann (1994), for example, claims that the embedding problem is consistent with simple utility maximization. One should place a higher nonuse value on water quality for a given lake when it is listed by itself than when it is last on a list with other lakes because the water quality of these other lakes is a substitute for the water quality of the given lake. But Hanemann fails to see the obvious. Listing the given lake by itself does not change the reality from listing many lakes. In either case there are the same number of lakes. The only way the Hanemann argument would hold is if people believe that only listed lakes are options for water quality improvement. But that cannot be the sole basis for the embedding effect. Diamond, Hausman, Lenard, and Denning (1993) in their study of wilderness areas found no substitution effects. One could also test the substitution effect directly by alternatively including and not including on the list items that people must know are alternative uses of their resources, such as charity.

4. This is particularly true when the solicitor is the same for all wilderness contributions.

5. Greene (1970) showed how a majority might benefit from a centralization of the financing of essentially local services.

6. The overwhelming support for this bill elsewhere makes even one Alaskan vote against it unusual, and makes three negative votes highly unlikely. The probability that the Alaskan vote is a result of chance is .0032. Controlling for the party mix of the Alaskan congressional delegation, the probability as a result of chance is .0024.

7. There is, however, one serious utilitarian argument that could be used against cost-benefit analysis. Many economists, such as Ng (2000) and Frank (1999), argue that private consumption has a significant negative externality not shared by public consumption. It increases one person's status at the expense of another's. This approach has often been used in advocating greater environmental expenditures. In that context it is not appropriate because voters supposedly have already taken the status impact of private consumption into account in determining the level of public expenditures. But the argument, if valid, would be a legitimate objection to the cost measures used in cost-benefit analysis.

8. The American Cancer Society (2001) reports that the survival rate for lung and bronchus cancer in 1989 was between 13 and 14 percent. The Statistical Abstract of the United States reports that chronic obstructive pulmonary deaths were 87 percent of the deaths from respiratory cancers in 1990 (U.S. Census 1992). The focus of the data about the Clean Air Act on cancer suggests that cancer deaths are more sensitive to air pollution than are other respiratory deaths compared to the relative number of deaths of the two. We

assume an equal sensitivity, an assumption that exaggerates the number of deaths attributable to air pollution prevented by the Clear Air Act.

9. One cannot use a t test for this difference because the distribution of value of life by uses banned under the Clean Air Act is clearly not normal. A chi-squared test cannot be used because Miller (1989) does not provide data for individual observations. Fortunately, the standard deviation in the Miller data is so small that we can use another procedure. The probability that the population mean value of life calculated from market behavior is greater than four standard deviations from the sample mean is vanishingly small. Eleven of the thirteen values of life in uses banned under the Clean Air Act are greater than the mean value of life determined by market behavior plus four standard deviations from the mean. The probability of that occurring by chance is less than 1 percent.

Summation

1. In fact, many of the variables such as church attendance that increase voting and charitable contributions decrease asymmetric "goodness." We do not discuss the role of conscience in the voting position case except when discussing lying about such positions, while we do deal with conscience in the charity and voting participation cases. That does not imply that it plays no role in the former. It just does not play a distinctive role. The main impact of conscience on voting positions is to create lagged responses. But those lags can also be generated by other processes.

Appendix 1

1.

$$\partial M/\partial g = Ps,$$
$$\P R/\partial g = Ps(1 + r)^2 / [(1 + r)^2 - (1 - P)] > \partial M/\partial g$$

Since $\partial a/\partial g = 1$,

$$\partial R/\partial a = \partial R/\partial g,$$
$$\partial F/\partial a = s[P^*P_2 + (1 - P^*)P] / \{1 - [1 - P + P^*(P - P_2)] / \{1 + r)^2\}.$$

If $P_2 > P$, then

$$\partial F/\partial a > \partial R/\partial a.$$

That condition will hold because P_2 = the ratio of partnerless favor initiators and reciprocators to those plus moochers. P = the ratio of partnerless favor initiators to all favor initiators, reciprocators and moochers.

Appendix 2

ı. The model is easily revised to take forgetfulness into account. Assume that all charitable contributions are forgotten over the period between favors to the same person. C will now be the one-period return to a moocher, given g_1. The relevant P for both the moocher equation and the determination of g_1 also changes. Only unmatched favor initiators at the beginning of the period will contribute to charity. P becomes the probability that those who are partnerless at the beginning of the period will stay unmatched before a particular individual's request. This change in the model will not affect the directional predictions we have made with the perpetual memory assumption.

Glossary

altruism: We focus on the motivation for behavior rather than its results. Altruism is defined as concern for the well-being of others, or in the language of economics, having the utility of others in one's own utility function. We assume the usual properties: the marginal utility of the well-being of others is positive and diminishing. We also assume that altruism is limited in the sense that at comparable income levels the marginal utility of the income of a person and his family is greater to him than the marginal utility of the income of anybody else; that is, he values the well-being of his family more than he values anybody else's well-being. Altruism is further narrowed by being concerned only with the utility of people directly affected by one's actions. For all of our purposes altruism will not include helping somebody because of the approval of some other person whom one loves.

asymmetric "goodness": For an important class of issues one signals "goodness" by advocating one side of the issue but not the other. These issues are those where group survival, compassion, and externalities produce advocacy on only one side of a political issue.

conscience: An internalization of social norms, a desire to follow social rules because one feels better by so doing.

externality: A consequence to somebody not involved in making a decision.

free-rider problem: A problem generated when a large group (not necessarily the total population) consumes a public good and there is no way to exclude a consumer who does not pay for the good. Clearly, this problem holds for self-interested individuals. It also holds for altruists who value their own family's utility more than the utility of others. Both would prefer that others pay for the public good.

"goodness": Trustworthiness toward people not in one's group as opposed to trustworthiness toward people in one's own group.

imitation: The imitation of another's political positions is, we believe, a signal that one wishes to engage in reciprocal relations with that individual.

marginal x: If x is, say, utility, marginal x is roughly the change in utility with a change in y (say income). A person maximizes utility by having the marginal values of y the same across all his consumption options.

morality signaling: Signaling one's trustworthiness to members of one's group who practice the group social rules by advocating those social rules and signaling to others general trustworthiness by being likely practitioners of those social rules.

operational social rules: Social rules that together with their enforcement machinery are such that individuals on the whole find it in their interest to obey them.

public good: Commodities that provide benefits to a large group of people at the same time. One person's consumption of the good does not detract from the benefits simultaneously accruing to other individuals from the same good. It should be emphasized that a public good need not require all to share its benefits; only a large group.

reciprocity: One person doing a favor for another person in response to an earlier favor from that person. The time delay is an important part of the concept as we use it.

regression coefficients: Also symbolized by b. The magnitude of the impact of one variable on another, holding the effects of other controlled variables constant. For our usual purpose there are only two important characteristics: (1) its sign; (2) whether the t value is large enough that it is statistically significant, that is, the sign could not have been produced by chance sampling fluctuations if there were no true relationship. We sometimes include regression equations. The numbers in those equations are the respective regression coefficients of the independent variable (next to the coefficient) on the dependent variable (on the left-hand side of the equation).

self-interest (economist's): Behavior that maximizes a utility function that does not include the well-being of non–family members as an argument.

self-interest (evolutionary): Behavior that maximizes in the long run the survival of a given trait possessed by an individual.

self-interest (narrow): Voting in terms of the consequences of the policies of candidates if their programs were enacted.

signaling: Indicating to someone else by some present act how one would behave in the future for that same or a different act.

survival (group): The survival of the group by way of individuals within the group possessing a particular trait. Maximizing group survival means maximizing the number in the group in the long run.

survival (individual): The survival of a trait carried by an individual either by culture or by gene. Maximizing individual survival means maximizing the number of individuals carrying that trait in the long run. The reason for that last qualifier is that long-run survival might be maximized by choosing, in the short run, quality of one's children over numbers.

two-sided "goodness": Where "goodness" advocates take one side of an issue and moralizers take another side.

trustworthiness: Begin with the probability that a person will reciprocate a given favor done for him by somebody else. Then form the weighted average of those probabilities over all likely favors, weighted by the importance a person attaches to a favor and the probability that one will need such a favor. This weighted average is the trustworthiness of one person as assessed by another. This summed over all individuals is general trustworthiness.

utility function: A list of the variables about which a person is concerned.

warm glow: Any nonaltruistic motivation for an action that benefits others at some material cost. Warm glow includes such obviously self-interested behavior as reputational motives as well as conscience and any other nonaltruistic motive.

References

ABAnetwork. 2000. *Legislative and Governmental Advocacy.* <www.abanetwork.org/poladv/legiss.pdf>. October 12, 2000.

Adamson, John. 1930. *A Short History of Education.* Cambridge: Cambridge University Press.

Alexander, Richard. 1987. *The Biology of Moral Systems.* New York: DeGruyter.

Alston, Richard, J. Kearl, and Michael Vaughan. 1992. "Is There a Consensus among Economists in the 1990's?" *American Economic Review* 82:203–9.

American Cancer Society. 2001. *Cancer Facts and Figures, 2001.* Atlanta.

American Red Cross. 1999. *Annual Financial Report.* New York.

Andreoni, James. 1990. "Impure Altruism and Donations to Public Goods: A Theory of Warm-Glow Giving." *Economic Journal* 100:464–77.

Asch, S. E. 1963. "Effects of Group Pressure upon the Modification of Judgments." In *Groups, Leadership, and Men,* ed. Harold Guetzkow. New York: Russell and Russell.

Axelrod, Robert. 1984. *The Evolution of Cooperation.* New York: Basic Books.

Bailey, Martin, Mancur Olson, and Paul Wonnacott. 1980. "The Marginal Utility of Income Does Not Increase: Borrowing, Lending, and Friedman Savage Gambles." *American Economic Review* 70:372–90.

Barkow, Jerome. 1992. "Beneath New Culture Is Old Psychology: Gossip and Social Stratification." In *The Adapted Mind,* ed. Jerome Barkow, Leda Cosmides, and John Tooby. Oxford: Oxford University Press.

Batson, C. Daniel. 1991. *The Altruism Question.* Hillsdale, N.J.: Lawrence Erlbaum.

Becker, Gary. 1971. *Economic Theory.* New York: Knopf.

———. 1976. "Altruism, Egoism, and Genetic Fitness: Economics and Sociobiology." *Journal of Economic Literature* 14:817–26.

Becker, Gary, and George Stigler. 1974. "Law Enforcement, Malfeasance, and the Compensation of Enforcers." *Journal of Legal Studies* 3:1–18.

Bennett, James, and William Orzechowski. 1983. "The Voting Behavior of Bureaucrats." *Public Choice* 41:271–83.

Berelson, Bernard. 1964. *Human Behavior.* New York: Harcourt, Brace and World.

Berelson, Bernard, Paul Lazarsfeld, and William McPhee. 1954. *Voting.* Chicago: University of Chicago Press.

Bernheim, B. Douglas. 1987. "Dissaving after Retirement: Testing the Pure Life Cycle Hypothesis." In *Issues in Pension Economics,* ed. Zvi Bodie, John Shoven, and David Wise. Chicago: University of Chicago Press.

Bernstein, Robert, Anita Chadha, and Robert Montjoy. 2001. "Overreporting Voting: Why It Happens and Why It Matters." *Public Opinion Quarterly* 65:22–44.

Bester, Helmut, and Werner Guth. 1998. "Is Altruism Evolutionarily Stable?" *Journal of Economic Behavior and Organization* 34:193–209.

Bischoping, Katherine, and Howard Schuman. 1992. "Pens and Polls in Nicaragua: An Analysis of the 1990 Pre-election Surveys." *American Journal of Political Science* 36:331–50.

Bishop, John, John Formby, and W. James Smith. 1991. "Incomplete Information, Income Redistribution, and Risk Averse Voter Behavior." *Public Choice* 68:41–55.

Boskin, Michael, and Martin Feldstein. 1978. "Effects of the Charitable Deduction on Contributions by Low Income and Middle Income Households: Evidence from the National Survey of Philanthropy." *Review of Economics and Statistics* 59:351–54.

Bowles, Samuel. 1998. "Cultural Group Selection and Human Social Structure: The Effects of Segmentation, Egalitarianism, and Conformism." University of Massachusetts at Amherst. Typescript.

Boyce, Rebecca, Thomas Brown, Gary McClelland, George Peterson, and William Schulze. 1992. "An Experimental Examination of Intrinsic Values as a Source of the WTA-WTP Disparity." *American Economic Review* 82:1366–73.

Boyd, Robert, and Peter Richardson. 1985. *Culture and the Evolutionary Process.* Chicago: University of Chicago Press.

Brandts, Jordi, and Arthur Schram. 2001. "Cooperation and Noise in Public Goods Experiments: Applying the Contribution Function Approach." *Journal of Public Economics* 79:399–427.

Brennan, Geoffrey, and James Buchanan. 1984. "Voter Choice and the Evaluation of Political Alternatives." *American Behavioral Scientist* 28:185–201.

Brennan, Geoffrey, and Alan Hamlin. 1998. "Expressive Voting and Electoral Equilibrium." *Public Choice* 95:149–75.

Browning, Edgar, and William Johnson. 1984. "The Trade-off between Equality and Efficiency." *Journal of Political Economy* 92:175–203.

Chomsky, Noam. 1989. *Necessary Illusions: Thought Control in Democratic Societies.* Boston: South End Press.

Clotfelter, Charles. 1985. *Federal Tax Policy and Charitable Giving.* Chicago: University of Chicago Press.

Coleman, James. 1990. *Foundations of Social Theory.* Cambridge: Harvard University Press.

Congressional Quarterly Weekly Report. 1979. 37:924–25. May 12.

———. 1980. 38:2552. August 23.

Constantelos, Demetrios. 1991. *Byzantine Philanthropy and Social Welfare.* 2d ed. New Rochelle, N.Y.: Caratzas.

Cosmides, Leda, and John Tooby. 1992. "Cognitive Adaptations for Social Exchange." In *The Adapted Mind,* ed. Jerome Barkow, Leda Cosmides, and John Tooby. Oxford: Oxford University Press.

Courant, Paul, Edward Gramlich, and Daniel Rubinfeld. 1980. "Why Voters Support Tax Limitation Amendments: The Michigan Case." *National Tax Journal* 33:1–20.

Damasio, Antonio. 1999. *The Feeling of What Happens.* New York: Harcourt Brace.

Dawkins, Richard. 1989. *The Selfish Gene.* Oxford: Oxford University Press.

Delli Carpini, Michael. 1984. "Scooping the Voters; The Consequences of the Network's Early Call of the 1980 Presidential Race." *Journal of Politics* 46:866–85.

Demsetz, Harold, and Kenneth Lehn. 1985. "The Structure of Corporate Ownership: Causes and Consequences." *Journal of Political Economy* 93:1155–77.

Desvousges, William, F. Reed Johnson, Richard Dunford, Kevin Boyle, Sara Hudson, and K. Nicole Wilson. 1993. "Measuring Natural Resource Damages with Contingent Valuation: Tests of Validity and Reliability." In *Contingent Valuation: A Critical Assessment,* ed. Jerry Hausman. Amsterdam: North Holland.

Diamond, Jared. 1997. *Guns, Germs, and Steel.* New York: Norton.

Diamond, Peter, and Jerry Hausman. 1993. "On Contingent Valuation Measurement of Nonuse Values." In *Contingent Valuation: A Critical Assessment,* ed. Jerry Hausman. Amsterdam: North Holland.

Diamond, Peter, Jerry Hausman, Gregory Leonard, and Mike Denning. 1993. "Does Contingent Valuation Measure Preferences? Experimental Evidence." In *Contingent Valuation: A Critical Assessment,* ed. Jerry Hausman. Amsterdam: North Holland.

Dineen, Terry, and Noreen Twail. 1997. *Federalism and Environmental Protection: Case Studies for Drinking Water and Ground Level Ozone.* Washington, D.C.: Congressional Budget Office.

Domb, Cyril. 1980. *Maaser Kesafim.* Jerusalem: Feldheim.

Downs, Anthony. 1957. *An Economic Theory of Democracy.* New York: Harper and Row.

Driesen, David. 1987. "The Societal Cost of Environmental Regulation: Beyond Cost-Benefit Analysis." *Ecology Law Quarterly* 242:545–617.

D'Souza, Dinesh. 1991. *Illiberal Education: The Politics of Race and Sex on Campus.* New York: Free Press.

Dunlap, Riley, George Gallup, and Alec Gallup. 1993. "Of Global Concern: Results of the Planetary Survey." *Environment* 35:7–39.

Durden, Gary, Jason Shogren, and Jonathan Silberman. 1991. "The Effects of Interest Groups on Coal Strip Mining Legislation." *Social Science Quarterly* 72:239–50.

Dye, Richard. 1978. "Personal Charitable Contributions: Tax Effects and Other Motives." In *Proceedings of the Seventieth Annual Conference on Taxation.* Columbus: National Tax Association–Tax Institute of America.

Ehrlich, Isaac. 1975. "The Deterrent Effect of Capital Punishment: A Question of Life and Death." *American Economic Review* 65:397–417.

Ehrlich, Isaac, and Zhiqiang Liu. 1999. "Sensitivity Analyses of the Deterrence Hypothesis: Let's Keep the Eco. in Econometrics." *Journal of Law and Economics* 42:455–87.

Elder, Harold. 1987. "Property Rights Structures and Criminal Courts: An Analysis of State Criminal Courts." *International Review of Law and Economics* 7:21–32.

Eliot, T. S. 1950. *The Cocktail Party.* New York: Harcourt, Brace.

Elster, Jon. 1984. *Ulysses and the Sirens: Studies in Rationality and Irrationality.* Rev. ed. Cambridge: Cambridge University Press.

———. 1998. "Emotions and Economic Theory." *Journal of Economic Literature* 36:47–74.

———. 1999. *Alchemies of the Mind: Rationality and the Emotions.* Cambridge: Cambridge University Press.

Enelow, James, and Melvin Hinich. 1984. *The Spatial Theory of Voting.* Cambridge: Cambridge University Press.

Eshel, Ian, Larry Samuelson, and Avner Shakel. 1998. "Altruists, Egoists, and Hooligans in a Local Interaction Model." *American Economic Review* 88:157–79.

Falk, Austin, and Timothy Nolan. 1996. *Patterns in Corporate Philanthropy.* Washington, D.C.: Capital Research Center.

Farber, Daniel. 1999. *Eco-pragmatism.* Chicago: University of Chicago Press.

Feenberg, Daniel. 1987. "Are Tax Price Models Really Identified? The Case of Charitable Giving." *National Tax Journal* 40:629–33.

Fehr, Ernst, and Simon Gachter. 2000. "Fairness and Retaliation: The Economics of Reciprocity." *Journal of Economic Perspectives* 14:159–81.

Filer, John, Lawrence Kenny, and Rebecca Morton. 1993. "Redistribution, Income, and Voting." *American Journal of Political Science* 37:63–67.

Fisher, Ronald. 1915. "The Evolution of Sexual Preference." *Eugenics Review* 7:184–92.

Foucault, Michel. 1980. *Power/Knowledge.* New York: Pantheon.

Frank, Robert. 1988. *Passions within Reason.* New York: Norton.

———. 1999. *Luxury Fever.* New York: Free Press.

Frank, Robert, Thomas Gilovich, and Dennis Regan. 1993. "Does Studying Economics Inhibit Cooperation?" *Journal of Economic Perspectives* 7:159–71.

Friedman, Milton. 1957. *A Theory of the Consumption Function.* Princeton: Princeton University Press.

Gallup, George. 1999. *The Gallup Poll.* Wilmington, Del.: Scholarly Resources.

Glaeser, Edward, David Laibson, and Bruce Sacerdote. 2000. "The Economic Approach to Social Capital." NBER Working Paper 7728. Cambridge: National Bureau of Economic Research.

Glaeser, Edward, David Laibson, Jose Scheinkman, and David Souter. 1999. "What Is Social Capital? The Determinants of Trust and Trustworthiness." NBER Working Paper 7216. Cambridge: National Bureau of Economic Research.

Glazer, Amihai, and Kai Konrad. 1996. "A Signaling Explanation for Charity." *American Economic Review* 86:1019–28.

Greene, Kenneth V. 1970. "Some Institutional Considerations in State-Local Fiscal Relations." *Public Choice* 9:1–18.

Greene, Kenneth V., and Phillip J. Nelson. 2002a. "If Extremists Vote, How Do They Express Themselves? An Empirical Test of an Expressive Theory of Voting." *Public Choice* 113:425–36.

———. 2002b. "Morality and the Political Process." In *Method and Morals in Constitutional Economics: Essays in Honor of James M. Buchanan,* ed. Geoffrey Brennan, Hartmut Kliemt, and Robert Tollison. New York: Springer-Verlag.

Greene, Kenneth V., and Oleg Nikolaev. 1999. "Voter Participation and the Redistributive State." *Public Choice* 98:213–26.

Griffin, James. 1986. *Well-Being: Its Meaning, Measurement, and Moral Importance.* Oxford: Clarendon Press.

Guth, James, John Green, Lyman Kellstedt, and Corwin Smidt. 1995. "Faith and the Environment: Religious Beliefs and Attitudes on Environmental Policy." *American Journal of Political Science* 39:364–82.

Hamilton, William. 1963. "The Evolution of Altruistic Behavior." *American Naturalist* 97:354–56.

Hanemann, W. Michael. 1994. "Valuing the Environment through Contingent Valuation." *Journal of Economic Perspectives* 8:19–43.

Harbaugh, William. 1996. "If People Vote Because They Like To, Then Why Do So Many of Them Lie?" *Public Choice* 89:63–76.

Havick, John. 1997. "Determinants of National Media Attention." *Journal of Communications* 47:97–109.

Hengstler, Gary. 1996. "In Political Year, ABA Policies Are Something to Talk About." *ABA Journal* 82:108–20.

Higgs, Robert. 1971. "Race, Skills, and Earnings: American Immigrants in 1909." *Journal of Economic History* 31:420–28.

Hirshleifer, Jack. 1994. "The Dark Side of the Force." *Economic Inquiry* 32:1–10.

Hoffman, Elisabeth, and Matthew Spitzer. 1982. "The Coase Theorem: Some Experimental Results." *Journal of Law and Economics* 25:73–98.

Holsey, Cheryl, and Thomas Borcherding. 1997. "Why Does Government's Share of National Income Grow? An Assessment of the Recent Literature on the U.S. Experience." In *Perspectives on Public Choice: A Handbook,* ed. Dennis Mueller. Cambridge: Cambridge University Press.

Jaarsma, Bert, Arthur van Winden, and Arthur Schram. 1985. "An Empirical Analysis of Voter Turnout in the Netherlands." Research Memorandum 8509. Faculty of Economics, University of Amsterdam.

———. 1986. "On the Voting Participation of Public Bureaucrats." *Public Choice* 48:183–87.

Jackson, John. 1983. "Election Night Reporting and Voter Turnout." *American Journal of Political Science* 27:613–35.

Kahn, Matthew, and John Matsusaka. 1997. "Demand for Environmental Goods: Evidence from Voting Patterns on California Initiatives." *Journal of Law and Economics* 40:137–73.

Kahneman, Daniel, and Amos Tversky. 1984. "Choices, Values, and Frames." *American Psychologist* 39:341–50.

Kalt, Joseph, and Mark Zupan. 1984. "Capture and Ideology in the Economic Theory of Politics." *American Economic Review* 74:279–300.

Kau, James, and Paul Rubin. 1979. "Self-Interest, Ideology, and Logrolling in Congressional Voting." *Journal of Law and Economics* 22:365–84.

———. 1982. *Congressmen, Constituents, and Contributors.* Boston: Martinus Nijhoff.

Keating, Barry, Robert Pitts, and David Appel. 1981. "United Way Contributions: Coercion, Charity, or Economic Self-Interest?" *Southern Economic Journal* 47:815–23.

Kellstedt, Lyman, and John Green. 1993. "Knowing God's Many People: Denominational Preference and Political Behavior." in *Rediscovering the Religious Factor in American Politics,* ed. Lyman Kellstedt and David Leege. Armonk, N.Y.: M. E. Sharpe.

Keneally, Thomas. 1998. *The Great Shame: A Story of the Irish in the Old World and the New.* New York: Talese.

Kors, Allan, and Harvey Silvergate. 1998. *The Shadow University: The Betrayal of Liberty on American Campuses.* New York: Free Press.

Kristov, Lorenzo, Peter Lindert, and Robert McClelland. 1992. "Pressure Groups and Redistribution." *Journal of Public Economics* 48:135–63.

Krueger, Anne. 1974. "The Political Economy of the Rent-Seeking Society." *American Economic Review* 64:291–303.

Kuran, Timur. 1995. *Private Truths, Public Lies: The Social Consequences of Behavior Falsification.* Cambridge: Harvard University Press.

———. 1997. "Moral Overload and Its Alleviation." In *Economics, Values, and Organization,* ed. Avner Ben-Ner and Louis Putterman. Cambridge: Cambridge University Press.

————. 1998. "Ethnic Norms and Their Transformation through Reputational Cascades." *Journal of Legal Studies* 27:623–59.

Laband, David, and Richard Beil. 1999. "Are Economists More Selfish Than Other Social Scientists?" *Public Choice* 100:85–101.

Lagemann, Ellen. 1989. *The Politics of Knowledge.* Middletown, Conn.: Wesleyan University Press.

Lapp, Miriam. 1999. "Incorporating Groups in a Rational Choice Explanation of Turnout: An Empirical Test." *Public Choice* 98:171–85.

Lawton, Leora, and Regina Bures. 2001. "Parental Divorce and the 'Switching' of Religious Identity." *Journal for the Scientific Study of Religion* 40:99–111.

Lee, Martin, and Norma Solomon. 1990. *Unreliable Sources.* New York: Carol Publishing Group.

Lenkowsky, Lawrence. 1999. "Seeing through the Left's False Lament." *Chronicle of Philanthropy,* April 8.

Levite, Allan. 1996. "Bias Basics." *National Review* 48:63–64.

Lichter, S. Robert, Stanley Rothman, and Linda Lichter. 1986. *The Media Elite.* New York: Hastings House.

Linsky, Martin. 1986. *How the Press Affects Federal Policy Making.* New York: Norton.

Lipset, Seymour, and Everett Ladd. 1971. "The Politics of American Political Scientists." *P.S.* 4:136–44.

Loewenstein, George. 2000. "Emotions in Economic Theory and Economic Behavior." *American Economic Review* 90:426–32.

Lott, John, and Lawrence Kenny. 1999. "Did Women's Suffrage Change the Size and Scope of Government?" *Journal of Political Economy* 107:1163–98.

Lowry, Robert. 1998. "Religion and the Demand for Membership in Environmental Citizen Groups." *Public Choice* 94:223–40.

Lumsden, Charles, and Edward Wilson. 1981. *Genes, Mind, and Culture.* Cambridge: Harvard University Press.

Madison, James. 1989. *Debates in the Federal Convention of 1787.* Ed. James McClellan and Martin Bradford. Richmond: James River Press.

Manski, Charles. 2000. "Economic Analysis of Social Interactions." *Journal of Economic Perspectives* 14:115–36.

Marsh, Allan. 1977. *Protest and Political Consciousness.* London: Sage.

Marsh, Catherine. 1984. "Back on the Bandwagon: The Effect of Opinion Polls on Public Opinion." *British Journal of Political Science* 15:51–74.

Marwell, Gerald, and Ruth Ames. 1981. "Economists Free Ride, Does Anyone Else? Experiments on the Provision of Public Goods." *Journal of Public Economics* 15:295–310.

Mikva, Abner. 1996. "Lawful Pursuits: Latest ABA Controversy Ignores History." *Texas Lawyer* (December) p. 20.

Milgrom, Paul. 1993. "Is Sympathy an Economic Value?" In *Contingent Valuation: A Critical Assessment,* ed. Jerry Hausman. New York: Elsevier.

Miller, Ted. 1989. "Willingness to Pay Comes of Age: Will the System Survive?" *Northwestern Law Review* 83:876–90.

Miller, Warren. 1988. *American National Election Studies Pre and Post Election Survey.* 2d ed. Ann Arbor: Inter-university Consortium for Political and Social Research.

Morgan, James. 1977. *A National Study of Philanthropy.* Ann Arbor: Inter-university Consortium for Political and Social Research.

Morris, Andrew. 1997. "Pesticides and Environmental Federalism: An Empirical and Qualitative Analysis of 824(c) Registrations." In *Environmental Federalism,* ed. by Terry L. Anderson and Peter J. Hill. Lanham, Md.: Rowman and Littlefield.

Moschis, George, and Roy Moore. 1979. "Decision Making among the Young." *Journal of Consumer Research* 6:101–12.

Mueller, Dennis. 1989. *Public Choice II.* Cambridge: Cambridge University Press.

Murphy, K., and N. Luther. 1997. "Assessing Honesty, Integrity, and Deception." In *The International Handbook of Selection and Assessment,* ed. Neil Anderson and Peter Herriot. Chister, England: Wiley.

National Opinion Research Center (NORC). 1986. *General Social Surveys, 1972–1986.* Ann Arbor: Inter-university Consortium for Political and Social Research.

———. 1996. *General Social Surveys, 1972–1996.* Ann Arbor: Inter-university Consortium for Political and Social Research.

Nelson, Phillip J. 1959. "Migration, Real Income, and Information." *Journal of Regional Science* 1:43–74.

———. 1994. "Voting and Imitation." *Economic Inquiry* 32:92–102.

Ng, Yew-Kwang. 2000. *Efficiency, Equality, and Public Policy.* New York: St. Martin's Press.

Nielson, Walderman. 1972. *The Big Foundations.* New York: Columbia University Press.

———. 1996. *Inside American Philanthropy.* Norman: University of Oklahoma Press.

Oates, Wallace. 1972. *Fiscal Federalism.* New York: Harcourt, Brace.

Oates, Wallace, and Robert Schwab. 1988. "Economic Competition between Jurisdictions." *Journal of Public Economics* 35:333–54.

Ofek, Haim. 2001. *Second Nature: Economic Origins of Human Evolution.* Cambridge: Cambridge University Press.

Olson, Mancur. 1982. *The Rise and Decline of Nations: Economic Growth, Stagflation, and Social Rigidities.* New Haven: Yale University Press.

Opaluch, James, and Thomas Grigalunas. 1991. *Ethical Values and Personal Preferences as Determinants of Nonuse Values: Implications for Natural Resource Damage Assessments.* Peacedale, R.I.: Economic Analysis.

Ostrom, Elinor. 2000. "Collective Action and the Evolution of Social Norms." *Journal of Economic Perspectives* 14:137–58.

Overbye, Elinor. 1995. "Explaining Welfare Spending." *Public Choice* 83:313–35.

Palfrey, Thomas, and Jeffrey Prisbrey. 1997. "Anomalous Behavior in Public Goods Experiments: How Much and Why?" *American Economic Review* 87:829–46.

Parry, Hugh, and Helen Crossley. 1950. "Validity of Responses to Survey Questions." *Public Opinion Quarterly* 14:61–80.

Peltzman, Sam. 1980. "The Growth of Government." *Journal of Law and Economics* 23:209–87.

———. 1984. "Constituent Interest and Congressional Voting." *Journal of Law and Economics* 27:181–210.

———. 1985. "An Economic Interpretation of the History of Congressional Voting in the Twentieth Century." *American Economic Review* 75:656–75.

Piven, Frances. 1971. *Regulating the Poor.* New York: Pantheon.

Podgers, James. 1992. "Which Way ABA? Pondering New Policy Directions." *ABA Journal* 78:60–69.

Poole, Keith, and Thomas Romer. 1985. "Patterns of Political Action Committee Contributions to the 1980 Campaigns for the United States House of Representatives." *Public Choice* 47:63–111.

Posner, Eric. 2000. *Law and Social Norms.* Cambridge: Harvard University Press.

Posner, Richard. 1980. "A Theory of Primitive Society, with Special Reference to Law." *Journal of Law and Economics* 23:1–53.

Price, George. 1972. "Extension of Covariance Selection Mathematics." *Annals of Human Genetics* 35:485–90.

Rabin, Matthew. 1998. "Psychology and Economics." *Journal of Economic Literature* 36:11–46.

Randolph, William. 1995. "Dynamic Income, Progressive Taxes, and the Timing of Charitable Contributions." *Journal of Political Economy* 103:709–38.

Reese, Stephen, Wayne Danielson, Pamela Shoemaker, Tsan-Kuo Chaug, and Huei-Ling Hsu. 1986. "Ethnicity of Interviewer Effects among Mexican Americans and Anglos." *Public Opinion Quarterly* 50:563–72.

Ridley, Matt. 1997. *The Origins of Virtue.* London: Penguin.

Robson, Arthur. 2001. "The Biological Basis of Economic Behavior." *Journal of Economic Literature* 39:11–33.

Sagoff, Mark. 1988. *The Economics of the Earth: Philosophy, Law, and the Environment.* Cambridge: Cambridge University Press.

Samuelson, William, and Richard Zeckhauser. 1988. "Status Quo Bias in Decision Making." *Journal of Risk and Uncertainty* 1:7–59.

Schuessler, Alexander. 2000. *A Logic of Expressive Choice.* Princeton: Princeton University Press.

Silver, Brian, Barbara Anderson, and Paul Abramson. 1986. "Who Overreports Voting?" *American Political Science Review* 80:613–24.

Smith, Adam. 1976. *The Theory of Moral Sentiments.* Oxford. Clarendon Press.

Sowell, Thomas. 1990. *Preferential Policies.* New York: Morrow.

———. 1995. *The Vision of the Anointed.* New York: Basic Books.

Spence, Michael. 1973. "Job Market Signaling." *Quarterly Journal of Economics* 87:355–74.

Stigler, George. 1965. *Essays in the History of Economics.* Chicago: University of Chicago Press.

———. 1971. "The Theory of Economic Regulation." *Bell Journal of Economics and Management Science* 2:3–21.

———. 1982. *The Economist as Preacher.* Chicago: University of Chicago Press.

Sudman, Seymour. 1986. "Do Exit Polls Influence Voting Behavior?" *Public Opinion Quarterly* 50:331–39.

Sunstein, Cass. 1997. *Free Markets and Social Justice.* Oxford: Oxford University Press.

Suro, Roberto. 1989. "Grass-Roots Groups Show Power Battling Pollution Close to Home." *New York Times,* July 2.

Sykes, Charles. 1990. *The Hollow Men.* Washington, D.C.: Regnery Gateway.

Tabarrok, Alexander, and Erik Helland. 1999. "Court Politics: The Political Economy of Tort Awards." *Journal of Law and Economics* 42:157–88.

Thaler, Richard. 1980. "Toward a Positive Theory of Consumer Choice." *Journal of Economic Behavior and Organization* 1:39–60.

Thaler, Richard, and H. M. Shefrin. 1981. "An Economic Theory of Self-Control." *Journal of Political Economy* 89:392–407.

Tiehan, Laura. 2001. "Tax Policy and Charitable Contributions of Money." *National Tax Journal* 54:707–19.

Timmerman, Kenneth. 2002. *Shakedown: Exposing the Real Jesse Jackson.* Washington, D.C.: Regency.

Toma, Eugenia. 1991. "Congressional Influence and the Supreme Court: The Budget as Signaling Device." *Journal of Legal Studies* 20:131–46.

Trow, Martin. 1975. *Teachers and Students: Aspects of American Higher Education.* New York: McGraw-Hill.

U.S. Census. 1960. *Statistical Abstract of the United States.* Washington, D.C.: Government Printing Office.

———. 1972. *Statistical Abstract of the United States.* Washington, D.C.: Government Printing Office.

———. 1973. *1970 Census of Population, Subject Reports, Earnings by Occupation and Education.* Washington, D.C.: Government Printing Office.

———. 1990. *Statistical Abstract of the United States.* Washington, D.C.: Government Printing Office.

———. 1992. *Statistical Abstract of the United States.* Washington, D.C.: Government Printing Office.

―――. 1999. *Statistical Abstract of the United States.* Washington, D.C.: Government Printing Office.

―――. 2000. *Statistical Abstract of the United States.* Washington, D.C.: Government Printing Office.

Van Houtven, George, and Maureen Cropper. 1996. "When Is a Life Too Costly to Save? The Evidence from U.S. Environmental Regulations." *Journal of Environmental Economics and Management* 30:348–68.

Wilcox, Derk. 1996. *The Left Guide.* Ann Arbor: Economics America.

―――. 1997. *The Right Guide.* Ann Arbor: Economics America.

Wilson, David, and Lee Allan Dugatkin. 1997. "Group Selection and Assortative Interactions." *American Naturalist* 149:336–51.

Wilson, David, and Elliot Sober. 1998. *Unto Others.* Cambridge: Harvard University Press.

Wilson, E. O. 1992. *The Diversity of Life.* Cambridge: Harvard University Press.

Wilson, James. 1993. *The Moral Sense.* New York: Macmillan.

Wright, Robert. 1994. *The Moral Animal.* New York: Vintage.

―――. 2000. *Non-Zero.* New York: Random House.

Yezer, Anthony, Robert Goldfarb, and Paul Poppen. 1996. "Does Studying Economics Discourage Cooperation? Watch What We Do, Not What We Say or How We Play." *Journal of Economic Perspectives* 10:177–86.

Index